01

MULTICULTURAL EDUCATION SERIES

James A. Banks, *Series Editor*

THE CHILDREN
ARE WATCHING

How the Media Teach About Diversity

Carlos E. Cortés

Teachers College, Columbia University
New York and London

Published by Teachers College Press, 1234 Amsterdam Avenue, New York,
NY 10027

Library of Congress Cataloging-in-Publication Data

Cortés, Carlos E.
    The children are watching : how the media teach about diversity / Carlos
    E. Cortés.
        p. cm. — (Multicultural education series)
    Includes bibliographical references and index.
    ISBN 0-8077-3938-3 (cloth : alk. paper) — ISBN 0-8077-3937-5 (paper : alk.
    paper)
        1. Multiculturalism in mass media.   2. Multicultural education.   3. Mass
    media and education.   I. Title.   II. Multicultural education series (New
    York, N.Y.)
P96.M83 C67 2000
306—dc21   99-057987

ISBN 0-8077-3937-5
ISBN 0-8077-3938-3

Printed on acid-free paper
Manufactured in the United States of America

07   06   05   04   03   02   01   00   8   7   6   5   4   3   2   1

To Laurel

My wife, my life, my love, my best friend

Contents

Part II: The Mass Media as Multicultural Curriculum

Part III: Media and Education in Contemporary Perspective

Part IV: Schooling in a Multiculturally Mediated World

Series Foreword

The nation's deepening ethnic texture, interracial tension and conflict, and the increasing percentage of students who speak a first language other than English make multicultural education imperative as the 21st century begins. The U.S. Bureau of the Census estimated that people of color made up 28% of the nation's population in 2000 (U.S. Bureau of the Census, 1998). The Census predicted that they would make up 38% of the nation's population in 2025 and 47% in 2050.

American classrooms are experiencing the largest influx of immigrant students since the beginning of the 20th century. About one million immigrants are making the United States their home each year (Martin & Midgley, 1999). More than six million legal immigrants settled in the United States between 1991 and 1996 (U.S. Bureau of the Census, 1998). A large but undetermined number of undocumented immigrants also enter the United States each year. The influence of an increasingly diverse population on the nation's schools, colleges, and universities is and will continue to be enormous.

In 1995, 35% of the students enrolled in public schools were students of color; this percentage is increasing each year, primarily because of the growth in the percentage of Latino students (Pratt & Rittenhouse, 1998). In some of the nation's largest cities and metropolitan areas, such as Chicago, Los Angeles, Washington, D.C., New York, Seattle, and San Francisco, half or more of the public school students are students of color. In California, the population of students of color in the public schools has exceeded the percentage of White students since the 1988/89 school year.

Language diversity is also increasing among the nation's student population. Fourteen percent of school-age youth lived in homes in which English was not the first language in 1990 (U.S. Bureau of the Census, 1998). Most teachers now in the classroom and in teacher education programs are likely to have students from diverse ethnic, racial, and language groups in their classrooms during their careers. This is true for both inner-city and suburban teachers.

An important goal of multicultural education is to improve race relations and to help all students acquire the knowledge, attitudes, and skills needed to participate in cross-cultural interactions and in personal, social, and civic action that will help make our nation more democratic and just. Multicultural education is consequently as important for middle-class White suburban students as it is for students of color who live in the inner-city. Multicultural education fosters the public good and the overarching goals of the commonwealth.

The major purpose of the *Multicultural Education Series* is to provide preservice educators, practicing educators, graduate students, and scholars with an interrelated and comprehensive set of books that summarizes and analyzes important research, theory, and practice related to the education of ethnic, racial, cultural, and language groups in the United States and the education of mainstream students about diversity. The books in the *Series* provide research, theoretical, and practical knowledge about the behaviors and learning characteristics of students of color, language minority students, and low-income students. They also provide knowledge about ways to improve academic achievement and race relations in educational settings.

The definition of multicultural education in the *Handbook of Research on Multicultural Education* (Banks & Banks, 1995) is used in the *Multicultural Education Series:* "multicultural education is a field of study designed to increase educational equity for all students that incorporates, for this purpose, content, concepts, principles, theories, and paradigms from history, the social and behavioral sciences, and particularly from ethnic studies and women studies" (p. xii). In the *Series*, as in the *Handbook*, multicultural education is considered a "metadiscipline."

The dimensions of multicultural education, developed by Banks (1995) and described in the *Handbook of Research on Multicultural Education*, provide the conceptual framework for the development of the books in the *Series*. They are: *content integration, the knowledge construction process, prejudice reduction, an equity pedagogy,* and *an empowering school culture and social structure.* To implement multicultural education effectively, teachers and administrators must attend to each of the five dimensions of multicultural education. They should use content from diverse groups when teaching concepts and skills, help students to understand how knowledge in the various disciplines is constructed, help students to develop positive intergroup attitudes and behaviors, and modify their teaching strategies so that students from different racial, cultural, language, and social-class groups will experience equal educational opportunities. The total environment and culture of the school must also be transformed so that students from diverse groups will experience equal status in the culture and life of the school.

Although the five dimensions of multicultural education are highly interrelated, each requires deliberate attention and focus. Each book in the series focuses on one or more of the dimensions, although each book deals with all of them to some extent because of the highly interrelated characteristics of the dimensions.

The Bluest Eye, Toni Morrison's first novel (1993), tells the tragic story of Pecola Breedlove, a young African American girl who wants blue eyes. The seminal research by Kenneth and Mamie Clark (1950)—and more recent research by Williams and Morland (1976) and Spencer (1982)—describes the ways in which young children often evaluate white more highly than black or brown. Children generalize their feelings about color to people. They accurately perceive the status of different racial groups within the larger society.

The representation of people and groups in the media is a cogent factor that influences children's perceptions, attitudes, and values. However, as Cortés points out in this incisive and engaging book, the influence of the media on student knowledge, attitudes, and beliefs is powerful but complex and difficult to predict; it is not straightforward and clear. The interpretations and meanings that children construct from media presentations are often quite different from those intended by the mediamaker, as well as from those constructed by parents and teachers. Cortés uses cogent examples from observations of his granddaughters to make this important point.

An astute observer of media and youth, Cortés helps readers to think deeply about education, diversity, and the media within a social context in which there are multiple influences on the socialization of youth. He eschews facile explanations about the effects of the media on children's beliefs and behaviors. Consequently, Cortés neither condemns nor defends images of diversity in the media but helps readers to understand their complex origins and effects.

Cortés' inviting writing style is a legacy of his days as a professional journalist. He personalizes this book with stories about his life and grandchildren. He blends the powerful insights of a master historian, the writing style of a seasoned journalist, and informative personal stories to create a significant book that will raise the level of the public conversation about the media and diversity and enrich the knowledge of its readers.

James A. Banks
Series Editor

References

Banks, J. A. (1995). Multicultural education: Historical development, dimensions, and practice. In J. A. Banks & C.A.M. Banks (Eds.), *Handbook of research on multicultural education* (pp. 3–24). New York: Macmillan.

Banks, J. A., & Banks, C.A.M. (Eds.). (1995). *Handbook of research on multicultural education.* New York: Macmillan.

Clark, K. B., & Clark, M. P. (1950). Emotional factors in racial identification and preference in Negro children. *Journal of Negro Education, 19,* 341–350.

Martin, P., & Midgley, E. (1999). Immigration to the United States. *Population Bulletin, 54*(2), 1–44. Washington, DC: Population Reference Bureau.

Morrison, T. (1993). *The bluest eye.* New York: Knopf.

Pratt, R., & Rittenhouse, G. (Eds.). (1998). *The condition of education: 1998.* Washington, DC: U.S. Government Printing Office.

Spencer, M. B. (1982). Personal and group identity of Black children: An alternative synthesis. *Genetic Psychology Monographs, 106,* 59–84.

United States Bureau of the Census. (1998). *Statistical abstract of the United States* (118th edition). Washington, DC: U.S. Government Printing Office.

Williams, J. E., & Morland, K. (1976). *Race, color and the young child.* Chapel Hill: The University of North Carolina Press.

Preface

This book has been simmering for a long time.

Maybe since I became enchanted by the media growing up in Kansas City, Missouri, gorging on Sunday afternoon triple features at a neighborhood movie theater or, along with my family, mesmerized by radio dramas, sometimes referred to as the "theater of the mind." I didn't get hooked on TV, because it didn't reach Kansas City until I was already in high school.

My fascination with the media continued over the years. While majoring in communications and public policy at the University of California, Berkeley, I edited the *Blue and Gold*, the school yearbook, and chaired the Student Publications Board, where I had my first experiences with pressure groups and censorship attempts. After working briefly for *Boxoffice Magazine*, a movie trade publication, I received an M.S. from Columbia Graduate School of Journalism as a preliminary step toward obtaining a degree in media law, a plan that got derailed. While there I also became stoked on New York theater, which led me to taking a public relations job with the American Shakespeare Festival.

Then came two years in the army, where again I did public relations, while also moonlighting as editor of the local newspaper's Sunday motion picture section. After completing my service, I spent two years in Phoenix editing a chain of weekly suburban newspapers. This was followed by a stint with the Associated Press, where every half hour for eight hours I had to write a five-minute radio newscast, to be sent out on the wire so that disc jockeys could read it between playing Elvis Presley and Bobby Darin.

Graduate school in Latin American history launched me on a career change that, at first, drew me away from the media, as I became a history professor at the University of California, Riverside. But at the beginning of the 1970s, during the early days of multicultural education, my media mania returned, but with a different purpose. The long-simmering pot became hotter as I increasingly recognized the enormous pedagogical implications of the media. Well before school educators ever began *talking* about multicultural education, the mass media *were* multicultural education—a chaotic, anarchic, semicoordinated, multivocal, usually unintended but nonetheless relentless flood of media textbooks on diversity, emanating from radios and television sets, inhabiting movie screens, and occupying the pages of newspapers and magazines.

That enveloping media multicultural curriculum guarantees that school educators do not have the power to decide *if* multicultural education will occur. It will . . . through the media, even if not in schools. Rather, school educators can only decide *whether or not* they will consciously participate and *how* they will participate in the inevitable process of teaching and learning about diversity.

For more than two decades I have been studying, teaching, writing about, and giving workshops on the relationship between the mass media and multicultural education. But only in the past few years have my ideas about that complex process really begun to gel. Only now have the myriad ingredients in my conceptual gumbo truly begun to form an integrated although still evolving whole.

The gumbo's still cooking. It probably always will be. Each week brings new insights, surprising variations on previously considered themes, and challenges to my current beliefs. But it's time to try to put it all together into a coherent, if inevitably changing, vision. So consider this a work in progress—in eternal progress—because my thinking about the role of the mass media in multicultural teaching and learning is constantly evolving . . . in fact, has evolved even as I have written this book.

The Book

This book is intended for educators, in the broadest sense of the word. Not just school educators, but all people, including parents and mediamakers, who touch the young and help shape their hearts and minds. I hope that it provides a better understanding of the inevitable role that the mass media play in the broad educational process, particularly in the ways that young people develop their beliefs and feelings about human diversity . . . themselves, others, and the social forces that envelop all of us. I also hope that it offers useful insights and ideas for grappling with the inevitable media teaching-learning process and for better understanding its implications for diversity-related education.

Think of this book as the ruminations of one who has worked and wallowed in the belly of the beast and would like to invite you to take a trip through its entrails. Part scholarship, part autobiography, part musings, part educational challenge, part effort to involve you in my personal search, this book engages some of the complexities and paradoxes of the triangular media–school–learner relationship. At times written from posi-

tions of intellectual distance or social commitment, at other times it reveals my personal struggles with this topic . . . as scholar, teacher, public
lecturer, workshop presenter, and most recently as a grandfather observing, contemplating, and contending with the interactions between the
media and two little inchoate minds.

The more that I read and think about the relationship between the
mass media and school education, particularly where diversity is concerned, the more I recognize the topic's tortuous complexities, puzzling
inconsistencies, tantalizing paradoxes, and constant surprises. This process of investigation has led me to the conclusion that school education
about diversity will *always* be self-limiting in its effectiveness if school
educators do not seriously engage the reality—the inevitability—of students learning about "otherness" through the media. And when I say
engage, I mean do more than complain about the media and lament their
impact. It does little good to recognize the mass media's multicultural
teaching power, particularly regarding the media treatment of different
social and cultural groups, if educators do not also draw upon that recognition to inform and transform their own teaching.

The book is divided into four sections. In the Prologue and Part I,
"An Introduction in Two Episodes," I provide an autobiographical setting
for the questions raised and addressed in the book. The Prologue describes the serendipitous incident that launched me on this line of inquiry.
In Chapter 1, I draw upon my experiences with my two oldest grandchildren, whose interaction with the media I have been observing for the past
half decade. Chapter 2 relates how I developed the concept of the "societal curriculum," the larger nonschool educational setting within which I
frame my media analysis.

Part II, "The Mass Media as Multicultural Curriculum," addresses
three basic long-range questions. How have mediamakers functioned as
multicultural curriculum developers and textbook creators? How have
the resulting media products served as public textbooks on diversity?
What and how have media consumers learned about diversity from these
multicultural textbooks?

Part III, "Media and Education in Contemporary Perspective," focuses on the current media scene. First, by means of a personal daily
journal, it scrutinizes one randomly selected month—October 1997—as
an example of the contemporary media multicultural curriculum. Then
based partly on an analysis of that journal, I draw tentative conclusions
about the overall nature of the contemporary media curriculum, discuss
the media curriculum's potential multicultural impact, and develop a theory of media-based multicultural learning.

While school implications are addressed throughout the book, Part

IV, "Schooling in a Multiculturally Mediated World," focuses directly on the issue of schools. What does it mean for schools to operate within an increasingly mediated world, including a world of inevitably mediated multicultural education? How can school educators become more knowledgeable about the complex, evolving media multicultural curriculum, more effectively address media-related school issues, and more transformatively integrate the media into their diversity-related educational efforts. This includes grappling with the inevitable issue of media-influenced stereotyping. Finally, what are the implications of cyberspace for media and school multicultural education?

Words

Throughout the book I use a few words in a manner somewhat at variance with ways that they are usually employed and understood. I do so because, as I developed my line of argument, I found that certain traditional uses of language have actually impeded and distorted our understanding of the educational process writ large. Only by recasting selected words and combinations could I engage these distortions and maintain a consistent thesis. Following are five of those terms—media, mediamakers, media textbooks, media curriculum, and school educators—and my reasons for using them as I do.

First the word *media* itself. I use that term in a comprehensive sense to mean all of the major forms of media, including newspapers, magazines, film, television, radio, and, as I discuss in the last chapter, the new cyberspace media. It is also used to encompass media that are often treated and analyzed dichotomously—for example, news versus entertainment, fictional versus nonfictional, mainstream versus alternative, and conservative versus liberal. There is scholarly literature on each of the various forms and categories of media, sometimes with specific attention to issues of diversity. In this book I am not interested in providing a detailed analysis of the *differences* among these media. Rather, I seek to tease out and reveal *common, deeper, underlying patterns* in the media treatment of diversity and, as a result, how these varying, sometimes conflicting, categories of media converge to form what I describe as a public curriculum on diversity.

This leads me to the next word, *mediamaker,* a term that I adopted simply because I could not find another word for the idea that I wish to convey. By mediamakers I simply mean those people who contribute substantively to the process of creating media content. As I argue throughout the book, media content (like school textbooks) is seldom the result of individual efforts. Increasingly it is the composite product of many minds and hands. A writer may pen an article or column, but others usually frame it in headlines, illustrate it with photos or other graphics, and place it in visual relationship to other elements in a newspaper or magazine. Movie directors (often used synonymously with filmmakers) usually get most of the credit for their films. Yet others, such as writers, producers, editors, and actors, also contribute heavily to the finished product. However, I have found no word that encompasses all of these contributors in all media. Therefore, I have adopted the term *mediamakers* as my shorthand to allow me to make broader generalizations about all of those involved significantly in the creation of media that deal with diversity.

This leads me to the next term, *media textbooks*. One of this book's central arguments is that media products—such as movies, television shows, newspapers, and talk radio segments—ultimately function as public textbooks. That is, whatever the pedagogical intention (or absence of intent) of mediamakers, their media products teach. When those products deal with diversity, they therefore *teach* about diversity. (The extent to which individual media consumers actually *learn* about diversity from specific media products is a different topic, which I address in Chapter 5.) In general parlance, the word *textbooks* is usually reserved for educational materials produced primarily for use in schools. However, a central thesis of the book is that, like school textbooks, mass media products, too, function pedagogically—sometimes intentionally, sometimes incidentally. Therefore, I have adopted the term *media textbooks* to apply to such mass media products.

Extending this line of analysis, I also refer to the composite of these various media textbooks as the *media curriculum,* comparable to the way that school textbooks contribute to that composite known as the school curriculum. The media curriculum operates alongside the school curriculum. Both curricula teach about diversity. Moreover, the media curriculum also functions as part of a larger phenomenon that I call the "societal curriculum," those other teaching dimensions of nonschool life, including families, peers, communities, religious institutions, and voluntary organizations.

This leads me to the final term, *school educators.* Having argued that there are both media and school textbooks and curricula, as well as positing that both mass media and schools are part of the broader process called education, it would have been inconsistent for me to fall back on the traditional, restricted use of the word *educators.* That is, using educators to apply only to teachers and others who contribute directly to education as it occurs in schools. Instead I have adopted the label *school educa-*

tors, juxtaposing them with *media educators,* those mediamakers who intentionally or unintentionally teach through the creation of media text-books.

I have three goals in using these terms. First, I want to challenge the traditional, artificially limiting, and thereby distorting use of such words as *textbooks* and *educators.* Second, I need to do so in order to maintain consistency and integrity in the development of my thesis. Finally, it provides me with a concise form for conveying some of the basic ideas of the book, particularly concerning the intersection of mass media and schools as part of the broader process of education.

Caveats

Beyond those who may experience some discomfort with the foregoing terms, there are two groups who will likely be disappointed with this book. First are those who lust for nonstop media-bashing. While you will find plenty of media criticism, it will be selective. I don't view the media writ large as the nemesis of school education, parental socialization, or societal values. An inevitable force, yes. Sometimes an ally, sometimes an antagonist to schools, most of the media are not insidious, antisocial monsters, a status conferred on them by critics from myriad ideological and group positions. Rather than bash, this book strives to provide a nuanced understanding of the multicultural dimensions of the media and the relationships of the media to education about diversity in the broadest sense, in contrast to widely disseminated, sometimes hysterical depictions of the media as unrelenting stereotypers or fire-breathing destroyers of mind and morality.

Second are those who want simple solutions and fool-proof classroom exercises. While the book provides some pedagogical ideas, it will not posit a string of definitive answers or easy "how-to" strategies for innoculating young people against the potentially noxious effects of the media on self-concept, intergroup perceptions, social harmony, or societal justice. However, I promise you a serious engagement with media-related issues of multicultural teaching and learning, an engagement that should help those interested in becoming more effective in fostering intergroup understanding and social equity by integrating the book's insights into transformative efforts at school, at home, in youth groups, or within religious institutions. My hope is that nobody who reads this book will want to—or be able to—continue educating just the way they've been doing.

Thanks

But before I proceed, I want to thank a number of people who have contributed to this book. Mark Anderson and Lore Kuehnert, my research assistants, for their determination in locating arcane materials and for their provocative conversations about the media. Jim Banks, my long-time cherished friend and compatriot in the struggle for greater equity and better understanding, for his encouragement, ideas, and criticisms. My supporters at Teachers College Press: Brian Ellerbeck, my editor, for his continuous, judicious advice; Wendy Schwartz, for her perceptive suggestions for strengthening the book; Karl Nyberg, for his thorough, careful editing of the manuscript; and Peter Ross Sieger, for helping me through the production process.

But most of all I want to thank the person who made this book possible . . . my loving, caring, and supportive life partner, my wife, Laurel. Thanks for all of those years when you didn't lose patience with me because I hadn't finished the book. Thanks for those evenings when you sacrificed TV shows you really wanted to see so that I could watch ones I just "had" to see for my research. Thanks for your forbearance for all of those times when, in the dark of the movie theater, I suddenly let go of your hand and started scribbling notes in order to capture thoughts I dared not lose.

Thanks for your intelligence and insight, your honesty and tenderness, your love and companionship. Without you there would have been no book. Without you there would have been no life.

Carlos E. Cortés
Riverside, California

It Began with the Gypsies

More than two decades ago, somewhere in the mists of time called the 1970s, I gave a year-long teacher-training course for a large urban school district on something—then so new—that it was just beginning to be called *multicultural education*.

The format was simple. Once a month I visited the community, spending two days with a group of about 70 teachers and administrators. My assignment—put on a good program. Their obligation—between each two-day session, try something new and multicultural in their classrooms, critique it, and discuss the results at the next session. This led to one of my "eureka" moments, a moment that would change both my thinking and my professional life.

One fourth-grade teacher decided to present a unit on Gypsies (more accurately, Rom). Why Gypsies? For one thing, the city had a sizable, concentrated Gypsy community. Second, she taught in a suburban school, distant from the Gypsy community and, to the best of her knowledge, with no Gypsy students. Finally, as far as she could tell, her students had never studied Gypsies (par for the course in American education). Ergo, the kids should provide the proverbial blank slates onto which she could etch Gypsy knowledge and initiate the process of Gypsy-related intercultural understanding.

To do this, she planned to employ many of the pedagogical strategies that are still multicultural education stock in trade for studying "other" cultures—stories, documents, film strips, posters, photographs, maps, movies, fact-filled handouts . . . even a field trip to the Gypsy community. But, after discussing her unit with me, we also decided that she should do one more thing. Before starting the unit, to make certain that the student mental slates were, indeed, blank, and to detect if there might be some "contaminating" prior knowledge, we decided that she should first ask the students what, if anything, they knew about Gypsies.

I will spare you the grisly details. Put succinctly, she discovered that her students—her ten-year-old students—not only knew *of* Gypsies, but knew quite a bit *about* them. For starters, Gypsies were weird, moved around alot, dressed strangely, sang, danced, stole, were dirty, told fortunes, kidnapped children, and used crystal balls. This brief warm-up exercise had quickly turned into an extended explosion of student perceptions of Gypsies. Where Gypsies were concerned, the teacher's expected multicultural blank slates simply did not exist.

This discovery necessitated an immediate pedagogical transformation. The teacher no longer merely had to help students learn about Gypsies. Following the Mark Twain adage, "Education consists mainly in what we have unlearned," she also now had to help them "unlearn" much of what they already knew. But first we needed to discover a bit more about the students.

After again discussing her unit with me, she expanded her class discussion from *what* the students knew to *how* and *where* they had learned what they knew. The most common single answer was parents. They had heard their parents (as well as other adult relatives) talk about Gypsies . . . as it turned out, usually in a deprecating manner. Students gave a variety of other less frequent answers, including incidental personal contact with Gypsies (generally accompanied by parental warnings against such contact).

Yet closely following parents, students most commonly cited the media, mainly television, as the source of their Gypsy knowledge. When asked to be more specific, students responded with answers ranging from children's cartoons (replete with strange and menacing Gypsy characters) to local TV newscasts to horror movies (many students recalled with chilling detail the Gypsy camp scenes from the 1941 Lon Chaney Jr., classic, *The Wolf Man*, which played regularly along with Frankenstein and Dracula movies on Saturday afternoon TV horrorthons).

The students' references to local TV newscasts proved baffling at first. Those of you who have reared children should contemplate the local-TV-news-watching proclivities of your nine- and ten-year-olds. How often did they dart into the room demanding that you turn on the local news? Had we come across some anomaly?

No. Further discussion clarified what was occurring. Their *parents* watched local news. Kids would wander in and out of the room while their parents were watching those newscasts, would catch glimpses of what happened to be on screen at the moment (sometimes stories about Gypsies), and, most importantly, would hear and absorb their parents' reactions to the news. In other words, while some of what kids learned about Gypsies came *directly* from their TV viewing and listening, other mediated Gypsy-learning occurred *indirectly*. That is, their learning was influenced by the ways that their parents reacted to, interpreted, and framed Gypsy news.

A follow-up class project—a very basic content analysis of Gypsy coverage in local TV newscasts—turned up the unsurprising fact that the two most frequent types of Gypsy stories concerned crime and cultural events like festivals and weddings. Is it any wonder that students gave some of the responses they did to the teacher's first question—What do you know about Gypsies?

When the teacher explained her findings in my multicultural education class, it set off an outburst of educational war stories. With a mixture of enthusiasm and consternation, other teachers shared their own struggles with what I shall simply call student media-based preexistent multicultural knowledge not just about Gypsies, but also about myriad other topics involving race, ethnicity, culture, gender, religion, and other diversity-related topics. Multicultural knowledge had become part of student cognitive and affective storehouses long before the teachers had decided that it was time to address specific diversity-related topics.

As an outgrowth of that course—particularly the experience of that one teacher who merely wanted to help her students develop a better understanding of Gypsies—I became fascinated by the topic of the mass media as a source of nonschool multicultural learning. Then and there I decided to make this a research focus. Little did I realize that my foray into the multicultural dimensions of the media would soon become a lifetime search, almost an obsession.

It was a search that later would come to involve my two oldest grandchildren, Holly and Melissa.

PART I

An Introduction in Two Episodes

CHAPTER I

Holly and Melissa's Multicultural Curriculum

Growing up, Holly and Melissa got multicultural education almost every day. Some days they got lessons on intergroup relations. Other days they were exposed to ideas on gender roles. Occasionally they immersed themselves in world cultures or cultural geography. Then, in fall 1997, Holly entered kindergarten, and education "officially" began.

Holly and her little sister Melissa (11 months younger), my two oldest grandchildren, spend lots of time with "grampushe" (their name for my wife, Laurel) and "granddy." Active, energetic, and creative, they spend most of their time with us playing with toys, enjoying books, doing jigsaw puzzles, painting, drawing, writing, talking, gallavanting in the backyard, visiting their friends, or going to the nearby park. But they do have their down times, when they relax in front of the television set.

When Holly and Melissa stay with us, we restrict their TV time. Sometimes we choose the programs or videos. On other occasions they pick their own entertainment, their own media curriculum . . . with our ultimate veto.

Actually, during their preschool years, their curricular requests went something like this: "We want to see *Pocahontas* (or Shirley Temple or *Aladdin* or *The Lion King* or *The Puzzle Place* or *Scooby Doo*)." They made these requests not because they wanted multicultural education or even knew that they were involved in multicultural learning. They just felt like watching one of their shows.

But wait a minute! That's not education. That's entertainment.

Half right. It is entertainment. But it is also education, because when they watch a video—or *Mr. Rogers* or *Sesame Street* or *Barney and Friends* or the *Teletubbies* or Saturday morning cartoons—Holly and Melissa are also learning about many things, including diversity. This happens whether or not the makers of these programs have any pedagogical goals. It also happens whether or not the little girls are actually aware that they are learning.

They learn about good and evil, right and wrong, life and death, villainy and heroism. They learn about family values from *The Lion King* and physical disabilities (later special abilities) from *Dumbo*. They learn about interpersonal, intergroup, and intercultural relations from *Pocahontas* and *The Puzzle Place*. They learn about gender relations from . . . well, from just about every show they see.

How do I know? Because I listen attentively and talk to them about their reactions to that "entertainment." Oh, yes, they learn, including things that I don't expect.

My "research design" has been simple. I often sit in the den while they watch their shows or videos. Because I want to discover what they *autonomously* extract from the videos, I restrain my natural teacher's inclination to ask questions in order to guide them. I do this because the very process of questioning and thereby provoking responses, while good pedagogically, would be obtrusive. It would pollute the relative purity of the direct interaction between these two developing minds and the media, as well as interfering with the spontaneity of their media-generated multicultural dialogue. My intervention would channel them in directions that I wanted, rather than allowing them to pursue directions that they themselves charted.

From an instructional perspective, it is important for parents and teachers to pose questions about the media, clarify and provide context, and try to mitigate deleterious messages that they think young people may be receiving. Although at times I did this, particularly in response to their questions and expressed reactions, my main goal was not pedagogical, but investigatory. I wanted to try to find out what these two little girls were extracting *on their own*, what they were constructing *between themselves*, and how they were reacting *without* my interference . . . unless, of course, they asked questions or initiated the discussion.

In other words, I wanted to discover what *they* were drawing autonomously from TV (including movies on videotape) and what actions might result from such viewing. This was my one chance to observe consciously, over an extended period of time, how two young children independently responded to the media without adult interference or guidance. It was as close as I could come to "unobtrusive measurement"—or at least as unobtrusive as a huge (to them) adult can be, even if silent. And I did find that my mere silent presence did influence their viewing habits. For example, during scenes of male-female affection, they would sometimes crawl under the den table so that I couldn't see their self-conscious reactions.

Watching Holly and Melissa, particularly during their preschool days, has been a revelation to me. Not that these two little girls are universal media children. But at least they are two, which is two more than most media scholars seem to have continuously observed, recorded, and analyzed over an extended period of time. Noting their reactions has increased my skepticism of most pundit and scholarly claims of what young people are learning from the media, especially assertions emanating from those who tend to project *their* hypercritical adult perceptions of the media onto young people. That tendency for people to overestimate the impact of media messages on others is sometimes referred to as the "third-person effect" (Davison, 1983). Relatively rare are studies based on actual observation of the response of young children to the media (Davies, 1997).

The following snapshots of Holly's and Melissa's media-derived multicultural learning hardly qualify as "thick description" (Geertz, 1973). However, they will give you an idea of what Laurel and I have observed as our two girls work their way through their own personal, idiosyncratic, semiself-selected media multicultural curriculum.

Shirley Temple

Let's start with lessons in gender behavior. One day Laurel and I heard Holly sobbing in the bathroom. We rushed in, only to be met with a faceful of joyous dimples reflecting back from the full-length wall mirror.

"What's wrong, sweetheart?" asked Laurel.

"Nothing. I'm just practicing my crying, like Shirley Temple. She cries when she's in trouble, and then people help her. I can do that, too."

Simply from watching Shirley Temple movies, Holly had already drawn a lesson on gender roles and behavior (Kohlberg & Ullian, 1974). Oh, well. After all, movies are just entertainment.

The Lion King

Throughout their preschool years, *The Lion King* became their most oft-selected video. It even crept into their language.

The Lion King provides an important example of a media product as textbook. Worldwide it has enjoyed the greatest sales of any movie video (at least until *Titanic*) and has become one of the world's all-time highest-grossing movies. It has also caught its lumps from critics concerned with its multicultural dimensions (Giroux, 1996).

Some criticized it as sexist. After all, a male is the head of the pride of lions, with his wife serving a minor supportive role. Pride leadership ultimately devolves upon their son, Simba, as it had previously upon his father, Mufassa. However, before Simba can assume that role after Mufassa's death, his evil Uncle Scar drives him into exile. After years of wandering in the wilderness, Simba encounters Nala, his long-lost girl-friend and wife-to-be. Failing at first to recognize each other, they engage in a battle royal, during which Nala gives as good as she gets. In fact, by the time that they finally recognize each other, she is on top of Simba. When we took Holly and Melissa to the store, the girls chose Nala, not Simba, T-shirts . . . with no sign of Simba envy.

Some criticized *The Lion King* as racist. The main targets were the secondary villains, the three hyenas, because they spoke in a kind of street patois (one of the voices was Whoopi Goldberg, another was Cheech Marin), which some critics concluded was Black speech (although not quite Ebonics). In other words, Black equals bad. Lost in this criticism was the fact that Mufassa, the elder Lion King, spoke perfect grammar with the resonant tones of the great James Earl Jones. Need I point out that Jones is Black?

And the Gay & Lesbian Alliance Against Defamation criticized the movie as homophobic. According to this argument, if the secondary villains, the hyenas, were surrogate Blacks, then the primary villain, Mufassa's nefarious, scheming, and murderous brother, Scar, was played as implicitly gay. He had no wife or kids. Also, I might inconveniently add, he had no male domestic partner. Just three hyena pals, whose relationship to Scar did not strike me as the least bit homoerotic. Moreover, as this line of criticism goes, Scar spoke in a decidedly effeminate (codedly homosexual) fashion. Maybe I'm betraying my unconscious heterosexual bias—or maybe I just lack sufficient multicultural sensitivity—but Scar did not seem effeminate to me. Supercilious, yes, with the type of weary, slothful speech sometimes used in the media to suggest British upper-class decadence. That his voice belonged to Jeremy Irons, who has made a career playing such self-absorbed elites, further buttressed this impression.

I certainly don't want to make light of these criticisms. The fact that *The Lion King* struck different viewers in these various ways cannot be summarily dismissed. However, apparently this is not what Holly and Melissa saw . . . or at least they said nothing that indicated this is what they saw. But the movie did have an impact . . . in some respects a troubling one.

One day, while watching the movie, Holly asked me, "Why did the wildebeests want to kill Mufassa?" In the movie, the jealous Scar hatches a plot to kill his brother, Mufassa, by having his allies, the hyenas, provoke a stampede of wildebeests into a narrow gorge where Scar has abandoned Simba. Informed that his son is in danger, Mufassa races into the gorge to save him. While Mufassa succeeds, he is then trampled to death after Scar pushes him off a cliff as he is trying to climb out of the gorge.

Holly's primary concern was not Mufassa's death, but the issue of volition. *"Why* did the wildebeests *want* to kill Mufassa?" I explained that they didn't *want* to kill Mufassa, but that he just happened to be in the way when the hyenas frightened them into stampeding. "Then why did the *hyenas* want to kill Mufassa?" Even as I gave my answer—the hyenas had stampeded the wildebeests because Scar had told them to do so— I realized that, like Oedipus, Holly would relentlessly continue asking questions in an effort to resolve her personal mystery. "But why did *Scar* want to kill Mufassa, his own brother? I don't want to kill Melissa."

It was only then that I recognized the extent of the moral questions that *The Lion King* had generated in that little seeking mind. What other lessons and dilemmas had this dark and fascinating movie generated for the girls?

Quite abruptly, Holly and Melissa decided that they were no longer interested in *The Lion King*. Their growing dislike of Scar had turned into fear. The movie had suddenly become too scary. But just as abruptly, a few months later, they returned to their old favorite. And this time, as Simba sadly looked down at his dead, trampled father, the little girls were smiling. I restrained myself from asking them why, but my perplexed look revealed my wordless question. "That's okay, granddad. He's not really dead. He's coming back later. It's the Circle of Life."

In truth, Mufassa does reappear later as a vision in Simba's quest to deal with his own personal dilemmas of growing into adulthood, assuming his responsibilities as head of the pride, and coming to grips with his role in his father's death. "The Circle of Life," the movie's theme song, had provided the girls with a metaphor and the language to grapple with both the events of the movie and maybe even with the concept of death itself.

On a lighter note, one day Melissa began whimpering because I had chastised her about something. Her consoling older sister turned to her and said, comfortingly, "That's okay. Hakuna matata." A tune sung by Simba and his two pals to cheer themselves up, "Hakuna Matata" means "no worries." It worked for Melissa as well as for Simba, because she grinned broadly and stopped whimpering. The girls' superficial imitative behavior may not be as dramatic as purported media-generated copycat killings. Nonetheless, it suggests the way that media surreptitiously become a part of language and action.

But, after all, *The Lion King* is just entertainment.

Pocahontas

Pocahontas proved even more problematic than *The Lion King* for Holly and Melissa. That movie, too, has been on the receiving end of multicultural criticism (for example, see Leslie, 1996; Sardar, 1996–1997). It does not accurately depict American Indian life. (Since when did cartoons accurately depict anything?) It does not tell the *true* story of Pocahontas and John Smith. (Did anyone really expect it would?) It ultimately represents Native Americans in a demeaning manner. Now that last criticism deserves closer scrutiny, particularly if it turns out that, indeed, some young people who view it develop a negative—or more negative—view of Indians (Tilton, 1994).

Let me return to my observable research universe of Holly and Melissa. Unlike adult critics, they have not expressed any particular concern about the movie's anthropological or historical fidelity. But *Pocahontas* has, in fact, turned out to be a multicultural textbook. Even at their young age, their textual interpretation has gone through phases.

When the girls began their *Pocahontas*-watching cycle, it tested the mettle of even this committed scholarly observer. One assault of the song, "Colors of the Wind," was more than enough for my ears. Unfortunately, many more were to come.

Given the amount of (mainly negative) multicultural analysis that *Pocahontas* has received (Kilpatrick, 1995; Lepore, 1996), I was prepared—I thought—for the little girls' probable initial responses. What questions would come first? Racial identity, ethnic conflict, intergroup love affairs? Wrong.

Holly, then three, opened the dialogue with an interrogatory thunderbolt: "Granddad, can I ask you something? Why are Pocahontas' b—bs" (deletion mine—a prominent part of the young Indian lass' anatomy) "so much bigger than _____'s?" (referring comparatively to a female member of our family). "Yeah," chimed in Melissa, then two. "They're even bigger than Barbie's." It was a pop-cultural gender one-two punch.

Don't ask me where the girls acquired that language. I have no idea. Maybe they picked it up incidentally from the media or maybe from some of their neighborhood or preschool peers. There is only so much informal learning that parents or grandparents can control (Harris, 1998). This even goes for fiercely protective parents, like film critic Michael Medved and psychologist Diane Medved (1998), who have severely restricted their children's media watching and carefully screened their children's friends. Yet they were aghast when one of their daughters informed them of the names of the Spice Girls . . . which she had learned at a Girl Scout meeting!

Gender difference (as well as intragender physical variation) was the first multicultural dimension of *Pocahontas* that attracted their attention . . . or at least the first dimension that they communicated to me. The issue of skin color—particularly the difference between Pocahontas and John Smith—did not arise until several months later.

The girls have always lived in racially mixed surroundings. They have noticed—sometimes even talked about—the fact that kids they know have different skin colors. So much for color blindness. However, our family made a conscious decision not to mention *racial categories* or engage in *racial labeling* around them. Aware that sooner or later they would pick these up—in school, from their friends, or maybe from the media—we would deal with them at that point, hopefully at a serendipitous developmental moment (Trubowitz, 1969). So when the girls met *Pocahontas*, they had given no evidence that racial categories had become part of their linguistic and perceptual structure. In other words, although not *color blind*, they were *race unaware* . . . or at least to the degree that we could infer from their verbal comments.

This coincides with Robyn Holmes's (1995) conclusions in *How Young Children Perceive Race*. After extensive observations of five racially and ethnically mixed kindergarten classes, Holmes concluded that even young children classified people by physical characteristics, including gender and skin color (white, brown, and black), as well as other ethnic dimensions (Japanese and Spanish). However, not all used American *racial* categories or the adult language of *racial* labeling. She pointed out that the children in her project "placed people into different categories primarily on the basis of skin color and the native language an individual spoke" (p. 41). Yet the mere noticing of these differences did not seem to result in prejudice or interracial conflict among the young people in her study. (For other interpretations of race awareness among preschool and kindergarten children, see, for example: Aboud, 1988; Goodman, 1952; Hatcher & Troyna, 1993; Hirschfeld, 1996; Katz, 1976; Ramsey, 1987.)

Pocahontas ultimately had a more deleterious multicultural effect on Holly and Melissa. At first they merely remarked about differences between the "Indians" (sometimes "savages") and the "sailors," including but not limited to the obvious, movie-emphasized distinctions in skin color. But somewhere along the line these seemingly neutral observations (and I emphasize, "seemingly," as I was not privy to what was going on in their minds) turned into value judgments. Indians (Pocahontas and a few others excepted) began to scare them because of what they wanted to do to John Smith. Indians were becoming part of their cognitive and attitudinal structure, at which point I could not hold back from intervening.

But, of course, *Pocahontas* is just entertainment.

O.J.

One day, shortly after she had turned three, Holly wandered into the kitchen and asked me in naive, puzzled, and chilling fashion, "Granddad, what's the N word?" When I interrogated her about the source of that question, she responded that she had just heard it on television.

A quick trip to the den clarified what had happened. The local TV news was on, they were discussing the O. J. Simpson trial, and one (or more) of the newspeople must have used that irritating pseudoeuphemism, "the N word." They had not said the N word, but they had said "the N word."

This puzzled Holly. We have several alphabet books, with a page of words and pictures devoted to each letter. In learning to read and write the alphabet, Holly had absorbed many words that started with each letter, including N. But if that was so, then how could there be *the* (meaning one) N word?

I had to make a quick developmental decision. Was she ready for a full explanation? Was it the right time for cutting open the apple to get to the core of the topic? For better or for worse, I decided that it was not the appropriate "teaching moment" for trying to initiate Holly and Melissa into the complexities of derogatory group epithets. So I punted. "I'll explain it to you later, sweetheart." "Oh," she responded, "when I'm four?" (her three-year-old's translation of "later"). "Yes, when you're four," I answered, obviously not meaning it.

So much for the N word. But what lingers in my mind is a question— What else did that inquisitive little mind draw from whatever she incidentally saw about the O. J. Simpson trial? Or, for that matter, what else has she drawn, in her own way, from other chance meetings with multiculturally laden newscasts?

Romance

Pocahontas, take two. As the girls' combination of fear and antipathy toward Indians receded, they readmitted that video into their multicultural curriculum. But the movie had taken on a new, more personal meaning.

One evening, without warning, Holly asked Laurel and me to leave the room. She didn't want us in the room during *that* part of the movie— the scene where Pocahontas and John Smith first express affection toward each other.

I don't want to get into cause-and-effect speculation. However, let me just say that Holly's desire for privacy with this video relationship— this intergroup relationship or, maybe in Holly's eyes, this inter-skin-color relationship—came at precisely the same time of her announcement of another relationship. Her two preschool boyfriends (twin brothers) had simultaneously asked her to marry them when they grew up. (Later she informed us that she *had* married them . . . both.) Had Pocahontas influenced Holly's reaction to their "proposal" or had their "proposal" influenced the way she viewed the Pocahontas-John Smith movie relationship?

Oh, let's not get carried away. After all, *Pocahontas* is just entertainment.

On the other hand, by the time she turned five, Holly had developed a fascination with the idea of romance, as well as with female traumas. Along with many of her kindergarten classmates, she was affected by the television coverage of Princess Diana's death. In fact, one day shortly thereafter, she announced that she wanted to be a princess when she grew up. The girls became enchanted with *Sleeping Beauty,* and, after they watched *The Karen Carpenter Story* with their mother, they felt the need to talk to us about her fatal eating problems. They loved Whitney Houston's 1997 multiracial television remake of Rodgers and Hammerstein's musical, *Cinderella,* although Holly opined that the prince seemed a bit silly running around the countryside trying to jam the lost slipper on women who looked nothing like Brandy (who played Cinderella). I'm not sure what role skin color played in that observation, as neither Holly nor Melissa mentioned it.

But possibly the most surprising (to us) media event was the evening that Holly wandered into the den just after Laurel had begun watching the 1997 British TV remake of *Jane Eyre.* Before Laurel realized it, Holly had become mesmerized . . . and watched the whole thing. Her fascination with mediated dimensions of male-female relations revealed the powerful role that this multicultural curriculum was already playing in her personal development. The next day Laurel overheard Holly relating the plot to Melissa with great drama and considerable nuance.

The Learners

But enough description. Let's cast this discussion in a broader light. Holly and Melissa are just ordinary little girls. Well, not so ordinary. After all, they are *my* grandchildren. But they are like other little girls and boys in that they are constantly learning—not just when, where, and what we adults want them to learn, certainly not just when, where, and what teachers, administrators, school boards, textbook publishers, or state curriculum adopters want them to learn.

And, like Holly and Melissa, much of what children learn outside of school, including through the media, will be multicultural—whether or not we want it, whether or not we notice it, whether or not we admit it.

CHAPTER 2

The Societal Curriculum

Gypsies. Holly and Melissa.

As these two examples illustrate, education—like lots of other stuff—happens. It happens even when we don't expect it, even where we don't want it, or even if we don't realize it.

Discussions of education usually, and erroneously, use schools and education as synonymous concepts. They aren't. Certainly schools contribute powerfully to education, but they don't monopolize that process, nor could they even if they wished (Postman, 1982). Students learn both in schools and outside of them, including learning about diversity. Among the schools' chief multicultural educational compatriots—collaborators, challengers, reinforcers, and competitors—are the mass media. As a result of the mass media, multicultural education occurs even though some school educators may finesse the topic of human diversity, while others consciously avoid certain aspects of it (Berry, 1980; Leifer, Gordon, & Graves, 1974; Leiss, Kline, & Jhally, 1986; Spring, 1992). Lilia Bartolomé and Donaldo Macedo (1997) went so far as to argue that:

> Academia needs to understand that the popular press and the mass media educate more people about issues regarding ethnicity and race than all other sources of education available to U.S. citizens. By shunning the mass media, educators are missing the obvious: that is, that more public education is done by the media than by teachers, professors, and anyone else. (p. 223)

The Societal Curriculum

While giving the multicultural education course that I discussed in the Prologue, particularly as a result of our rich, extended discussions about the mass media and other nonschool multicultural learning, three words obtruded in my head—"the societal curriculum." From that nonschool curriculum, students learn about myriad topics, including diversity. This occurs regardless of the desires or concerns, hopes or fears of teachers, administrators, and school boards, sometimes irrespective of the intentions or awareness of the developers and disseminators of that nonschool curriculum (Phinney & Rotheram, 1987).

I tried out my "societal curriculum" idea on the class. Bingo! Not only did it lead to the best and most intense discussions of the entire course, but it inspired me to write a small exploratory article, "The Societal Curriculum and the School Curriculum: Allies or Antagonists?," which appeared in the April 1979 *Educational Leadership* (Cortés, 1979). Of the more than 100 articles I have written throughout my academic career, few have provoked more response than this brief, exploratory, five-page think-piece. Letters and phone calls poured in (fortunately this occurred before the E-mail era, or I might never have logged off).

It was not that I had said anything profound. People, including students, learn outside of school. Big deal! No, it was the packaging—"the societal curriculum"—that seemed to reverberate, because it framed the obvious as a dual curricular construct, with nonschool and school teaching as parallel, interacting, and sometimes competing forces. It also provided a conceptual tool for examining the relationship between these two curricula, which proved particularly useful when considering the topic of diversity.

I later defined the societal curriculum as "that massive, ongoing, informal curriculum of families, peer groups, neighborhoods, churches, organizations, institutions, mass media, and other socializing forces that educate all of us throughout our lives" (Cortés, 1981, p. 24). I also subdivided it into four intersecting, interacting categories:

(1) *the immediate curriculum*—home, family, peers, and neighborhood;
(2) *the institutional curriculum*—those organizations and institutions with whom people interact and from which they learn, like youth groups, religious institutions, and voluntary associations;
(3) *the serendipitous curriculum*—random personal experiences, such as chance interactions with strangers or visits to foreign countries;
(4) *the media curriculum*—the mass media, in its myriad forms.

Through their interactions with the mass media, as well as through other dimensions of the societal curriculum, young people learn language, acquire culture, obtain cross-cultural knowledge (leave aside the question of accuracy), develop beliefs, hone perceptions, internalize attitudes, and observe patterns of behavior (Cortés, 1992). They learn about groups to which they and others belong. They learn about variations within as well as between groups.

They learn about physical appearance, gender differences and relations, meanings of race, experiences of different ethnic groups, the existence of different religions and belief systems, myriad variations of cultural practices, intergroup conflict and cooperation, and the multitude of languages spoken within the United States and around the world. They learn about their nation, other countries, and various regions of the world.

In short, through the societal curriculum, all students receive a multicultural education, whether or not schools actively or consciously participate in that process. As a major dimension of nonschool teaching, the media curriculum on diversity is omnipresent. The only way to avoid it is to avoid the media . . . all of them.

Mass Media and Schools

Analogies are treacherous and always imperfect. As Heracleitus pointed out, "Upon those who step into the same rivers different and ever different waters flow down"—sometimes colloquialized into "You can't step into the same river twice." Yet let me suggest a few rough parallels between the mass media and the school curriculum.

Taken individually, specific elements of the mass media—for example, a movie, magazine, rap song, talk radio segment, or TV show—function like school textbooks . . . or at least like textbook sections, supplementary reading, or other types of educational materials. Taken as a whole, the mass media function like a school curriculum. Yet, like much of the school curriculum, the media curriculum is chaotic, inconsistent, multivocal, in many respects unplanned and uncoordinated, laden with conflicting messages, and offering myriad perspectives. This does not mean, however, that all perspectives enjoy equal exposure or equitable access to dissemination.

Both mass media and school curricula—including their myriad text materials—rely on teams for creation and dissemination. Media textbooks and curricula involve writers, editors, directors, producers, reporters, anchorpersons, columnists, talk show hosts, actors, photographers and, of course, owners—from movie studio heads to newspaper chain magnates, who involve themselves to varying degrees in media curriculum design. In April 1999, for the first time, a majority of the Pulitzer Prizes in journalism went to collectives (staffs and editorial boards), not to individual reporters (Meyer, 1999).

School materials result from the efforts of writers, editors, designers, artists, copyreaders, and publishers. Moreover, school curricula are developed, mandated, implemented, and modified in various ways by teachers, curriculum specialists, education goal-setters, accountability assessors, education code writers, administrators, and school boards.

Both kinds of textbooks and curricula—mass media and school—are developed for markets and provide something for consumers. Media try to deliver information, entertainment, and occasionally art; textbooks and school curricula try to deliver education (information, ideas, skills, and values). Yet both kinds of textbooks and curricula often deliver far more and far different things than their creators may intend, than their disseminators may realize, or than their ultimate recipients—audiences and students—may recognize (Grossberg, Wartella, & Whitney, 1998).

Education scholars have addressed the surreptitious, sometimes unintended, and often unanticipated dimensions and consequences of textbooks, curricula, and other aspects of the schooling process. In doing so they have applied such labels as "the hidden curriculum." That curriculum, however, is not always hidden, although it may not be fully recognized. Rather, the metaphor suggests a schooling process—particularly ideas and values that are taught, if not always learned—that is neither explicitly prescribed by educational decision makers nor always consciously implemented by textbook writers, curriculum developers, teachers, or administrators.

The mass media curriculum, too, contains comparably "hidden" dimensions. Also, like schools, because of the myriad participants in the creation and dissemination of media textbooks, that curriculum contains multifaceted, argumentative elements that send mixed and sometimes conflicting messages. At times the media strive for truth, accuracy, and balance, while at other times they consciously distort for purposes of sensationalism, commercialism, and ideological message transmission.

Moreover, that so-called hidden curriculum is often so "unhidden," so highly visible, sometimes so blatant that the media receive a continuous public battering for their supposed or at least their potential learning impact. In their article, "Television and Socialization of Young Children," Aletha Huston and John Wright (1996) pointed out, "Public figures, the popular press, and many individuals believe that television is the root of almost every social evil from declining test scores to the loss of 'family values'" (p. 37).

Yet despite the constant barrage of public criticism of the media curriculum—criticism often originating within or disseminated by the media themselves—much of media teaching remains hidden in one sense. Its more subtle messages generally go unnoticed, even when learned and sometimes acted upon. Moreover, the mass media function as a teaching force whether or not individuals involved in the process of creation or dissemination realize that they are writing such textbooks or participating as teachers, including about the subject of diversity. As Gordon Berry (1980) wrote:

> It is important to suggest that, while one of the major missions of commercial television is to entertain, the effect of that entertainment is to provide social learning messages that reach children just as those associated with the planned curriculum of an educational institution do. The only differences are that commercial programs are not intended to instruct and are essentially unplanned in terms of the learning experiences they provide. (p. 78)

From Teaching to Learning

But what about the other side of the educational equation, learning as contrasted to teaching? Media-based multicultural learning may occur whether or not learners approach the media as a source of knowledge and information and whether or not they are aware of that learning (Small, 1992). To further complicate matters, it is doubtful that any media learners are so relentlessly metacognitive that they *always* recognize how previous multicultural experiences—including mass media exposure to diversity—may be influencing the meanings they consciously or unconsciously construct from their ongoing interactions with the media (Cortés, 1995).

A note of caution. The mass media curriculum is far too complex for simplistic divisions of most media multicultural textbooks into dualistic good-bad or positive-negative categories. Media may foster or erode group pride, while reinforcing or weakening intragroup connections through the repetition of themes, messages, and images (Allen & Hatchett, 1986). They sometimes contribute to intergroup understanding through insightful, nuanced examinations of diverse experiences, cultures, issues, and problems, but at other times exacerbate intergroup misunderstanding through the repeated presentation of derogatory stereotypes, inflammatory hyperbole, and an overemphasis on demeaning (often violent) themes about selected groups or nations (Keen, 1986; MacDonald, 1992; Shaheen, 1984). By influencing public norms, perceptions, expectations, hopes, fears, desires, and angsts about diversity, the mass media play a powerful role in the social construction of knowledge about race, ethnicity, religion, gender, culture, sexual orientation, and other aspects of diversity.

Entertainment Media as Education

Multicultural education permeates all aspects of the mass media. From a teaching-learning perspective, this reality devalues efforts to arbitrarily separate, dichotomize, categorize, segregate, or sequester individual media textbooks as either information or entertainment, fact or fiction, reality or make-believe. Certainly audiences learn from programs and publications intended to provide news, information, analysis, and fact. But they also learn from media presumably made primarily to entertain (as well as to make money).

Moreover, mediamakers have blurred that supposed—probably always illusory—dividing line between information and entertainment. As a result, audiences have difficulty distinguishing between these admittedly dubious traditional categories. For example, a 1989 survey revealed that 50% of U.S. television viewers considered the hybrid show *America's Most Wanted* to be a news program, while 28% considered it entertainment (Rosenstiel, 1989).

While some mediamakers publicly adopt the sometimes cynical posture that they merely offer entertainment, in fact they simultaneously teach, whether intentionally or incidentally (Rosenstone, 1995). Reverse the equation again. Whatever the stated or unstated goals of the makers, audiences learn from and construct knowledge based on both fictional and nonfictional media sources, although in the case of fictional media they are less likely to realize that such media-based learning is occurring. This has special application to children, who are even more likely to blur those sources (Nikken & Peeters, 1988).

This is hardly a contemporary idea. After all, Plato recognized the power of fictional narrative when he asserted, "Those who tell the stories also rule the society." In his *Republic,* he expressed particular concern with the impact of stories on children: "Then shall we so easily let the children hear just any tales fashioned by just anyone and take into their souls opinions for the most part opposite to those we'll suppose they must have when they are grown up?" (1968, pp. 54–55).

Fast forward. In a more recent, media-based formulation of Plato's argument, Ariel Dorfman argued in *The Empire's Old Clothes: What the Lone Ranger, Babar, and Other Innocent Heroes Do to Our Minds* (1983):

> Industrially produced fiction has become one of the primary shapers of our emotions and our intellect in the 20th Century. Although these stories are supposed to merely entertain us, they constantly give us a secret education. We are not only taught certain styles of violence, the latest fashions, and sex roles by TV, movies, magazines, and comic strips; we are also taught how to

succeed, how to love, how to buy, how to conquer, how to forget the past and suppress the future. We are taught, more than anything else, how not to rebel. (p. ix)

A Global Issue

The *degree* to which media actually *inculcate* multicultural knowledge, perceptions, and stereotypes can be debated. Beyond debate, however, is the fact that they *contribute* to the construction of beliefs and attitudes about diversity. This is not merely an American but a global concern. In June 1998, when cultural representatives of 18 African, European, and Latin American nations met with Canadian officials in Ottawa to develop a plan for muting Hollywood's influence, one issue addressed was how to stop the media from inflaming interethnic antagonisms.

Governments fear and government opponents look hopefully to the entertainment media. Richard Attenborough's 1987 antiapartheid film, *Cry Freedom*, celebrated the friendship between South African Black Consciousness Movement leader Steve Biko and liberal White South African newspaper editor Donald Woods. On July 29, 1988, the day that the movie opened in 30 packed South African theaters, government officials confiscated it, fearing its teaching power about national racial conditions. More recently, the 1997 feature film *Seven Years at Tibet*, which dealt with the young Dalai Lama, drew a vigorous if somewhat hyperbolic pedagogical response. Referring to the movie's star, one Tibetan refugee enthused, "With what Brad Pitt has done for the Tibetan cause, we are very happy. Sometimes one man does make a difference" (Higgins, 1997, sec. E, p. 2).

Concerns about the teaching power of the media, particularly the entertainment media, erupt constantly in the United States. Feminist concerns that Fox's hit series, *Ally McBeal*, might be undermining the image of professional women. Greek American concerns that the possible appearance of superstar Antonio Banderas as the lead in the proposed film biography of the hated General Mustafa Kemal Ataturk, considered the founder of modern Turkey, might glorify him. Arab American concerns that the 1998 film, *The Siege*, might heighten antagonisms against them. African American concerns that the (short-lived) TV "comedy" series, *The Secret Diary of Desmond Pfeiffer*, made light of slavery. The National Coalition for the Protection of Children and Families's concerns that Adrian Lyne's 1998 film version of *Lolita* might create sympathy for pedophiles. The Christian Action Network's concerns over the growing number of movie and television gay teenagers, reflected in its call for network TV to add a "homosexual content" designation to its program rating system.

And on and on and on. From across often-conflicting ideological camps and interest groups, concerned media inspectors agree on two basic points. Media teach and media consumers learn.

Yet the challenge comes in attempting to identify precisely what the media have taught and assessing what different individuals, groups, or nations have actually learned. In his book, *Images of American Life: A History of Ideological Management in Schools, Movies, Radio, and Television,* Joel Spring (1992) argued, "Of course, we have no way of knowing the actual influence of schools, movies, radio, and television on the average American. But we can speculate on what people may have learned" (p. 1). While research and analysis do permit us to do more than speculate, Spring did correctly point out the need for restraint in making assertions about media-based learning.

But there is one final complicating and mitigating factor that must be considered when assessing the media curriculum. As teachers, the media do not operate independently from the other, nonmedia components of the societal curriculum. In particular, those other components play two fundamental media-related roles—as gatekeepers and as spin doctors. Most salient for school educators are the ways that parents, along with other family members and peers (Harris, 1998), function in these two roles.

Parents as Media Gatekeepers

In mass media scholarship, gatekeepers are traditionally considered to be decision makers who influence what ultimately becomes media content. These could be reporters who choose which elements to include in a story, editors who select among competing stories submitted for publication, radio talk show hosts who decide when to continue with or cut off a caller, or those who contribute to content decisions of a TV newscast.

Other components of the societal curriculum may also play—or try to play—a media gatekeeping role. Religious institutions or affiliated organizations sometimes attempt to influence the media habits of their followers. Among the most concerted efforts was the Legion of Decency, the Catholic organization that for decades rated movies, indicating those that Catholics should not see because of objectionable content (Black, 1994, 1998). At various times, local, state, or federal government censorship has impeded dissemination of media textbooks, particularly motion pictures.

Parents, other family members, and peers also serve as gatekeepers. Of particular importance for young children are parents, who may help select what media they see, listen to, or read (Desmond, Singer, Singer,

Calam, & Colimore, 1985). (I'm not discounting the powerful pressures of five-year-olds chanting, "We want to watch the *Teletubbies*" . . . or fill in the blanks with your own oft-heard chants.) Parents also select the magazines and newspapers that enter the house, which thereby become readily accessible for their children. (Long before she could read, Melissa became a devotee of *National Geographic,* constantly asking me to explain photos that fascinated her.)

In reviewing the extant scholarship on television and children, Huston and Wright (1996) drew some revealing conclusions. First, when parents and children watch television together, they usually view shows that reflect parental priorities, not the priorities of children. As a result, children often end up viewing programs that parents want to watch, not those that children would choose if they were alone. (Holly didn't choose *Jane Eyre*. She just wandered into the den and became mesmerized.)

Siblings, too, influence each other's viewing habits. Yet their influence appears to operate in contrarian directions. Older siblings influence younger ones, causing them to "graduate" more quickly from so-called children's programming. But the process also works in reverse. Younger children affect their older siblings' viewing habits, drawing the latter into watching shows oriented toward a younger audience.

Such intrafamilial gatekeeping inevitably influences media multicultural teaching and learning. Parents are likely to select television programs (as well as turn on radio shows and subscribe to magazines and newspapers) that meet their interests, reflect their values, strike responsive attitudinal chords, or at least connect in some ways with their predispositions, concerns, or visions of the world around them. This includes their beliefs, attitudes, and values about diversity. For example, parents will probably choose newscasts, commentators, or talk shows that provide preferred patterns of news selection, deliver news the way they like to have it framed, and offer interpretations that concur with their beliefs, including the framing and interpretation of diversity-related topics.

Parents as Spin Doctors

But parents not only influence *what* media their children consume. They also influence *how* children process, interpret, and internalize the media they are consuming. In doing so, parents participate alongside other societal curriculum individuals and organizations as both gatekeepers and media "spin doctors."

Media spin doctors are those professionals who specialize in telling audiences (including other mediamakers) what they ought to think about what they themselves have just seen, heard, or read. Think of political candidate handlers, television commentators, radio talk show hosts, and journalistic pundits who enter the fray immediately following presidential debates. You may have watched these debates yourselves, but spin doctors try to emphasize what they want you to recall and to create frames that they want you to use when interpreting the just-viewed proceedings.

In doing so, media spin doctors illustrate a process that Paul Lazarsfeld described a half-century ago in his two-step flow model of media communication and reception (Lazarsfeld, Berelson, & Gaudet, 1944). According to that formulation, much of media learning comes not *directly* from audience contact with the media, but *indirectly* through the interpretive intercession of other parties, particularly respected opinion leaders.

Increasingly, these interceding influentials are themselves part of the media, using their media-based positions of power to interpret *other* media that you may or may not have read, heard, or seen. Take, for example, reviewers or critics who tell you what to think and feel about a particular TV show or movie that you have not yet seen and may never see . . . including those dealing with diversity. Isn't that one of the ways that you decide whether or not you want to watch? Or talk show hosts who interpret newspaper stories, magazine articles, or published opinion pieces— for example, about some race relations incident—that most of their listeners have not read. Or newspaper columnists who react to, synthesize, or interpret televised governmental events—for example, congressional hearings on affirmative action, immigration, or sexual harassment.

Parents, siblings, and peers also serve as spin doctors, albeit of a less formal variety. They may teach directly, sharing their opinions about a piece of media or a media-related story that the children have just seen, heard, or read . . . validating or contradicting it, reinforcing or challenging it, explaining or elaborating on it, framing or reframing it. Parents and other family members may also discuss media-spread "stuff" to which their children have not yet been exposed, consciously seeking to interpret those unconsumed media products and messages. Other times they may talk about that stuff not *to* their children, yet within their earshot. (Some developmental psychologists opine that as much as 90% of young children's learning may be "incidental" as a result of overheard conversations.) Still other times they may respond to their children's questions or comments about a piece of media.

Siblings and peers also play that role. How often we have heard our little mutual spin doctors, Holly and Melissa, talking intensely about multicultural dimensions of television programs and videos: intergroup conflict in *Pocahontas;* cultural aspects of *Aladdin;* or gender relations in *The Lion King* and *Cinderella.*

In their research survey, Huston and Wright (1996) found that when adults inject their interpretations while watching programs along with young people, the latter tend to learn *more* from the programs. Through an empirical study of 30 first-grade students in Urbana, Illinois, James Walling (1976) determined that parental interaction fostered "incidental learning" from television about such things as social roles. Moreover, he concluded that such children "were more likely to employ the 'incidentally learned' material in daily life problem solving situations than did children who *did not* interact with parents or children who did not watch TV at all" (p. 22). It takes no great leap of faith to recognize how this adult interpretation affects the child learning process as part of nonschool multicultural education.

As they comment on television shows with diversity-related content, parents are likely to express—maybe even try to inculcate their children with—their own values and interpretations. Such interpretations will often go beyond the specific content of these programs to include commentary about broader aspects of societal diversity. This commentary may include parental attitudes and beliefs, hopes and fears, and praise and condemnation, as well as their stereotypes about specific groupings of people . . . racial, ethnic, gender, religious, or sexual orientation groupings, for example.

Consider the possibilities: a chance comment about a television show that addresses gender relations; a spontaneous reaction to a news story about sexual orientation; a response to a documentary about religion, particularly about a religion different from those of the parents; an unthinking (or intentional) use of racial or ethnic epithets while watching a situation comedy. All of these are examples of parental coparticipation in the process of media multicultural education.

In short, even if they fail to realize it, parents, as well as peers and other family members, play a role in the media-based multicultural knowledge construction process of K–12 students. By serving as gatekeepers through the selection (and efforts at prohibition) of media material and as spin doctors through the interpretation of and commentary upon media content, such family and peer group opinion leaders influence (not necessarily determine) how young people receive, react to, process, and internalize media multicultural messages and construct multicultural knowledge.

Conclusion

The mass media curriculum exists, and young people will learn from it (Minow, 1995). Because of the omnipresence of the societal curriculum, school educators simply cannot control multicultural education. Like lots of things, it will happen, whether or not schools participate.

Therefore, school educators confront an unavoidable choice. Will they participate effectively and constructively in the inevitable process of multicultural education? Or will they opt out, leaving multicultural education to the whims of mass media curriculum developers and other components of the societal curriculum?

PART II

The Mass Media as Multicultural Curriculum

CHAPTER 3

Mediamakers as Multicultural Curriculum Developers

Let's be clear about Chapters 3 and 4. They concern teaching, not learning. This chapter addresses media creation—mediamakers as intentional or unintentional multicultural teachers, textbook writers, and curriculum developers. Chapter 4 examines content—the disseminated mass media as a multicultural curriculum—by looking at media products as intended or unintended multicultural textbooks. We'll get around to learning in Chapter 5.

I reemphasize the division between teaching and learning because so many professional and amateur media analysts—scholars, journalists, commentators, school educators, group spokespeople, and certainly lots of politicians—talk about the media as if what *they* see, interpret, and conclude about media content must be what everyone else is seeing, interpreting, concluding, and therefore learning from it . . . the third-person effect. (Holly and Melissa provide me with constant reality checks against that fallacy!)

Certainly the mass media have teaching power, or else I wouldn't be writing this book. But beware of making unwarranted assumptions that your (or my) individual, idiosyncratic, culturally influenced perceptions of a particular media product (or media in general) must be mirrored by others. This can become particularly ludicrous when it involves adults asserting dogmatically and arrogantly what young people must be learning from the media. Each individual's perceptions will likely be shared by some others . . . but who knows how many?

Media teaching (in fact, all teaching) has two dimensions—input and output. First input, which we can consider through some inevitably imperfect but nonetheless suggestive media-school analogies.

Publishers and school boards, media producers and educational bureaucrats all organize, work with finances, and make broad decisions about content and "delivery systems." Media directors and school superintendents, media editors and school principals attempt to coordinate and orchestrate their respective systems. Operating within industry, governmental, pressure group, and other types of constraints, screenwriters and textbook writers, journalists and curriculum developers create texts to be delivered. Newscasters and teachers, actors and professors—all are involved in the actual delivery (or, if some educators prefer, the exploration or facilitation) of content (Spring, 1992).

Then there is the output dimension . . . the content itself. Once envisioned, once created, once produced, once recorded, once printed, once passed through final editing—or final cut—content exists. Whether popular magazines or textbooks, feature films or CD-ROM educational materials, TV sitcoms or duplicated classroom handouts, "squawk radio" complaint sessions or textbook-promoted class discussions, advertising-laden network newscasts disseminated to temporary (we hope) couch potatoes or advertising-laden Channel One classroom newscasts disseminated to desk potatoes, content quickly takes on a life of its own. In terms of dissemination, usage, manner of reception, or learning impact, content may operate independently from—even contrary to—the goals or visions of its creators.

Content can be observed, scrutinized, celebrated, criticized, processed, accepted, or rejected. It may be ignored, learned from (although learners may extract quite different messages from the same mass media or school text), and partially forgotten or recalled (often transformed in the process). Individual learning may stray far from—in fact, may conflict with and confound—the intentions of content creators.

Content Creators: The Media Writ Large

There is a long scholarly and popular tradition of analyzing what goes into creating mass media products. From single sheet newspapers to "gangsta rap" CDs, from general interest magazines to TV sitcoms, from silent movies to seldom-silent radio talk show hosts, the mass media have drawn attention from analysts interested in the process of creating and disseminating media (Postman, 1985).

Here, however, we are concerned with the creation and dissemination of media multicultural content. How have mediamakers addressed the topic of diversity in its many dimensions? How and why have they generated different kinds of multicultural images and messages? When it comes to the dissemination of multicultural content and ideas, media creators vary (Fisher & Lowenstein, 1967; Rubin, 1980; Wilson & Gutiérrez, 1995).

Some mediamakers intentionally try to teach about race, ethnicity, and other aspects of diversity—for example, through movies like *Schindler's List*, *Guess Who's Coming to Dinner*, and *Lone Star*, or TV docudramas such as the 1997 *Buffalo Soldiers*. Others teach incidentally, such as by publishing news stories that happen to have multicultural dimensions or by including ethnic characters in movie or television narratives without any particular goal of ethnic image-making or message-sending. Yet whatever the mediamakers' intentions, their media may teach simply because these products become available as texts from which people can learn (Diawara, 1992). In considering mediamakers, we can look at the media at large, a particular media industry, or individual components of the media.

Some scholars have argued that media content creation should be addressed in structural terms of the media at large, including the societal context in which the media operate (Gandy, 1998; Gitlin, 1979). According to this line of analysis, that larger societal context may have far greater impact on content creation than the conscious goals or attitudes of individual creators. As Stuart Hall (1981) wrote:

> If the media function in a systematically racist manner, it is not because they are run and organized exclusively by active racists; this is a category mistake. This would be equivalent to saying that you could change the character of the capitalist state by replacing its personnel. Whereas the media, like the state, have a structure, a set of practices which are not reducible to the individuals who staff them. What defines how the media function is the result of a set of complex, often contradictory, social relations; not the personal inclinations of its members. (p. 46)

When it comes to diversity, media creators vary in the specifics of their depictions, images, or narratives. However, this difference of perspective seldom breaks the ideological boundaries erected by reigning folk wisdom or generalized societal beliefs about diversity.

Take, for example, the case of World War II. That war provided a dramatic demonstration of how the media at large sometimes adopt a relatively lockstep approach to the treatment of a critical public issue, including its multicultural dimensions, even while providing variations in the specificity of their messages. When called upon by the federal government to support World War II mobilization, the American media consciously created a pro-war multicultural curriculum.

Recorded music, broadcast on the radio (commercial TV did not arrive until after the war), ridiculed and dehumanized the enemy, particularly the Japanese. Newspapers and radio programs made Rosie the Riveter the symbol of the government's appeal for women to take their place on the assembly line in support of the war effort. Hollywood cranked out movie after movie featuring multiethnic military units, each containing at least one Grabowski, one Ginsberg, one González, and one Graziano . . . a message that Americans of all backgrounds have fought for their country in the past and should be happy to do so now (Koppes & Black, 1987). Even Charlie Chan movies became textbooks on multicultural patriotism by emphasizing that the redoubtable Chinese American detective was vigorously "not Japanese" (Chin, 1973).

With government encouragement, operating in a societal context of virtually universal public support of the war effort, most American mediamakers—regardless of varying beliefs about such diversity-related matters as legal segregation, gays in the military, and the societal role of women—came up with a set of common messages based on and (temporarily) bounded by a reigning national ideology. They produced, in short, a transitory wartime media multicultural core curriculum. In contrast, paralleling deep public divisions, such a consensus failed to emerge among the media during the war in Vietnam.

Yet ideologies change, sometimes rapidly. The wartime media may have appealed to Rosie the Riveter to take her place on the assembly line, but they generally made a rapid postwar about-face, calling on Rosie to return home, raise her family, and leave jobs to their rightful possessors, men. With such renewed hegemonic societal ideologies in place, media messages even reverted with consistency. While media manipulation by a core of conspirators can exist, centralized plots are unnecessary when societal ideologies reign supreme—what has been labeled "soft hegemony" (Liebes, 1997).

Content Creators: Media Industries

One can also focus on specific media industries, as do some analysts and career (or recreational) complainers. Some critics of the media, including politicians and special-interest pressure groups, have proclaimed that specific media industries have consciously set out to influence multicultural thinking. Yet, while they have discovered a few spent shells lying about, neither critics nor scholars have convincingly revealed many mediawide or even single industrywide smoking guns of mediamaker multicultural educational intentions.

Industrywide content codes serve as revealing sources of evidence. Yet even here it is difficult to separate the degree to which these codes reflect true industry beliefs from the degree to which they reflect defensive responses to external political or economic pressures . . . or fears of pressures. In this respect, such codes can be likened to textbook guidelines or curriculum frameworks adopted by educational agencies, often under pressure from different publics or interest groups.

Media codes tend to be internally produced (although government entities sometimes come up with their own do's and don'ts). In contrast, school textbook and curricular guidelines tend to emerge from different levels of government or from private schools, although occasionally publishers develop internal guidelines, such as rules for what labels should be used for specific groups—Latino or Hispanic, American Indian or Native American.

Exemplary was the Motion Picture Production Code, created within the Motion Picture Producers and Distributors of America. Written by a Jesuit priest appointed by a Presbyterian elder (Will Hays, MPPDA President) for use by (predominantly) Jewish studio heads to make movies for heavily Protestant audiences, the so-called Hays Code was grudgingly adopted in 1934 by the film industry as its movie textbook content guidelines. That action came in response to pressure from religious groups (mainly Catholic), as well as fears of federal government censorship and antimonopoly actions. Hollywood filmmakers had to follow its do's and don'ts in order to earn the Production Code Administration's official Seal of Approval for commercial exhibition.

Some of the Hays Code's provisions applied directly to diversity or had serious multicultural implications, particularly in the treatment of gender relations. However, with one major exception—its injunction that "Miscegenation (sex relationship between the white and black races) is forbidden"—even this critical document does not provide evidence of any industrywide concern about the treatment of ethnic and racial diversity.

For example, Section V of the Code stated that "the Production Code Administration may take cognizance of the fact that the following words and phrases are obviously offensive to the patrons of motion pictures in the United States and *more particularly* [emphasis mine] to the patrons of motion pictures in foreign countries: Chink, Dago, Frog, Greaser, Hunkie, Kike, Nigger, Spig, Wop, Yid" (Stanley & Steinberg, 1976, p. 83). The code's emphasis on the concerns of patrons in foreign countries suggests that the commercial issue of overseas ticket sales provided a stronger imperative than did the moral issues of ethnic sensitivities or the potential impact of movies on intergroup relations.

Yet even within the movie industry there were variations. For example, in its early years, Warner Brothers movie studio took a special interest in making social problem films, which often dealt with discrimination, racial inequality, and antiethnic bigotry. In contrast, certain studios avoided such controversial issues as box-office poison.

Content Creators: Individual Mediamakers

Finally, one can move from mediawide or industrywide analyses and examine more limited media collaborations around specific themes, concerns, issues, or products. Some individual newspapers, magazines, stations, and even movie studios, as well as editors, writers, producers, and directors, have acted upon their own multicultural beliefs, sometimes in ideological lockstep with others.

At one time, Jewish movie studio heads took steps to reduce the screen visibility of Jewish Americans. Intent on emphasizing assimilation and reducing the significance of their ethnic distinctiveness, these moguls muted the Jewish presence within the movie curriculum, particularly during the rise of European anti-Semitism in the 1930s (Gabler, 1988). Even when an iconic Jewish figure did reach the screen, as in the sound-breaking 1927 film *The Jazz Singer,* the story focused on his movement *away from* the ghetto and into the American mainstream (Rogin, 1996).

In contrast, particularly since the late 1960s, many filmmakers have emphasized the movie exploration of their own ethnic groups. Creators like Spike Lee, Edward James Olmos, Wayne Wang, Paul Mazursky, Woody Allen, and Martin Scorsese have made such films central to their careers. For them, the screen has provided an opportunity to ruminate publicly and, incidentally, instruct other Americans about their ethnic heritages (hooks, 1996; Lourdeaux, 1990; Noriega, 1992).

Alternative independent film movements, not just individual filmmakers, have occasionally arisen around selected multicultural themes and issues, such as Black "race movies" (Cripps, 1978) and Yiddish films of the 1920s and 1930s. Jewish American moviemakers in the Yiddish film movement provided a sharp contrast with major studio heads. According to most scholars of the Yiddish film movement, its leaders ideologically opposed the assimilationist values espoused by Hollywood's Jewish moguls. Instead they created a competing multicultural curriculum (better yet, a single-group ethnic studies curriculum) that consciously emphasized the celebration and maintenance of Jewish culture (Goldberg, 1983; Goldman, 1983; Hoberman, 1991). (For a contrarian view that asserts an assimilationist bent for Yiddish filmmakers, see Cohen, 1998.)

Similar variations have occurred in other sectors of the media. The mainstream press has long been paralleled by a multifaceted ethnic and religious press (Hoover, 1998; Miller, 1987). Thomas Leonard (1998) compared the treatment of the 1898 Cuban-Spanish-American War in the mainstream press and the Black press, then numbering about 150 weeklies. While the mainstream press said little about racial tensions within the American military, this theme appeared regularly in the Black press, often in the form of letters from Black servicemen.

Today major network television must increasingly vie with cable narrowcasting, some of it targeted toward specific audiences, such as Christians, Blacks, and Spanish-speaking Latinos, while the Ethnic-American Broadcasting Company offers programming in a variety of languages, including Arabic, Tagalog, and Greek. In recorded music, the generalized all-American hit parade has given way to a multicultural musical spectrum, often ethnic or religious. In some communities, non-English-speaking radio stations have captured the top rung of listenership. As of 1998, Spanish-language Univisión had become the nation's fifth largest TV network, while an African American, Tom Joyner, had the highest rated urban morning radio show in the country. Along with African American filmmakers, Black hip-hop and rap singers have created a radio-disseminated multicultural curriculum that features personal interpretations of selected dimensions of African American life, experiences, perceptions, and frustrations.

Over the years, individual mediamakers have consciously tried to influence societal attitudes about diversity or toward specific ethnic groups through their media textbooks. For example, some makers of films and TV shows have tried to combine entertainment with an effort to reduce bigotry by challenging ethnic prejudice. This occurred often in the immediate post-World War II era, where bigotry was condemned by movie textbooks like *Home of the Brave* (African Americans), *A Medal for Benny* (Mexican Americans), *Broken Arrow* (American Indians), *Saturday's Hero* (Polish Americans), *Crossfire* (Jewish Americans), and *Knock on Any Door* (Italian Americans).

Some mediamakers have used their products to try to deliver broader multicultural messages, such as celebrating ethnic diversity as an element of American society or presenting cultural diversity as an integral part of American national character, culture, and values. In contrast, other mediamakers have consciously traded on antiethnic bigotry. In the movies, such a process began during the early silent era in the unapologetically and unsubtly anti-Mexican "greaser" movies (like *The Greaser's Revenge*), the parade of Indian savage movies, and even film classics like D. W. Griffith's *The Birth of a Nation*, which featured some of the most despicable depictions of African Americans ever to reach the screen.

Some mediamakers have switched multicultural positions, occasionally accompanied by public mea culpas about their past media textbook sins. After decades of making movies that demonized American Indians so that John Wayne (occasionally aided by the U.S. Cavalry) could ride to the rescue, the eminent director John Ford issued a public apology via his 1964 film, *Cheyenne Autumn*. As Ford lamented during a 1963 interview:

> I had wanted to make it for a long time. I've killed more Indians than Custer, Beecher and Chivington put together. . . . There are two sides to every story, but I wanted to show their point of view for a change. Let's face it, we've treated them very badly—it's a blot on our shield: we've cheated and robbed, killed, murdered, massacred and everything else, but they kill one white man and, God, out come the troops. (Bogdanovich, 1968, p. 104)

No longer savages, Indians (at least the Cheyenne) emerged as decent people who only wanted to retain their ancestral ways, opposed by now-evil White men. Such publicly proclaimed multicultural mea culpas are rare. Yet they reveal the self-recognition by at least some mediamakers that they do function as teachers and, therefore, bear some pedagogical—not just commercial and artistic—responsibility for their products.

Limits on Mediamakers

Mediamakers, however, operate within imposed limits. In that sense they share dilemmas with creators of school educational materials. Let's consider four such limits and their effect on media multicultural education: internal constraints; audiences; pressure groups; and ideological conflicts.

Internal Constraints. Neither mediamakers nor school textbook writers operate with full autonomy *within* their respective industries. Textbook authors often find that their original conceptions become severely modified, sometimes seriously undermined, even drastically distorted in the development and production process. This is increasingly true as the growth of in-house textbook creation—or subcontracting of textbook creation— often transforms "official" authorship into little more than window dressing. Likewise, media authors often find that the final product fails to mirror their original conceptions. As a result, images, depictions, and messages—including those dealing with diversity—that ultimately appear in media or school textbooks may or may not represent the best expression of a creator's intent.

For example, from the swarm of Hollywood and television autobiographies and published interviews emerges a pattern of creative people often burdened with the sense that their films and shows could have been better, should have been better, would have been better . . . if they had only had more time, more money, more control over the final product, or countless other "if onlys." And, I might add, when retrospectively reconsidering their past products, some mediamakers have expressed the wish, "If I had only had more sensitivity" at the time.

Or take the relationship between print media stories, headlines, and visuals. A story is written and then edited, sometimes significantly. A headline and sometimes visuals are added. The end result may differ significantly from the original article. Consider the following two examples.

1. A January 6, 1998, newspaper headline announced that "Gingrich wants end to bilingual education." Yet the story said nothing of the sort. Rather, it reported that House Speaker Newt Gingrich had merely *criticized* bilingual education as part of a broader speech (Hines, 1998).

2. A June 20, 1998, newspaper story analyzed the firings of *Boston Globe* columnist Patricia Smith and *New Republic* reporter Stephen Glass for inventing quotations, people, and places in their writings (Getlin, 1998). Yet only one photo appeared, that of Smith, an African American. At that point I knew nothing about Glass's racial or ethnic identity, nor to this day do I know why only Smith was chosen or why both of their pictures did not appear. Whatever the reasons, that single photo gave a firm, if possibly unintended, racial tilt to the article.

Audiences. Mediamakers sometimes base their product on multicultural assumptions about audiences. In doing so they draw upon presumed audience predispositions in order to elicit media-conditioned emotional responses. For example, TV and film textbook makers often manipulate viewer fears by providing an ethnic menace based on existent societal stereotypes, including media-ingrained icons of ethnic threats.

In traditional Western movies, this threat might be represented by a band of Indians who mysteriously appear over the horizon, menacingly near a wagon train or isolated family farm. Sometimes audience premonition can be provoked merely by a smoke signal accompanied by the ominous beating of tom-toms. In contemporary urban crime dramas, the same (particularly White) audience dread may be elicited by showing a lone White woman or couple encountering a large group—presumably a violence-bent gang—of young Latinos or African Americans striding down the street at night.

Imagine, if you can, motion picture history as decades of full-length Willie Horton ads ... but for different purposes. Willie Horton had a short but powerful TV career, helping to elect George Bush to the presidency in 1988, as the latter's mediamakers "played the race card" with supreme effectiveness in destroying the candidacy of Michael Dukakis. This was intergroup pedagogy with an electoral purpose ... and it worked.

Generally, however, makers of movies and TV shows lack such clear pedagogical intentions or behavioral goals. But no less than the Willie Horton ad creators, they repeatedly play the race card to provoke audience responses, such as race-based fear and apprehension.

Or go to the other extreme. Rather than chills, some entertainment mediamakers go for cheap intercultural laughs. Techniques include anointing characters with "odd" surnames, showing a crowd of Japanese tourists with cameras, or, in *The End* (1978), featuring an asylum inmate who first admits that he strangled his father because he was "too Polish" and then proceeds to unleash a string of scurilous Polish jokes.

As non-Whites become an increasing part of the U.S. population— according to some estimates, they will comprise roughly half of it by the middle of the twenty-first century—media are trying to adjust, with sometimes controversial results. In an attempt to shore up the *Los Angeles Times* readership, Publisher Mark Willes generated a veritable firestorm when he announced that he wanted more stories about and quotations from minorities and women (Bannon, 1998). *USA Today* tried and then junked a system for keeping a numerical record of minority quotations.

While trading on and manipulating presumed audience predispositions, mediamakers simultaneously teach multiculturally by reinforcing such audience beliefs (including stereotypes). They thereby create more fertile ground for other mediamakers to harvest media-reinforced intergroup knowledge and perceptions. In terms of multicultural teaching/learning, the media function simultaneously as chicken and egg, a continuously swirling circle that often becomes multiculturally vicious.

Pressure Groups. The media function in a world of external pressure groups, including both government and private entities. The latter— watchdog groups, ratings groups, protest groups, ethnic, religious, women's, and sexual orientation organizations, and multigroup coalitions—have often tried and sometimes succeeded in influencing media treatment of diversity (Alwood, 1996; Lewels, 1974; Shoemaker & Reese, 1991). Even when protests fail to modify content, they sometimes influence packaging, as when in 1997 ABC added a warning, "Due to adult content, parental discretion is advised," to the beginning of selected *Ellen* episodes that dealt with lesbian relations. Occasionally protests influence networks not to rerun a show, as may have happened following protests against a *Seinfeld* episode in which a Puerto Rican flag was set on fire and then stomped on.

Protest groups range widely in ideological positions and group interests. They include religion-based groups like the Traditional Values Coalition, Focus on the Family, and the Legion of Decency. They encompass ethnic protest groups like the Italian-American Anti-Defamation Committee, the Anti-Defamation League of B'nai B'rith, and the Polish-American Guardian Society, as well as such groups as the National Organization for Women and the Gay & Lesbian Alliance against Defamation.

Sometimes protests expose intragroup wrangles. In 1997, the Catholic League for Religious and Civil Rights launched an attack on the new TV dramatic series, *Nothing Sacred*, concerning an independent young priest. Yet Catholics, including priests, were involved in the creation and production of the series. When *Boston* magazine published a generally laudatory 1998 profile of Harvard professor Henry Louis Gates Jr., and then titled it "Head Negro in Charge" (which also appeared on the cover), African American religious leaders split openly—on television—over whether or not the magazine should apologize for the title.

Protest groups also arise from within the ranks of the media themselves. These are often formal organizations or informal associations dedicated to improving the media image of specific groups or the media curricular treatment of certain diversity-related themes. Yet, due to the power of hierarchy, the internal protest arena is hardly a free marketplace of ideas. One National Association of Black Journalists report indicated that nearly one-third of African American journalists feared that they could hurt their own careers by bringing up racial issues in their articles (Bartolomé & Macedo, 1997).

Then there is government. If the federal government threatens censorship or hints at breaking up one of the many monopolistic industry arrangements, media outlets or entire media industries sometimes take steps to demonstrate that they can police themselves. If other nations raise too much of a fuss, particularly if they threaten to cut off movie imports or subscriptions to U.S. TV products, media organizations often appease them with content modifications (Vasey, 1997).

A particularly revealing case study is *Amos 'n' Andy*, the enormously popular radio comedy, later a short-running TV series (Ely, 1991). The radio show was written by two White men, who also played all of the roles using their versions of Black dialect and accents. But when *Amos 'n' Andy* made the switch from radio to television, it didn't take so-called political correctness to suggest that African American actors should play those roles. Yet the TV adaptation became the target of Black protest groups, who felt that it ridiculed and stereotyped African Americans as conniving, semi-intelligent, morally vacuous lowlifes. The protest worked, and the show soon disappeared from the small screen.

In retrospect, *Amos 'n' Andy* seems stereotypically tame, particularly when compared to some of contemporary television's Black sitcoms. And in terms of being derogatory, compare it to some of the Black comedians on cable, who seem incapable of uttering a single line without using the word "nigger" at least once, launching at least one four-letter word, or—in the case of male comedians—referring to an African American woman as other than a bitch or a whore. What kind of multicultural curriculum are they writing and disseminating? What different kinds of messages might Black audiences *and* non-Black audiences be deriving from such shows? And where are the pressure groups?

Ideological Conflicts. Both the media industry and individual mediamakers have embodied reigning or at least competing societal beliefs and ideologies concerning diversity. Some mediamakers support affirmative action; others oppose it. Some champion immigration; others want to raise the barriers. Mediamakers have taken varying positions on such multicultural subjects as homosexuality, sexual harassment, interracial marriage, the intersection of church and state, and making English the official language. These divisions simultaneously reflect, refract, reframe, and influence larger societal clashes and intergroup tensions.

Moreover, they give birth to armed camps of critics, who try to portray the media (writ large) as a pedagogical monolith. Take, for example, many self-righteous conservative radio talk-show hosts who rant incessantly about that ultimate stereotype, the so-called liberalmedia (one word, as some find it nearly impossible to utter the word media without attaching *liberal* to the front). Or the contrarian but comparably self-righteous Marxist critics, who obsess about the U.S. media as a nearly lockstep tool of capitalist manipulation.

Yet the media have never been the curricular monolith claimed by critics of various and conflicting ideological persuasions (Condit, 1994). This is precisely why *all* of these critics can find plenty of evidence to "prove" that they are right. With some 1,500 TV stations, 12,000 radio stations, 11,000 magazines, 1,500 daily newspapers, and 100 cable services, the U.S. media are so diverse that virtually any critic can find myriad examples to support a personal interpretive position.

In fact, criticizing the media has become one of the nation's easiest avocations. If you believe something about the media, look long enough and you'll find plenty of examples to support your claim. This is particularly true if you simultaneously ignore media evidence that goes *contrary* to your claim. Columnist Cal Thomas (1998) provided an unintended (I think) parody of this penchant toward stereotyping the media when he wrote:

> Most of the big media subscribe to certain prejudices. They include, but are not limited to, biases about big corporations (they are evil), white people (they are racists until proved otherwise), males (they are sexists), Republicans (they are shills for big business and insensitive to the poor), the seriously religious (they are ignorant) and America (a bad country that does bad things to innocent people). (p. A-14)

If Thomas were correct, then why do so many groups protest against the media treatment of women, minorities, and the poor, particularly immigrants (Rivers, 1996)? I should also mention that I read Thomas's column in one of those "big media" newspapers that he blasted, and I'm sure it appeared in many more.

Because of the widespread selective use of evidence, digging of ideological foxholes, and issuing of blanket condemnations of the media, I decided that in my analysis of the media multicultural curriculum I would go beyond assessing the *differences* among media critics. Rather, I looked for the analytical *convergences* among ideological opponents and representatives of diverse interest groups. Where do conservatives and liberals *agree* in their interpretations of the media? Marxist and right-wing ideologues? Feminists and antifeminists? Civil rights activists and die-hard racists? Homosexuals and homophobes? Spokepeople for different racial, ethnic, and religious groups?

These convergences of interpretations allow us to tease out the deeper forces at work in shaping the development of the media multicultural curriculum (Gitlin, 1979; Hall, 1982). Out of this cacaphony, I have identified a series of basic, more resilient, intersecting factors that have tended to shape the media treatment of diversity. Let's consider three such factors: commercialism, tradition, and convention.

Commercialism

Most mediamakers are in the business of selling a product—their product. They repeat themes or approaches that they believe audiences want or at least will accept. Conversely, they tend to avoid themes that they believe audiences will not accept and, therefore, will not pay money to read, listen to, or view.

For years some critics complained that African Americans were invisible on TV. Even when they did appear in TV dramas, they did so mainly to commit crimes (a problem for White heroes to solve). No longer. Today network TV is loaded with Black situation comedies (you judge whether or not this amounts to multicultural curricular progress). At one time Black-White buddy movies like the 1958 *The Defiant Ones* (Sidney Poitier and Tony Curtis) or TV series like *I Spy* (Bill Cosby and Robert Culp) were considered avant-garde, pioneering, even iconoclastic. Today they litter the screen, such as in police melodramas like TV's *Homicide: Life on the Street* and the popular Mel Gibson-Danny Glover *Lethal Weapon* movie series.

The reason? Commercialism. African Americans, who seem to gravitate to shows with Blacks in the cast, now view television at higher rates than do Whites and form a major part of the moviegoing audience. Moreover, with Blacks comprising nearly one-fourth of HBO subscribers as of summer 1998, that cable channel has become heavily involved in producing original movies on African Americans (for example, *The Tuskegee Airmen, Miss Evers' Boys, A Lesson Before Dying,* and *Don King: Only in America*). Discussing the pedagogical importance of such shows for Whites, Charles Richardson, President of Triad Communications, stated:

> It doesn't go in one ear and out the other, it goes in one ear and stays. We look at film as entertainment on the surface and, secondarily, as food for our subconscious. It's important and great that the opportunities that seem to be showing up are varied. Because all these people going to movies are getting this input. And the next time they interact with someone of a different race, they might have a frame of reference that will be positively drawn from these kinds of films. (Hornaday, 1998, p. F-27)

What about local television news, a major multicultural curriculum about the surrounding community? Travel from city to city and you will generally find the same types of multicultural stories—crime, ethnic controversies, and debates about such "hot button" diversity-related issues as affirmative action and bilingual education. These are the stuff that mediamakers think audiences want, meaning higher competitive ratings and advertising rates. Similar concerns influence the print media, particularly as recent years have seen the erosion of the fabled "wall" between news and business departments.

Diversity makes it into the media curriculum primarily when mediamakers decide that diversity sells. It tends to find a place in that curriculum as long as it can be framed to fit what mediamakers think will be commercially effective. In these respects, mediamakers closely resemble school textbook creators (Perlmutter, 1997).

Tradition

If it ain't broke, why fix it? If mediamakers believe that certain traditions or formulae work—meaning they attract audiences—they will continue to follow them, usually disregarding their social or pedagogical ramifications.

For decades, hostile Indians functioned as the assembly-line menace in Western movies made primarily for White audiences. Then the declining popularity of the Western genre, growing Native American protests, and emerging viewer sensitivities about the media treatment of Indians combined to consign these "hostiles" to old movie cable channels. In recent years, Native Americans have made a modest movie and TV comeback. But the "hostiles" have now become the "nobles"—as in "noble savages"—whether in TNT's string of paint-by-the-numbers Indian biographies, in big screen epics like *Dances with Wolves* or *The Last of the Mohicans,* or even in contemporary social dramas, where nobility becomes modernized into stoicism and spirituality.

It is too early to ascertain whether or not a new Indian media tradition has emerged. My guess is that Native American chic will just be a red flash in the White man's media textbook pan—that is, unless it survives its ultimate test, long-range box-office or viewer commercialism.

Or take the Prince Charming tradition. Despite feminist attacks on the media preoccupation with portraying women's self-fulfillment and happiness as being dependent upon finding a man, that genre appears to be holding its own. One of the 1982 movie box-office smashes was Taylor Hackford's *An Officer and a Gentleman,* a clever updating of the traditional story starring Richard Gere as Prince Charming (now Zack) and Debra Winger as Cinderella (now Paula). (I could just as well have used Snow White as my trope, but it struck me as somewhat inappropriate. Postmodern Paula may have been White, but she was hardly as pure as snow, considering the amount of time that she and Zack spent participating premaritally in presumably unsafe sex.)

In *Officer,* the looking-for-Prince-Charming tradition became transformed into Puget Sound factory girls trying to snag naval officer candidates in the nearby flight training school to escape their dead-end lower-middle-class lives. Although released nearly two decades after the beginning of the feminist critical onslaught against such screen fantasies, the movie drew huge, adoring, and enraptured audiences of both women and men.

But the mediamakers did not simply provide a Cinderella in modern dress. In a token bow to contemporary feminism, they included a pre-Citadel female officer candidate, who ultimately wins her wings by proving that she can do a man's job. Yet even this success is tainted. To clear her most formidable hurdle, a rope climb over a high wooden wall, she succeeds only when verbally encouraged and accompanied by a fellow male candidate.

The mediamakers also both responded to contemporary "celebrating diversity" chic and reinforced the larger, societally popular textbook message of the ultimate healing power of racial desegregation. World War II movies featured multiethnic, but seldom multiracial, units. (In truth, the American military was not desegregated until after World War II.) In contrast, Zack's class prominently features officer candidates of diverse skin colors and ethnic surnames (Zack himself is half Irish and half Italian). And who should be the drill sergeant who holds their collective fates in the palm of his hand? An African American, played in Academy Award-winning fashion by Lou Gossett Jr.

With tough, demanding exterior, yet soft, sensitive inner core, Gossett prods, demands, bullies, cajoles, and ultimately delivers a sharp kick to the groin to help Gere complete his training and earn his officer's commission . . . a Black man helping a White (Irish-Italian ethnic) boy become a man. Diversity triumphs. Multiculturalism works. Except, of course, for one of the media's safe targets, Polish Americans, represented by Paula's crude, hairy, inarticulate stepfather (no wicked stepmothers for feminist-era Cinderellas). Moreover, the film celebrated diversity *without* sacrificing tradition. *Officer* still gave us the Prince Charming we have come to know, love, and expect. Can't disappoint the tradition-impaired.

Predictably, Zack breaks up with Paula, who goes back to her life of factory drudgery and hopes that the next officer class will offer better pickings. (Paula, herself, is the offspring of an officer candidate who left her mother pregnant while he went off to military glory.)

But wait! In the closing scene, who should stride into the deafening factory, more natty than Pat Riley in an Armani suit, his white officer's uniform more than a sufficient substitute for Prince Charming's usual white horse? None other than Zack, who surprises Paula, lifts her into his arms, and, with musical crescendo, carries her off into a glorious future (at least until the first time he cheats on her). Paula's mother looks on with tearful happiness, while Paula's sexpot pal, Lynette, who had faked a pregnancy to entrap her officer candidate prey and later drove him to suicide when he flunked out of officer school, shouts the immortal movie-ending line, "Way to go, Paula! Way to go!"

When Laurel and I first saw the movie (I must admit we still enjoy it), dozens of young women in the audience shouted, "Way to go, Paula" along with Lynette. Intrigued, the following week I asked students in my History of the Mass Media class, "What is the last line in *An Officer and a Gentleman*?" Almost to a woman (and man), they answered back, "Way to go, Paula!"

Tradition is a powerful force. Mediamakers defy it at their risk . . . and they usually don't. Revisionism and innovation *within* the constraints of tradition are fine. But only the truly adventurous break the deeper barriers of tradition.

Convention

Convention is tradition writ large. Or tradition internalized to the point of mental laziness. Or tradition transformed into knee-jerk responses. Or tradition converted into mindlessness.

If there's a movie criminal, why not call him Codianni? We've been awarding Italian surnames to screen criminals for a long time, so why change now?

If there's a maid, make her Hispanic. If she speaks English, give her an accent and make her English garbled. And, of course, call her María.

If our news staff is covering the barrio or ghetto, what should we show? Why not crime? Isn't that what you mainly find there, what we've been covering for a long time, and what our viewers seem to expect? And if we don't do it and one of our competitors does, viewers might switch channels.

This happened during the O. J. Simpson criminal trial. Stations reduced coverage at their own risk . . . and sometimes with loss of ratings. Radio and TV talk shows bombarded listeners with O. J. trivia. Yet the public—readers, listeners, and viewers—bears much of the blame for such mediamaker actions.

A revealing case of mediamaker convention occurred with the meteoric rise of golfer Tiger Woods. Like most other people, I have never met nor seen Tiger Woods, but merely know him as a "mediated" figure. In the 1997 Masters Tournament, the precocious, ferocious, and charismatic young Woods stunned even the nongolfing world with his overwhelming triumph in that prestigious event, whose final coronation day enjoyed one of the largest viewing audiences in televised golf history.

But the significance of Woods's victory went well beyond sports. As journalists proclaimed, he was the first African American golfer to win the prestigious Masters, long viewed as one of the Whitest tournaments in a traditionally White sport. (It took years after the Professional Golfers' Association had dropped its "Caucasians Only" policy before Blacks even *played* in the Masters.)

But wait a minute. Was Woods *really* African American? Or was he the first Asian American golfer to win the Masters? There's the rub. For Tiger Woods defies American racial categorizing and labeling conventions . . . including those used by mediamakers (Chiong, 1998).

Woods's racial/ethnic roots contain various lines—Black, Thai, Chinese, American Indian, and White. Sorry to say, from the perspective of "my people," he apparently has no Hispanic ancestry . . . but "my people" have already won the Masters. For blood percentage devotees (remember, the United States has a long tradition—including legal tradition—of arbitrarily making racial assignments based on blood percentages or the presence of any traces of blood from proscribed lines), Woods's predominant ancestry is Thai . . . but so what?

Tiger Woods becoming the first Thai American golfer to win the Masters has no visceral sociohistorical significance. It lacks the pith and poignancy of his becoming the first African American champion. As one who lived for nearly two years in Augusta, Georgia (site of the tournament) and once covered the tournament (for a *Sport Magazine* article on Art Wall, who won that year), I found myself sobbing as the Tiger strode onto the eighteenth green to make history.

This wasn't just golf history, which he certainly made by crushing his opposition and setting a tournament record. It was American history . . . multicultural history. For this victory occurred in the heart of Dixie, in a mythic, long racially restrictive golf tournament—meaning restricted against African Americans, because Asians and Latinos had played there at least as far back as the 1950s. (Note: in Asia, where athletes like Tiger Woods and Chinese American tennis star Michael Chang are legends, the media trumpeted the fact that this was the first *Asian* victory at the Masters. Moreover, Korean golfer Se Ri Pak, the newest sensation on the women's professional circuit, is known in Asia as "the female Tiger Woods.")

For the media to have ignored race would have been to ignore history. Yet in their coverage, mediamakers periodically fell into lazy convention. In fact, some print press writers (or editors) continued to label Woods *simply* as a Black golfer, ignoring his multiracial heritage. In doing so, they remained mired in the conventional American linguistic comfort zone of categorizing people as single race when they are, in fact, multiracial. Simultaneously, those mediamakers reinforced the traditional American construction of racial categories.

The Tiger himself has contributed to media curricular complexity both through his many interviews and the Nike marketing campaign. When asked how he categorizes himself racially, Woods sometimes responds that he identifies himself as Cablinasian, a conflation of Caucasian, Black, Indian, and Asian. Sorry, but I can't take that too seriously.

When he walked off Augusta's eighteenth green, Tiger immediately hugged Lee Elder (who in 1975 had become the first Black to play in the Masters) and reportedly whispered, "Thanks for making this possible." And, when Nike "showed him the (endorsement) money," it played the dual race card in its marketing campaign. On the home front, Nike ran a provocative, controversial, and highly effective newspaper ad featuring Woods and proclaiming, "There are still golf courses in the United States that I am not allowed to play because of the color of my skin" (presumably it wasn't because they didn't allow Cablinasians). Yet in Asia, the world's fastest growing golf market, Nike trumpets Woods's Thai ancestry. I'm sure that this cerebral young man, supported by parents with a deep sense of history and culture, has a solid sense of his *multiple* identities. Moreover, he recognizes his place in America's multicultural history and the role of media coverage as part of America's public multicultural curriculum.

By now you may be thinking that I'm making too much of the multicultural teaching significance of the Tiger Woods phenomenon. Yet on April 14—the day after Woods's victory—I surfed talk radio to see if the Tiger curriculum had intertextual legs. It did. I immediately encountered a talk show devoting an hour to the media racial labeling of Tiger Woods. The callers—mainly White, I think, although I may be accused of auditory stereotyping—almost unanimously unloaded on sports announcers and writers as divisive for bringing race into their coverage. Some even resorted to that knee-jerk platitude of wishful historical amnesia, "Why don't we just talk about him as a member of the human race?" Tell that to the next Black or Latino man who gets stopped by the police while driving or jogging through a predominantly White neighborhood because he "fits the profile"—meaning the police "profile" of those darker members of the human race who aren't normally seen in those environs.

These callers wanted the media suddenly, abruptly, and consciously to ignore the historical significance of the event. The past had become irritatingly inconvenient. Yet I'll bet some of those same callers would turn apoplectic if someone suggested that we should forget Pearl Harbor on December 7, eradicate the Fourth of July, or trash Memorial Day . . . all based on remembering, not ignoring, history.

The Tiger-spawned, media-disseminated multicultural curriculum also spilled over into schools. For at least two months, the Tiger Woods media coverage came up spontaneously from participants in my multicultural education workshops. It did so both because students were talking about it, sometimes in the classroom, and because teachers, who are also lifelong, if often unaware, media multicultural learners, wanted to talk about it.

At one school, a teacher asked what might be the most significant question regarding the topic—when will we stop including race in the coverage of professional golf? My answer—when professional golf truly becomes so integrated that the racial identity of its participants is no longer a story. When is the last time you heard an NBA announcer shout, "Michael Jordan, the African American guard of the Chicago Bulls, just made a three-point shot?"

But in recent years I have read stories or heard announcers comment about the first American-born Black to play in the National Hockey League (with the Edmonton Oilers), the first Mexican-born player in the National Basketball Association (with the Phoenix Suns), and Japanese and Korean pitchers in major league baseball. Those identifications enjoy significance because they amount to historical breakthroughs and deserve to become part of the media multicultural curriculum.

But slothful conventions still reign, sometimes with unintentionally ironic results. In August 1998, a magnificent ebony-skinned golfer named V. J. Singh won the prestigious Professional Golfers Association tournament. During the coverage, I didn't hear or read one racial reference to him. Yet a week later on a sports talk show, an announcer referred to Singh as an African American (actually, he was born in Fiji of Indian subcontinent ancestry). Elevating error into irony, the announcer remarked how good it was that nobody had raised "race" in the Singh coverage, as compared to Woods at the Masters. Yet this announcer had done just that . . . raised "race," distortingly. Convention had triumphed over complexity in the media multicultural curriculum.

Then there is the "both sides of an issue" convention, a reflection of the deeply rooted American tendency to look at issues in a dichotomous, either/or manner. "Both sides" has become the default function of both interpersonal and mediated American discourse. When mediamakers frame issues, they seldom call for examining *multiple* perspectives. The popular *Crossfire* insists on polarizing every issue by bringing you perspectives from the left and from the right. Even Jesse Jackson, champion of the rainbow coalition, calls his TV talk show *Both Sides*.

John Dewey's "pernicious dualisms" have attained the status of an American ideology, even when *multi*cultural matters are being addressed. Are you for or against affirmative action? (Don't confuse things by bringing up the wide-ranging nature of affirmative action programs). Are you for or against bilingual education? (Don't complicate matters by mentioning the various types of programs lumped under the bilingual education rubric.)

Possibly no linguistic practice is more polarizing and multiculturally destructive than the "both sides" default convention used by mediamakers, and, often, by school educators. It functions as an invitation—at times, almost a command—to divide into two opposing camps. The subtleties of multiperspective thinking are inconvenient obstacles to be eliminated.

A Life of Their Own

But the role of media creation, including the dissemination of the created product, has its limits. Like creators of school materials, mediamakers ultimately lose control of their multicultural textbooks. Once media products appear, they often become "permanent" parts of the media multicultural curriculum, with time seriously transforming their meanings for consumers in different eras.

Mediamakers primarily direct their products at contemporary audiences—readers, viewers, and listeners. Yet once in existence, these products become timeless textbooks. Students can go back and read old newspapers and magazines. Movies, TV shows, and recorded music may be disseminated and digested for decades.

Old movies, for example, have been transformed by television and cable into ongoing living room textbooks. Each showing and viewing becomes temporally further removed from the historical, cultural, societal, and global context in which the films were made and originally screened. In fact, school textbooks enjoy a far shorter pedagogical "shelf life" than movie reruns on television.

Thus, beyond the question of mediamakers as multicultural curriculum developers, media products take on virtual lives of their own. This brings us to the second major dimension of the analysis of the media multicultural curriculum—the issue of media content.

CHAPTER 4

Media Products as Multicultural Textbooks

So just what has the mass media curriculum taught about diversity? What multicultural pedagogical riches lie in those mass media textbooks? What messages have the media disseminated about individual groups, about relations among groups, and about the intersection of diversity with American institutions and socioeconomic forces? Have there been basic media curricular patterns? In what respects have these patterns operated in concert or in conflict?

In the area of diversity, content analysis has been the favorite haunt of mass media scholars, analysts, critics, and protesters. Responses to the question, "What have the media taught?" range from careful (as well as careless) scholarly content analyses to cursory journalistic reactions, from pompous pontificating to political posturing, from jargon-ridden academic treatises to emotion-ridden demagoguery. However, most responses to the multicultural content of mass media textbooks have displayed three general characteristics: single group focus, absence of comparative context, and limited temporal coverage.

Single Group Analyses

First, most content analyses, ranging from rigorous to impressionistic, deal with the media treatment of individual groups—women, gays, people with disabilities, or selected racial, ethnic, religious, national, geographical, or cultural groups. Take discussions of race, ethnicity, and foreignness. Such group studies usually focus on a single ethnic group, such as Chinese Americans; a broader constellation of related ethnic groups, such as Asian Americans; a single foreign nation, such as China; or a single foreign area, such as Asia. Occasional studies try to link the related ethnic and foreign cultures, such as Asian Americans and Asians (Wong, 1978).

There is also a parallel and sometimes intersecting literature on the media treatment of gender—mainly about women, occasionally about men, sometimes comparing the depictions of women and men (Haskell, 1987; Rosen, 1973; Tasker, 1998). Still smaller bodies of literature deal with media and other multicultural groups: religious groups or religions themselves (Friedman, 1982; Keyser & Keyser, 1984), sexual orientation (Russo, 1987), geographical regions (Billings, Norman, & Ledford, 1999), and people with disabilities (Norden, 1994).

Tight single-group studies serve a purpose. We need to know how the media depict specific groups. Moreover, such knowledge provides the building blocks for larger generalizations about the media multicultural curriculum. In some respects this is comparable to schools, where books, units, or even courses on individual groups may form part of multicultural education, even as we also strive for multicultural curricular integration and broader diversity-based generalizations.

Absence of Comparative Context

Second, because most studies focus on particular subject groups or areas, only sporadically are efforts made to place such unigroup content analyses in comparative context. For example, studies of the media treatment of a particular ethnic group generally devote cursory attention, if any, to the comparative media treatment of other ethnic groups.

Despite its value, the unigroup approach to media content analysis contains the seeds of potential problems. For example, such analyses sometimes lead to false assertions or implied assumptions that the media's (usually derogatory) treatment of Group X is unique (meaning uniquely negative). While in some cases those assertions may be true, only through comparative analysis can this be ascertained.

Have the media treated other groups in a similar way? Unless that issue is addressed, assertions of uniqueness of treatment are unconvincing even though they may appeal to those lusting for "proof" of media stereotyping. Comparative multicultural analysis may reveal that such treatment was not group-specific and that, during a particular era, the media were giving similar treatment to some or many other ethnic groups or cultures or, for that matter, to Americans in general.

But the reverse can also occur. A comparative analysis may reveal unique patterns of single group treatment that might not "obtrude" in a unigroup analysis. A type of relationship, a story-line pattern, or a repeatedly used adjective that might escape notice in a unigroup analysis may be revealed, heightened, or confirmed through a comparative approach.

Years ago I was struck by what appeared to be a media pattern of using the adjective "sleepy" to refer to small Latin American towns. You know, "sleepy" as in "siestas are us." "Sleepy" found its way into newspaper articles, television newscasts, travel magazines, even cruise line ads. In fact, I once spoke at a major international education conference in San Antonio. One of the conference's daily newsletters went so far as to invert the usage, referring to "not-so-sleepy" San Antonio, thereby implying that San Antonio was an aberration to the general rule for locales with heavy concentrations of Latin Americans or U.S. Latinos.

Comparative analysis confirmed my hypothesis. What about villages and small towns in other parts of the world? Are the mass media equal opportunity disseminators of the small-town sleepiness image? It turns out that they aren't. While an occasional "sleepy" does find its way into media references to small European, African, Asian, or non-Hispanic U.S. towns, it does not occur with Latino regularity. These towns and villages tend to be quaint or picturesque, squalid or poverty-ridden, crime-free or crime-ridden, neighborly or friendly . . . but not sleepy. The media have generally reserved "sleepy" for denizens of small Latin American towns and, sometimes, for rural U.S. Latino communities. While a unigroup analysis can *suggest* such treatment patterns, only a comparative analysis can *confirm* it.

Short-term Analyses

Third, most media content analyses provide highly selective, temporally limited snapshots of media treatment. Some studies involve attempts to examine systematically and comprehensively the *long-term chronological* development of the movie, television, or other media treatment of the target group or culture (Cripps, 1977; Friar & Friar, 1972; Leab, 1975; MacDonald, 1992; Pettit, 1980). But most studies avoid the extended, sometimes tedious work that goes into such a longitudinal analysis.

These snapshot studies have value—for example, in-depth analyses of one or a handful of individual movies or television series (Caso, 1980; Dates & Barlow, 1990; Friedman, 1991; Fuchs, 1993; Toplin, 1993). They may provide provocative and revealing—if time-constrained—insights. They may also provide building blocks for developing and testing hypotheses about long-range media treatment.

However, there is a tendency toward overgeneralizing on the basis of one or several snapshots. This usually consists of assertions of broad long-term generalizations about media treatment of specific groups or other diversity-related topics. Or it may lead to grandiose claims about timeless images, messages, and stereotypes based on a relatively small number of fragmentary, overly selective, or temporally restricted examples.

In this book I eschew group-by-group analysis. Rather, I address media textbooks by attempting to tease out multicultural *patterns*. In general, I have concluded that, over time, the mass media have provided five distinct but interrelated *types* of multicultural content.

1. Media *present information* about individual groups and broader multicultural topics.
2. Media *organize information and ideas* about constituent societal groups and other aspects of diversity.
3. Media *disseminate values* about groups, intergroup relations, other dimensions of multiculturalism, and diversity itself.
4. Media *address audience expectations* about diversity, including specific topics and groups.
5. Media *provide models for behavior* for members of individual groups, for the treatment of members of other groups, and for ways of dealing with diversity.

Information

The mass media deluge readers, viewers, and listeners with information, including multicultural information. In his book, *Information Anxiety,* Richard Saul Wurman (1989) posited that the amount of information now doubled every half decade. For example, he argued that a single current weekday issue of the *New York Times* contained more information than the average resident of seventeenth-century England was likely to encounter in a lifetime. And that was before the true Internet information explosion. Less than a decade later, David Shenk (1997) would refer to that information overload as *Data Smog.*

Mediated information may be accurate or inaccurate. It may be presented within a context that facilitates comprehensibility or misleads the audience. It may be multifaceted or simplistic, nuanced or stereotypical. It may be packaged as news or presented in the form of entertainment. It may be offered as either fact or fiction.

Consumers may take a jaundiced view of certain specific sources among news media or mediamakers. Yet, in general, they tend to consider newspapers, magazines, nonfiction books, radio and television news, and documentary films as information providers. That information, of course, has been selected, organized, edited, filtered, and contextualized in ways that contribute to its varying accuracy and quality.

What about the entertainment media? Anecdotal evidence abounds, often in the form of "war stories" from teachers, concerning how students have gleaned information—including multicultural information—from the fictional media. For example, one Massachusetts high school teacher was introducing her students to the study of Nazi Germany. Upon inquiring, she learned with consternation that, while her students already knew some "stuff" about Nazi Germany, many of them had acquired much of their basic knowledge from the television comedy series, *Hogan's Heroes* (Chartock, 1978).

Even teachers extract multicultural information from the media . . . after all, teachers are people, too. I will never forget a workshop I gave in which the tedious subject of Cleopatra's "race" arose. In the midst of the increasingly active give and take over whether or not Cleopatra was Black, one teacher brought the discussion to an ominous, stupefying halt with the seriously uttered question, "How could Cleopatra have been Black? Elizabeth Taylor played her in the movie." In short, fictional mass media, such as magazine stories, TV sitcoms, and feature films become sources from which consumers may draw information.

Regardless of the type of source, media contribute to individual viewer/reader/listener pools of information, even if recipients are unaware of some of the information that is growing in those pools. It is this media-selected, media-delivered information upon which people rely for much of their knowledge about human diversity (Naficy & Gabriel, 1993; O'Barr, 1994).

None of us can develop in-depth knowledge about every racial or ethnic group, nation, culture, or religion on the basis of personal experience or even school learning. Nor can we travel into the past. Therefore, we obviously must rely on mediating forms of communication—what historian Daniel Boorstin (1961) termed the *pseudoenvironment*—for most of our learning about today's world as well as the past. Steven Spielberg's 1998 epic *Saving Private Ryan* may well become a primary textbook on World War II for today's young people, while his 1997 *Amistad* could become one of their major sources of knowledge about the trans-Atlantic slave trade (Beck, 1998).

But how accurate is that mediated information? Who knows? We don't spend our lives cross-checking each bit of multicultural information spread by the media. We all rely on the media, even as we sometimes criticize them for their perceived biases, distortions, or stereotyping.

Moreover, the issue of media multicultural information goes well beyond the question of accuracy (Keever, Martindale, & Weston, 1997). Take the factor of repetition. In news, even if each and every story about a group and its members were accurate in and of itself, the constant reiteration of certain themes might contribute to a group public image (Heller, 1992). Similarly, the repetition of a particular set of group images by the entertainment media can further add to viewers' pools of "knowledge." Now what if news and entertainment treatments of a group coincide? In that case, they would tend to reinforce each other. Once again, the issue is not accuracy, but frequency.

So let's look at a few "snapshots" of information about diversity presented by the mass media, in this case one media category, television. These "snapshots" are drawn from Sherry Browne Graves's (1996) research review, "Diversity on Television," in which she highlighted some of the conclusions about television content reached by various scholars. But remember that these conclusions are, themselves, time-constrained and may not be as valid concerning today's TV multicultural curriculum as when the research was conducted.

1. People of color were seldom shown in advertisements as the only group endorsing a product. However, commercials regularly showed only White Americans. There was one major exception—during "niche" shows about a specific racial/ethnic group, presumably targeted at that group audience, such as viewers of predominantly Black situation comedies.
2. During the 1980s, Hispanics comprised only 1 percent of families on prime-time television. Yet, during that decade, the Hispanic population rose from 9 to 12% of the total United States population.
3. Little girl-oriented advertisements for items other than food presented a racially segregated world. They seldom showed White and visibly non-White girls playing together with the advertised item.
4. In fictional television between 1955 and 1986, Latinos were twice as likely as European Americans to be shown as law breakers and four times as likely as African Americans. Conversely, Asian Americans were shown as victims of violence four times as often as they were depicted as strong and assertive.
5. Various studies revealed that, among visibly racial/ethnic characters, men appeared twice or three times as often as women.
6. Interracial contact among television characters was more likely to occur in job-related situations than in social situations, while race relations were seldom discussed.
7. Most conflict among youth occurred *within* a racial/ethnic group rather than between members of *different* racial/ethnic groups.
8. The most continuous, positive TV interracial contact occurred on

public television in such children's shows as *Sesame Street, Barney and Friends,* and *Reading Rainbow.* In these shows, race relations were sometimes explicitly discussed.

These snapshots deal not with learning, but with *content.* However, they suggest the variety of diversity-related information presented to consumers. The mass media, then, are omnipresent sources of multicultural information.

Organization of Ideas

Beyond simply providing multicultural information—a deluge of data and images—the mass media also help organize and disseminate ideas about that information (Abt & Seesholtz, 1998; Barnhurst & Mutz, 1997; Dorfman & Woodruff, 1998). Through this process, they influence viewer, reader, and listener cognitive structures—the ways that media consumers perceive, receive, think about, interpret, and remember. In short, they transform, not just inform, helping to shape the way consumers process and organize media-disseminated multicultural information and ideas (Adoni & Mane, 1984).

This organizing dimension of media multicultural education can be seen most clearly in those aspects of the media that function primarily to influence consumers' ideas—newspaper editorials, magazine columns, media advertising, television commentators, and radio talk show hosts. They relentlessly bombard consumers with opinions (and sometimes facts), while also attempting to convince them how to organize and interpret information. Think of the many diversity-related subjects that the media try to organize for viewers—topics ranging from affirmative action to desegregation, Official English to sexual harassment, gay and lesbian marriage to immigration, political correctness or the role of race in the O. J. Simpson trial . . . even multicultural education itself. Take the latter.

Columnists and talk show hosts fill periodicals and airwaves with diatribes against multicultural education, even as the misinformation that they disseminate suggests that they have probably never read a serious book written by someone involved in the field. Rather, their sources—when they bother to mention them—are usually other diatribes against multicultural education, which they redisseminate at face value. To further the irony, particularly on talk radio, some antimulticulturalism hosts take pains to announce *their own* group identities—"speaking as a Black . . . as a woman . . . as a Christian"—as if these were special credentials to legitimize their criticisms of multiculturalism and multicultural education.

Yet even multicultural education has fared better than some other diversity-related aspects of education. Bilingual education has become a favorite whipping boy for media pundits who seem unconcerned with the extensive research done in that field (August & Hakuta, 1998). Or take the sensationalistic way that most of the media organized the public curriculum concerning the Oakland (California) school board's 1996 vote on using Ebonics as one strategy for helping African American students gain command over mainstream English (Watson, 1998).

But beyond those explicitly idea-organizing aspects of the media, there are more subtle examples of such information-framing. In writing a news story, a journalist may attempt to provide a balanced interpretation of a complex diversity-related topic, sometimes by including varieties of perspectives and voices. Yet a headline or magazine cover will grab the reader even before eyes are laid on the story itself, suggesting what interpretive framework should be used in reading the story.

In May 1992, rioting broke out in South Central Los Angeles following the jury verdict exonerating the policemen who beat Black motorist Rodney King. The cover of the May 11 *U.S. News & World Report* succinctly organized the event for readers: "After the Rodney King Verdict. RACE AND RAGE, Black vs. White: The New Fears. Cops in the Crossfire." Yet one week later, the May 18 *Newsweek* provided a far different framing, with a cover that read, "Beyond Black & White: Rethinking Race and Crime in America." What a difference a week makes! The traditional knee-jerk Black-White media convention had given way to a reframing based on the recognition that this was a multicultural, not a biracial, event.

Then there is media narrative as a form of organizing multicultural information (Gregg, 1998). Fictional and nonfictional narratives perform the same roles that folk stories and fairy tales have done for years, helping consumers make sense of the world—often the world that they only know through the media pseudoenvironment (Bettleheim, 1976). Reporting in 1977 that there had been more than 2,300 research papers on television and human behavior, social psychologist George Comstock (1977) addressed the issue of social structures:

> Several writers have argued that television is a powerful reinforcer of the status quo. The ostensible mechanisms are the effects of its portrayals on public expectations and perceptions. Television portrayals and particularly violent drama are said to assign roles of authority, power, success, failure, dependence, and vulnerability in a manner that matches the real-life social

hierarchy, thereby strengthening that hierarchy by increasing its acknowl-
edgement among the public and by failing to provide positive images for
members of social categories occupying a subservient position. Content
analyses of television drama support the contention that portrayals reflect
normative status. (pp. 20–21)

To the degree that the media assert the normality of social hierar-
chies—be they racial, ethnic, gender, religious, sexual orientation, or
other types—they serve to reinforce the legitimacy of those relationships.
To the degree that they display or reiterate intergroup taboos, they serve
to reify the naturalness of those societal norms and attitudes.

When news media continually reflect and present specific patterns
of thinking about individual groups or other aspects of diversity, they
help to shape reader and viewer mental and attitudinal frameworks for
organizing future information and ideas about these topics (Hartmann &
Husband, 1972; Hawkins & Pingree, 1981). When the entertainment media repeatedly depict interethnic or racial dominance or subservience,
they contribute to the formation or reinforcement of viewer schema for
perceiving those relationships (Bernardi, 1998). When news and entertainment media coincide in their patterns of portraying members of specific groups in limited spheres of action, they create and reify cognitive
structures and emotional predispositions for absorbing future images
into a meaningful, consistent, if distorted, conceptual framework (Wiegman, 1989).

For example, in a study of the comparative treatment of Blacks and
Whites by Chicago local television news, communications scholar Robert
Entman (1990) concluded that:

In the stories analyzed, crime reporting made blacks look particularly threat-
ening, while coverage of politics exaggerated the degree to which black politicians (as compared to white ones) practice special interest politics. These
images would feed the first two components of modern racism, anti-black
affect and resistance to blacks' political demands. On the other hand, the
positive dimension of the news, the presence of black anchors and other
authority figures, may simultaneously engender an impression that racial
discrimination is no longer a problem. . . . (p. 342)

By influencing the multicultural organizational schemas of viewers, readers, and listeners, the media go well beyond spreading information (and
misinformation) about diversity.

Values

So let's keep going "beyond." Beyond organizing and contributing to reception schema, media also disseminate values (Hilmes, 1997; Miller, 1998). These include values about diversity and diverse groups (Chan, 1998). In that respect, media share a pedagogical space with school textbooks. As Jean Anyon (1979) wrote:

> Social agencies, such as the schools, the media, and government, whose functions include the dissemination of information, are major sources of knowledge that is both available and socially approved. If the views embedded in the information disseminated by these agencies predispose people to accept some values and not others, support some groups' activities and not others, and exclude some choices as unacceptable, then they provide invisible intellectual, internalized, and perhaps unconscious boundaries to social choice. (p. 383)

Since their advent, mass media have been lauded for their capacity to shape "positive" or pro-social values and criticized for their threat of fostering "negative" or antisocial values. Hardly a week goes by without some politician, protest group, advocacy organization, special interest coalition, or even critic within the media raising the issue of the media's influence on some aspect of values.

Values concerning the use of violence. Family values (usually framed as whether or not the media support or undermine family values, without specifying whose version of family values). Values about sexual behavior (at what age, between whom, and the relationship to marriage). Smoking (particularly with the widespread reemergence of smoking by major characters in motion pictures). Religion (usually framed according to the simplistic either/or convention of whether the media are for or against religion, while generally avoiding the more fundamental issue of *what* or *whose* religion different media may be for or against). Gender roles (often framed as whether the media reinforce or challenge traditional or more liberated gender roles). Homosexuality (usually fears or cheers that the increasing number of gay characters on network television series and the frequent discussion of homosexuality on TV talk shows has helped spread the so-called homosexual agenda) (Gamson, 1998). Race and ethnicity (whether the media disseminate positive or negative images about different groups).

Sociologist Herbert Gans (1967) likened television to schools and television programs to school courses:

[A]llmost all TV programs and magazine fiction teach something about American society. For example, *Batman* is, from this vantage point, a course in criminology that describes how a superhuman aristocrat does a better job eradicating crime than do public officials. Similarly, *The Beverly Hillbillies* offers a course in social stratification and applied economics, teaching that with money, uneducated and uncultured people can do pretty well in American society, and can easily outwit more sophisticated and more powerful middle-class types. . . . And even the innocuous family situation comedies such as *Ozzie and Harriet* deal occasionally with ethical problems encountered on a neighborhood level. . . . Although the schools argue that they are the major transmitter of society's moral values, the mass media offer a great deal more content on this topic. (pp. 21–22)

The concern over the media's role in disseminating values can be seen over the years in book titles. For example, the Payne Fund studies of motion picture impact, published during the 1930s, included Henry James Forman's (1933) provocatively titled *Our Movie Made Children.* Even more recently, media historian Robert Sklar (1975) upped the titular ante in suggesting the role of movies in disseminating values when he selected *Movie-Made America* as the title for his widely read cultural history of U.S. motion pictures. In fact, however, Sklar's seminal work did not adopt the deterministic "hypodermic needle effect" position of some of the Payne Fund Studies (Jarvis, 1991).

The list of those who have taken their shots at the media as values creators continues to grow. In 1992, movie critic Michael Medved (1992) weighed in with a provocative but heavy-handed diatribe entitled *Hollywood v. America: Popular Culture and the War on Traditional Values.* While Medved failed to make a convincing case in support of the book's hyperbolic title, he nonetheless provided a compelling argument that nonfiction films and television do function as values educators. Of course, so do the rest of the mass media, of which Medved is an active contributor through his movie reviews and talk-show hosting.

Sometimes media become the site for curricular warfare over values. On May 3, 1998, NBC ran *The Long Island Incident,* a TV docudrama about the December 7, 1993 one-man shooting rampage on a New York commuter train, which left six dead and 19 wounded. Concerned over the show's pro-gun-control values lesson, the National Rifle Association countered with its own pro-gun-ownership values textbook. This came via full-page newspaper ads, with the bold-faced heading, "A TERRIBLE PRICE TO PAY FOR RATINGS," consisting of a letter signed by NRA First Vice President Charlton Heston, himself a movie star.

The widespread concern about media as values textbooks emanates from myriad ideological camps. Yet relatively few commentators have addressed the issue of *diversity-related* values compared, for example, to the flood of criticism of the media as disseminators of sex-and-violence antisocial values. Occasionally, however, we find documents that suggest awareness of the media's role in disseminating multicultural values.

Let's return to the Motion Picture Production Code (the Hays Code), adopted by the movie industry in 1934. It provides a primer on Hollywood's response to public concerns over the motion picture industry's role in teaching values. For example, one of the code's value positions, its opposition to interracial love, appeared in Section II, Rule 6, which read, "Miscegenation (sex relationship between the white and black races) is forbidden." Until that rule was deleted in 1956, Hollywood drummed home the repeated values message that miscegenation should be avoided, not only between "the white and black races," but also between Whites and other people categorized as "colored." In those rare screen instances where interracial love or sex occurred or seemed about to occur, disaster must follow—failure, punishment, death, or other types of retribution (Cortés, 1991).

To an extent this values element of the Hollywood movie curriculum reflected widespread American social mores. When surveys conducted for Gunnar Myrdal's (1944) classic, *An American Dilemma: The Negro Problem and Modern Democracy,* asked southern White men what discriminatory lines must be maintained, their most common answer was "the bar against intermarriage and sexual intercourse involving white women" (p. 60). Moreover, similar Anglo (non-Hispanic White) opposition to intermarriage with Mexican Americans was documented through interviews for economist Paul Taylor's (1930) study of Mexican labor in the United States. For example, in defense of prohibiting Mexican and Mexican American students from attending the local school, one south Texas Anglo tenant farmer proclaimed:

> Because a damned greaser is not fit to sit side of a white girl. Anybody who wants to get into trouble around here can just try to put them in the same school. A man would rather his daughter was dead than that she should marry a Mexican. (p. 389)

Opposition to interracial marriage became legally codified in 36 states in the form of antimiscegenation laws forbidding people classified as racially different from intermarrying. Since these laws were passed at the state level, not federally, each law addressed antimiscegenation in its own idiosyncratic way, creating a legal crazy quilt. Each prohibited different racial combinations (most commonly Black-White), defined racial categorizations in different ways (one-eighth, one-sixteenth, one-thirty-second, or one drop of "Black blood"), or drew various specific intergroup lines (for example, forbidding White-Chinese but not White-Asian marriages). Not until 1967, in the case of *Loving v. Virginia*, did the U.S. Supreme Court eliminate this chaos by striking down all antimiscegenation statutes. Only then could all (heterosexual) Americans legally marry the person they loved, regardless of racial background.

On the other hand, as not all states had antimiscegenation laws, interracial marriage had long occurred in the United States. Yet Hollywood elevated antimiscegenation values lessons over the presentation of interracial marital realities. In adopting this pattern of portrayals, moviemakers functioned simultaneously as learners (reacting to the presence of such social mores among many Americans, particularly ticket-buying White Americans), as teachers of values (creating these antimiscegenation "curriculum guidelines" and consistently transmitting this "thou-shall-not" marital lesson to the viewing public), and as profits-at-all-costs commercialists (fearing that movies with interracial love might not "sell" to White audiences, particularly in the South) (Cripps, 1970).

Since the 1967 elimination of antimiscegenation laws, interracial love has developed into a "hot" topic not only in the movies, but also in other areas of the mass media. Hardly a week goes by that some newspaper columnist, wire service, national magazine, or radio talk show host does not discuss the issue of the racial categorization of racially mixed people . . . the offspring of interracial liaisons. Moviemakers now recognize that interracial love (if effectively marketed) can actually sell tickets. In some cases, such as Stanley Kramer's *Guess Who's Coming to Dinner* (1967), released in the same year as the Loving decision, and Spike Lee's *Jungle Fever* (1991), such love provided the focus of the movie. In addition, films like *Waiting to Exhale* (1995) and *Year of the Dragon* (1985) used interracial love as an important subtext.

Yet possibly the most revealing dimension of the fictional treatment of interracial love has been the growing number of films and TV shows, including daytime soap operas (Bramlett-Solomon & Farwell, 1996), in which such love simply occurs, with little or no mention of the issue of race. Let the image, the very physical presence of the actors, send the values message without having to rely on words. Whether intentionally or unintentionally, such shows disseminate the value that interracial love is normal . . . or at least not as abnormal as taught in the past. This values lesson parallels the declining, although still existent, societal opposition to interracial dating and marriage.

Expectations

In *Hollywood v. America*, film critic Michael Medved (1992) argued, "If nothing else, repeated exposure to media images serves to alter our perceptions of the society in which we live and to gradually shape what we accept—and expect—from our fellow citizens" (p. xxiii). I agree. Mass media do help shape expectations.

Saving Private Ryan undoubtedly has influenced what viewers expect from war, in contrast to the comparatively sanitized expectations disseminated by World War II-era movies. *Murphy Brown* may have influenced women's expectations about breast cancer. In August 1998, when President Clinton announced that the United States had bombed terrorist support sites in Afghanistan and Sudan, and, in December of that year, when it bombed Iraq, some mediamakers (and members of Congress) quickly launched a "Wag the Dog" hypothesis, based on expectations drawn from the 1997 movie of the same name.

What about public expectations concerning diversity? In 1998, Parents and Friends of Ex-Gays, the Christian Coalition, the Family Research Council, and other conservative groups certainly hoped to influence expectations about gays and lesbians when they ran newspaper ads with headlines like, "We're standing for the truth that homosexuals can change."

Race and ethnicity? One study suggested that, as of the late 1970s, prime-time television drama, situation comedies, and movies continued to reinforce racially separatist expectations (Weigel, Loomis, & Soja, 1980). That study concluded that cross-racial interactions comprised only 2 percent of the time in which characters were on screen. Moreover, in comparison to White-White interactions, Black-White relations on fictional television were more formal, involved less intimacy, and included less shared decision-making.

The Hays Code also provides examples of the creation of expectations. Ruling Hollywood since 1934, before beginning its slow decline in the mid-1950s and suffering extinction in 1968, the Hays Code ordained that crime could not pay in American films. All screen criminals ultimately had to receive their just desserts. So it came as a shock to expecting audiences when a criminal mastermind (played by Steve McQueen) flew away to Europe to enjoy the fruits of his brilliantly engineered bank robberies as the 1968 film, *The Thomas Crown Affair*, came to an end.

With the burying of the Hays Code, Hollywood moved from a crime-cannot-pay to a crime-may-or-may-not-pay position of expectation shaping. Ironically and unfortunately, this more permissive instructional position concerning the expected results of criminality occurred parallel with the rise in ethnic theme films spurred by the civil rights movements of the 1960s and the new pluralism revival of ethnic consciousness of the early 1970s. This resulted in a flood of movies with ethnics as the principal perpetrators of crime.

Since the late 1960s, for example, Italian Americans have become nearly synonymous with screen crime, particularly since the 1972 release of the epic film, *The Godfather*. This has contributed to audience expectations that Italian American characters are likely to be involved in some aspect of violence or criminality (Tomasulo, 1996). Simultaneously, it has fostered predispositions among news media consumers to expect—or, more temperately, to consider the possibility—that Italian-surnamed public figures might . . . just might . . . have criminal connections. (Democratic Vice Presidential candidate Geraldine Ferraro faced this problem during the 1984 presidential election, in this case suffering from the media-highlighted focus on the business dealings of her husband.)

Recognizing the effectiveness of this expectation-setting agenda, makers of movies and television shows now often slap Italian surnames on criminal characters, even when their ethnicity has no plot significance, in order to connect with presumed audience stereotypical predispositions. At the same time, documentaries on Italian American criminals continue to be hot draws on cable TV. When Italian American megastar Frank Sinatra died in May 1998, retrospectives on his life highlighted his reputed mafia connections.

One of the most bizarrely revealing illustrations of media expectations involving Italian Americans came in an April 20, 1998 *Sports Illustrated* story about a young African American high school student who had decided to enter the National Basketball Association draft. His name was Korleone Young. Given his first name, *Sports Illustrated* could not resist writing an article entitled "Young Guns," featuring a chart comparing Korleone Young with Michael Corleone, the mob boss of *The Godfather* series. Among the comparisons: that both of them shot with their right hands; and that while Korleone Young's ambition was "to bury jumpers in the Meadowlands," Michael Corleone's ambition was "to bury stoolies in the Meadowlands" ("Young Guns," April 20, 1998, p. 26).

Or how about sexual orientation? During a June 1997, cross-country flight, I observed firsthand an example of media expectations in action. The airline was showing a variety of short television segments, including an episode from *Ellen*—not the coming-out episode. But it might as well have been. The minute the show came on, just about every earphone-less person around me began talking about *the* episode, what the airline episode "must" be about, and, ultimately, their own opinion on Ellen coming out, as well as, of course, homosexuality in general. What actually occurred in the flight-shown episode was irrelevant. Spurred by the visual image, nonlistening viewer expectations about *Ellen* had taken over.

Models for Behavior

Finally, mass media provide models for behavior (Kniveton, 1976). You don't need to take it to the extremes of the gentle gardener of the novel, later movie, *Being There* (1979), who learned almost everything he knew from TV. Simply consider the fact that "product placement" in major motion pictures has become a growth industry, as companies and advertising agencies vie to have their products used by heroes and heroines to promote greater sales. Even comic books now charge as high as six figures to integrate products into their stories.

Anecdotal evidence abounds concerning the impact of media role-modeling. Television and movies provide myriad examples of how entertainment media have influenced behavior. They have added to the American vernacular ("Go ahead, make my day," "Show me the money," or "Make him an offer he can't refuse"). Law school applications skyrocketed during the first four years of the TV hit series, *L. A. Law.* When *Happy Days*'s Fonzie obtained a library card, real-life library card applications leaped 500%. Maybe most fascinating is that Jim Thome, all-star first baseman for the Cleveland Indians, reportedly altered his batting stance based on watching Robert Redford in the movie, *The Natural.*

Talk radio has also gotten into the role-modeling act. Rush Limbaugh has enriched the American English language in various ways—ergo, "ditto heads" and "mega dittos." Yet he provided a different kind of verbal role-modeling for a southern California Catholic high school student, who was disciplined for referring to the teaching nuns as "femi-Nazis," another Rushism.

Most critics of the media focus on what they perceive as the media's role-modeling of inappropriate sexual or violence-related behavior (or, more recently, smoking by Joe Camel and, increasingly, by lead characters in feature films—according to some estimates, at four times the national smoking rate). Many young people now suffer from what has been termed "Slight Trigger Disease," the tendency to do physical battle over minor bumps or perceived "wrong" looks. According to James Kauffman and Harold Burbach (1997), they may be doing what they see adults do, often transmitted to them through the media:

They see popular sports figures who seem to be always on edge, talking trash, scowling at close calls, and flashing intimidating looks at their opponents ... politicians reflexively demeaning each other ... television talk show hosts encouraging guests to abuse each other verbally, often over trivial issues. (p. 322)

The media also role model behavior related to diversity. Aware of the possibility of imitation—some would claim a likelihood of imitation—protesters regularly rail against the release of youth gang films or movies with interracial violence (Willis, 1997). Such protests have occurred continually since the 1970s with films involving ethnic gangs, such as *The Warriors* (1979), *Colors* (1988), and *Boyz N the Hood* (1991), for fear that young people would imitate the screen gang violence. Based on such fears, even Magic Johnson's Los Angeles theater complex refused to show the 1998 urban movie *Belly*. Although a few fights have broken out near theaters that showed these and similar films, massive waves of imitative gang violence have not occurred, which has come as a shock to those who proclaimed such deterministic positions about media impact.

Even greater concern has been expressed over gangsta rap. What are the possible behavioral ramifications of such lyrics as "I'm 'bout to bust some shots off. I'm 'bout to dust some cops off," or "It's a deadly game of baseball, so when they try to pull you over shoot 'em in the face, ya'll" (Slater, 1998)?

But let's consider some dimensions that are not framed as potential cause-and-effect provocation to action. Some critical theorists argue that media fostering of "nonchange"—or at a least reduction in the speed of change—may constitute the most important behavior-related aspect of the media. From this perspective, interracial buddy movies and desegregated TV news teams may actually retard the process of social change. Rather than role-modeling integration, they may surreptitiously suggest that social change is occurring so rapidly and normally that additional special efforts are unnecessary.

Then there is the issue of "disinhibiting effects." Instead of asking whether or not the media model behavior by guiding and provoking people into action, we also need to consider their potential for removing inhibitions to previously repressed actions.

Many movies celebrate vigilantism (for example, the *Death Wish* series). Do they contribute to societal violence by removing inhibitions to imitative behavior, or do they reduce violence by providing viewers a catharsis for pent-up frustrations? Do flicks with teenage sex make such activity appear normative or "safe," thereby contributing to teenage promiscuity (as well as pregnancy) by "disinhibiting" such behavior, or do they provide a vicarious substitute for the real thing? Does the cable dissemination of African American comedians who repeatedly use the word "nigger" in their routines unwittingly lower public inhibitions against employing this brutalizing word, thereby unintentionally legitimizing its use by non-Blacks?

Fear of media-influenced behavior has even penetrated the legal system. In Detroit, a White police officer was convicted of murder for beating a Black motorist to death. Nearly five years later, the Michigan Supreme Court reversed the conviction. One of the major factors in the reversal was that jurors had watched the movie *Malcolm X* during the course of the trial!

Mass Media Curriculum as Message System

The mass media multicultural curriculum, then, involves far more than simply the creation and dissemination of group images. It involves the transmission of information (correct or incorrect, balanced or distorted, contextualized or stereotypical). It involves the organization of information and ideas. It involves the disseminating and influencing of values and attitudes. It involves the shaping and reinforcing of expectations. And it involves the providing of models for action and the disinhibiting of other actions. In short, through multicultural content, the mass media have contributed significantly to the corpus of American thinking, feeling, and acting in the realm of diversity.

The operative word here is *contribute*, not cause. Some might take comfort (or gain demagogic mileage) by blaming the mass media for being *the* single culprit or bearing *sole* responsibility for many of society's ills, including bigotry, intergroup misunderstanding, and group stereotyping. I can't count the number of times that I have heard, "It's the media's fault" proffered as the simplistic explanation for a complex issue, often countered by media apologists with the equally simplistic, "But that's not the *real* problem," as if every issue must be boiled down to an argument over *the* single cause.

The mass media seldom singularly *cause* anything. But that doesn't absolve them of responsibility for their *contributions* both to social ills and to the improvement of societal conditions, including in the realm of diversity. But to get a better idea of how the media contribute, we need to move beyond content and examine the other side of the teaching-learning multicultural equation. What have people actually learned about diversity from the media? That is the subject of Chapter 5.

Mass Media and
Multicultural Learning

So now it's time to look at the legendary bottom line. Even while recognizing that mediamakers teach by creating public textbooks on diversity and that these textbooks disseminate multicultural content, what have people—particularly students and young students-to-be—actually learned from this media curriculum? Unfortunately, clear, simple answers do not exist (Postman, 1982; Real, 1977; Wartella & Reeves, 1985).

All school educators know that teaching and learning are not synonymous. We teach. Then, often to our chagrin, we discover through examinations or other forms of assessment that great variations exist in the extent, content, and quality of student learning ... including variations in learning through school multicultural education (Banks, 1991; 1993). That same gap applies to media teaching and reader/viewer/listener learning from the media (Schwoch, White, & Reilly, 1992). Once a media textbook is published, played, broadcast, or screened, audiences become part of the teaching/learning process. This includes young learners.

Case in point—the popular television show, *Mighty Morphin Power Rangers*. From a diversity perspective, the show models multicultural integration, emphasizing the value of cooperation among teenagers of diverse racial and ethnic backgrounds in the struggle against evil. On the other hand, in this struggle, the rangers often use martial arts, even though the show provides caveats that such techniques should be used only in self-defense.

But what messages do young viewers learn, particularly the main target audience, ages 9 to 12, according to the producers? Do they learn interracial cooperation and that violence should be used only for self-defense? Moreover, whatever its *purported* audience, the show has attained a cult following even among preschoolers, particularly boys. According to Tannis MacBeth (1996):

> Parents and teachers of preschool and elementary school children in Canada, the United Kingdom, the United States, and Scandinavia have expressed

considerable and widespread displeasure with the program because of the way young children behave after watching it, including the use of imitative violence. (p. 27)

Learning, in short, does not necessarily conform to either the teaching goals or the nonteaching claims of mediamakers. Once a media product is published or projected, consumers "read" that product, including its treatment of diversity (Abercrombie & Longhurst, 1998; Webster & Phalen, 1997). They may react as conscious, analytical learners, pondering the media's treatment of race, ethnicity, gender, culture, religion, and other aspects of diversity. They may make an effort to integrate thoughtfully and critically this learning into their own personal ideational frameworks, attitudinal structures, and value systems.

On the other hand, they may uncritically absorb or viscerally reject different multicultural lessons. They may react and learn by unconsciously relating these new ideas to their existent knowledge, perceptions, attitudes, values, and mental schema. Whether or not readers, listeners, and viewers are aware of that learning process, any piece of media has the capacity to contribute to an individual's multicultural corpus.

News vs. Entertainment

Consumers are more likely to be aware that they are learning (or supposed to be learning) from the news media, including such variations as TV and film documentaries. After all, they select news media *in order to learn*, whether that learning involves weather predictions, stock market reports, the latest discrimination law suit, or who (including ethnic identity) has been involved in the latest drive-by shooting or carjacking.

News media consumers recognize that they are encountering "information," although accuracy, bias, and packaging will vary. Yet they are unlikely to be aware of *all* of the ways that such "information" is adding to, reinforcing, or challenging their mental schema, worldviews, or deeper value systems. Only on rare occasions do we encounter an O. J. Simpson case where people and pundits continuously scrutinize how media consumers of different genders and racial backgrounds actually react to and draw conclusions based on media coverage of a diversity-related event.

The entertainment media present a different type of learning dilemma. Consumers usually watch entertainment TV, go to movies, or listen to music to be diverted, not informed. Therefore, as contrasted to their experience with news media, they are generally less aware that learning may be taking place. Yet both research and anecdotal evidence have demonstrated that people do learn from the entertainment media. Even the preamble of the Motion Picture Production Code (adopted by the industry in 1934) described its official position as follows:

> Hence, though regarding motion pictures primarily as entertainment without any explicit purpose of teaching or propaganda, they know that the motion picture within its own field of entertainment may be directly responsible for spiritual or moral progress, for higher types of social life, and for much correct thinking. (Stanley & Steinberg, 1976, p. 80)

Let's apply this to multicultural learning. Stretched over time, entertainment media-based learning may occur in various ways. Consider some of the possibilities.

Consumers may be influenced in their thinking about diversity by depictions of racially and religiously diverse male and female characters—including those of different sexual orientations—in situation comedies or crime movies. They may become more accepting of, or conversely, more angry about different types of interpersonal and intergroup relations as a result of the entertainment media treatment of love, friendship, conflict, and power imbalances involving persons of different genders, ethnic backgrounds, or sexual orientations. Their attitudes and expectations about diversity may be affected by the depiction of relations between ethnic individuals and various societal institutions, such as the police and schools. They may become more accustomed to desegregated settings or, conversely, become more antagonistic toward the overwhelming presence of "otherness" as a result of viewing the increasingly multiethnic, gender-mixed composition of screen hospitals, banks, schools, and other places of work. According to some scholars, media consumers learn more from background information and images than from those details that attract their conscious attention (Krugman, 1971).

Whether or not the mediamaker intends it, whether or not the viewer is aware of it, a television series or feature film may well serve as a multicultural textbook. As part of the media multicultural curriculum, these entertainment textbooks may contribute to a viewer's corpus of knowledge, attitudes, and mental structures concerning myriad aspects of diversity.

You have probably noticed—and possibly have become irritated with—how often I insert the word "may." Certainly I would sound more authoritative if I asserted, unflinchingly, with self-confident certainty, that media consumers do (not may) learn certain things about diversity, invariably ingest stereotypes, or predictably develop prejudices from their media consumption experiences. Many authors and pundits adopt this smug, dogmatic stance. I won't because we don't know—and may *never* know—the precise broad-scale impact of the mass media on multicultural or any other type of learning. As Garth Jowett and James Linton (1980) noted:

> Most of the research on movie influence deals with individual movies, but it is the cumulative effect of years of viewing movies which so far defies adequate measurement and which is of real interest in any assessment of the movies' impact on society and culture. (p. 10)

Or as pointed out by Steven Chaffee (1997), "Experiments do show that fantasy violence produces aggressive behavior in young children, but no one has followed a panel of, say, kindergarteners over the years to see if heavy early exposure to cartoon violence leads to aggressive adolescents or adults" (p. 172).

Although precision in identifying long-range, media-based multicultural learning remains elusive, research demonstrates that media do *contribute* to stereotypes and other kinds of multicultural learning (Gilman, 1985). Yet audiences filter in conscious and unconscious ways. Viewers bring widely varying sets of experiences, cognitive frameworks, and expectations to the media reception process (consider diverse reactions of audiences and critics to the same movie or TV show). Listeners have deeply imbedded values and beliefs (including prejudices) that influence media curricular choices or reactions to the same media source (hence varying listener responses to the same talk show pundit). Readers differ greatly in what knowledge they bring as they engage print media multicultural textbooks.

Therefore "may" remains a "must" when talking about media impact or media-based learning. There is overwhelming evidence that media multicultural education—both teaching and learning—has been extensive, continuous, and powerful. Yet caution must temper assertions concerning the precise content of audience learning (Korzenny, Ting-Toomey, & Schiff, 1992).

The Media Impact Debate: Polarization and Pomposity

To a degree, scholarly and popular analyses of the societal impact of the media have become polarized. In one camp sit the "all-powerful media" critics, who treat the media as virtually irrepressible forces, relentlessly inculcating audiences with their values. Some interpreters have adopted a nearly deterministic position, drawing direct causal (sometimes uni-causal) links between media and the development of individual, group, and national beliefs, attitudes, and behavior. Rampant in many early media studies, this common trap of media determinism is sometimes referred to as the "hypodermic needle" or "magic bullet" media effect. (In contemporary computerese, this phenomenon is sometimes called the "learner-as-bucket" theory.)

One analyst described television as the new "Pied Piper" because of what was deemed to be its enormous effect on children (Shayon, 1952). Marie Winn (1977) even used the title *The Plug-In Drug* for her book on television. While the hypodermic needle effect is now scorned by most scholars, it remains a popular assumption of many antimedia protest groups, political demagogues, and assorted haranguers. It has also served as a premise for many influential authors like Betty Friedan (1963), who argued that post-World War II media were instrumental in constructing women's visions and aspirations.

Since media all-powerfulness is assumed, little concrete evidence of media impact on learning is necessary. Dedicated media bashers of the all-powerful school merely need to look at a media example, draw their own conclusions as to what it says, and then assert that this is what consumers must be learning from it. Media content (teaching, as they see it) becomes synonymous with audience impact (learning). In the area of schooling, this would be analogous to analyzing textbooks and lectures instead of directly assessing student learning. Imagine if teachers tried to get away with this . . . using lectures, lesson plans, textbooks, and syllabi to "prove" what students are learning!

In opposition to the media determinism camp stand the "limited-impact" analysts, who downplay media influence on audiences. They present a number of arguments. Media merely reflect social consensus (as opposed to forging it). They simply satisfy audience desires (a knee-jerk mediamaker defense of the paparazzi in the wake of Princess Diana's death). Audiences are consumer activists, who continually, actively construct their own meanings from the media and thereby thwart the pedagogical intentions of mediamakers—in contemporary media studies jargon, they subvert the dominant or hegemonic readings of a piece of media (Jenkins, 1992).

Those who take these limited-influence positions consist of two basic groups. First are mediamakers. Newsmakers sometimes defend sensationalistic feeding frenzies or a fixation on violent crime by claiming that they merely "reflect" the world around them, as if they were passively holding up mirrors. Or they argue that they merely provide a "window" on the world, as if they simply opened the shades and let the world flow in, ignoring their gatekeeping and spin-doctoring roles of news selection and framing.

In the realm of fictional media, the common claim of mediamakers is that they merely entertain, sometimes even denying the entertainment media's teaching potential (Medved, 1992). (Then why do marketers compete so vigorously to place their products in feature films? When James Bond switched from an Aston Martin to a BMW sports car in the 1995 flick *GoldenEye,* the latter's sales skyrocketed, as did the sales of Ray-Ban sunglasses after Tommy Lee Jones and Will Smith wore them in *Men in Black.*)

Second are proponents of certain varieties of "reception theory," particularly those who assert that media readers, viewers, and listeners control the teaching-learning equation (Williams, 1995). Some even claim that movies and entertainment TV shows have *no* intrinsic meaning. Audiences provide it all.

Other scholars champion the idea of "oppositional readings." Translated into English, this means that audiences consciously select and modify what enters their hearts and minds. That is, they continuously contest the mediamaker's position (hegemonic reading), constantly provide their own interpretations, and emerge victorious in the struggle for meaning construction, a stark contrast with the passive victims of media manipulation posited by the all-powerful media proponents (Fajes, 1984).

Let's look at this multiculturally. What happens when people watch television shows that portray members of a particular group? When it comes to groups about which consumers have limited firsthand knowledge, they would be more likely to view these portrayals as at least somewhat representative. However, when they view shows that depict members of their own group or groups with which they are familiar, they might tend to become more critical, possibly supplying such "oppositional readings," particularly if those portrayals conflict with their own personal experiences or previous mediated learning (Lichter & Lichter, 1988).

Some consumers are downright subversive, supplying their own ironic twists to the content. Gays have employed that kind of subversion through their own group-based reinterpretations of such media-disseminated pop classics as Judy Garland's "Somewhere Over the Rainbow" and Doris Day's "Secret Love" ("Now I shouted from the highest hill . . .").

In characterizing these two competing positions, I don't want to leave the false impression of radical intransigence. One can view media as a powerful teaching force (I do) without becoming a hypodermic-needle determinist. And one can also recognize the inevitability of alternative interpretations and knowledge construction (once again, I do) without becoming a radical constructivist (Berger & Luckman, 1966).

In fact, most media scholars occupy a multifaceted middle ground (Rogers, 1994; Ross, 1998), expressed concisely by Richard Dyer (1986): "Audiences cannot make media images mean anything they want to, but they can select from the complexity of the image the meanings and feelings, the variations, inflections and contradictions, that work for them" (p. 5). Analysts recognize that both fictional and nonfictional media have an impact, which is why there has been such a hue and cry about cigarette ads targeted at young people and about the recent increase in smoking by lead characters in feature films. Yet they generally realize that this impact falls short of being as all-powerful and deterministic as the magic bullet folks tend to argue. From this broad middle ground has emerged research that provides some revealing insights (Huston, Donnerstein, Fairchild, Feshbach, Katz, Murray, Rubinstein, Wilcox, & Zuckerman, 1992; Tichi, 1992). In diversity-related scholarship, consideration of media impact has generally fallen into three admittedly intertwined categories: empirical, projective, and theoretical.

Media-based Learning: An Empirical Perspective

There has been sporadic empirical scholarship on the multicultural impact of media—for example, on group-derived self-identity, intragroup thinking, and intergroup perceptions. Most of that scholarship has focused on the entertainment media, usually examining the short-range effects of specific films or television shows, often conducted in experimental settings. Even though results vary in their specifics, they do coalesce convincingly around two basic conclusions, providing some—but only some—solace for the two warring camps.

First, media do influence intergroup, intragroup, and self-perceptions, as well as thinking about other aspects of diversity. Turn it around. Consumers do learn about race, ethnicity, gender, religion, and other dimensions of diversity from both nonfiction and entertainment media.

Second, the nature of that influence varies. Individual readers, listeners, and viewers provide a key variable concerning the extent, content, and tenacity of that conscious or unconscious learning. In short, scholarship confirms that social science axiom, *"Some* people are influenced by *some* media, at *some* time."* As Tannis MacBeth (1996) stated in the introduction to her edited volume, *Tuning in to Young Viewers: Social Science Perspectives on Television,* "Many different groups of experts, brought together over the years, have reached the conclusion that, although no single study can be definitive, the body of research evidence indicates that television does have some effects on some viewers under some circumstances" (p. 3).

Take the issue of prejudice. Media sometimes reinforce it, while at other times modifying such attitudes (Raths & Trager, 1948). Consider the following two examples.

One pioneering study involved the classic 1915 silent film, *The Birth of a Nation*, infamous for its degrading portrayal of African Americans during the post-Civil War Reconstruction era. This study concluded that when White students viewed *Birth* as part of their courses on U.S. history, student prejudice toward African Americans increased (Peterson & Thurstone, 1933).

But media, including entertainment media, can also reduce prejudice, even if audiences fail to realize it. Some scholars found that the 1947 anti-anti-Semitism film, *Gentleman's Agreement*, had a prejudice-reducing effect . . . at least in the short run (Middleton, 1960). According to one study (Rosen, 1948), students who saw the film reported improved attitudes toward Jews. Ironically, most of the surveyed students simultaneously *denied* that the film had been a factor in changing their attitudes. As with most media-based learning—especially when the entertainment media are involved—those student viewers had not recognized their own learning processes.

One of the most extensive—and controversial—efforts to explore directly and empirically the impact of the entertainment media on audience learning occurred in the early 1930s. Carried out by leading sociologists, psychologists, and educators located principally at the University of Chicago, this examination focused on movies, resulting in the 12-volume Payne Fund studies (Jowett, Jarvie, & Fuller, 1996).

The Payne Fund project began in response to often hysterical public expressions of concern about the effects of movies—especially the impact of filmed crime, sex, and violence—on young people. It served as a kind of forerunner to the current tidal wave of accusations and political posturing concerning the sex-and-violence influence of film, television, and recorded music. (I am not championing media sex and violence or ignoring the legitimacy of such concerns. Rather, I am referring to the over-the-top and often politically expedient nature of many such attacks, with their underlying hypodermic needle assumptions.)

The various Payne Fund projects came to differing conclusions. Some researchers argued that movies had to be viewed as only one influence operating alongside others, not stand-alone, all-powerful causes of thinking and behavior. But the public—particularly powerful politicians—literally demanded that the scholars reach absolute conclusions about movie impact. Pressure was exerted on them to create action agendas, not end their studies with predictable calls for more research. Fearful of being viewed as too academically cautious, some of the scholars went beyond the bounds of their evidence in their conclusions and recommendations. Moreover, the project summary, *Our Movie Made Children*, written by journalist H. J. Forman (1933), made ever more sweeping claims. This combination brought much of their research into scholarly ill repute.

In truth, today some of their methodologies seem empirically crude. Yet their research results—as contrasted with their often poorly grounded cries of alarm and calls for action—did provide compelling evidence (although not precise determination) of learning, including learning about diversity. However, such research virtually ended in the late 1940s with the advent of television, as communications scholars turned their impact-study attention to television, the new kid on the media block.

Today most such research focuses on media and violence (Gerbner & Gross, 1976). Yet occasionally there are studies involving diversity. For example, one such study (Johnston & Ettema, 1982) indicated that the popular educational TV show, *Freestyle,* modified young viewers' beliefs about what girls and boys were able to and supposed to do. Moreover, it suggested that this value change also led to more limited behavioral change.

However, there has been frustration with the failure of such narrow cause-and-effect approaches, often conducted in controlled settings, to reveal more than *limited* and *short-range* media effects on attitudes and overt behavior. In addition, there are concerns about the degree to which media impact discovered in a laboratory setting can be validly projected onto natural media-consumption situations (Chaffee & Hochheimer, 1985; Hall, 1982; Rogers, Dearing, and Bregman, 1993). Instead, researchers have looked for other ways to assess the teaching-learning relationship between media and consumers. These alternative impact models include uses-and-gratifications, agenda-setting, and reception analysis.

Uses and Gratifications

Uses-and-gratifications research emphasizes the conscious volition of media consumers, who select specific media because they serve useful functions for them or provide certain personal gratifications (Tan & Tan, 1979). This includes readers of various ethnic, religious, or women's publications and regular viewers of Spanish-language, Black-oriented, or Christian-based television networks, as well as foreign residents who make a special effort to read newspapers and magazines from their home countries (Ríos & Gaines, 1997; Sampedro, 1998). To illustrate the wide variation in media uses and gratifications, I need only point out that, according to some early 1998 listenership surveys, the two most popular national radio talk shows were Howard Stern and Dr. Laura Schlessinger, sometimes referred to as "Stern and Sterner."

Uses-and-gratifications scholarship has provided insights into what different *groups* of Americans have sought, done with, and drawn from the media. Take gender. By the time they enter school, boys exceed girls in the amount of time spent watching television. And what programs do boys watch during that extra television time? Shows like sports and action adventures (Alvarez, Huston, Wright, & Kerkman, 1988).

Or take race. Some studies have concluded that Black children, more than White children, consider entertainment TV to be an important source of learning about the world. According to these scholars, many Black children find television to be a curriculum on behavior with the opposite sex and other types of social adaptation (Atkin, Greenberg, & McDermott, 1978; Gerson, 1966). Moreover, TV shows with Black characters—particularly Black situation comedies—tend to be viewed more frequently by African Americans than by other Americans (Graves, 1996; Liss, 1981). You decide what lessons on behavior these televised textbooks might provide. (According to the Nielsen ratings, during its 1997–1998 final season, the hit TV series *Seinfeld* ranked 50th among Black viewers. Conversely, *Between Brothers*, the most popular TV show among Blacks, ranked 112th among White viewers!)

Agenda-setting

Agenda-setting research began with the principle that the media may not be able to tell audiences what to think, but they can tell consumers what to think about (Kosicki, 1993). By restricting the flow of ideas, the media can limit consumer propensity to think about and ability to talk knowledgeably about certain issues. Agenda-setting scholars later expanded beyond the "what to think *about*" domain, demonstrating the added ability of the media to *frame* public issues and to prime the public on how to think about them (Goffman, 1974; Scheufele, 1999; Ynegar & Kinder, 1987). As argued by Maxwell McCombs and Donald Shaw (1993):

> Agenda setting is considerably more than the classical assertion that the news tells us *what to think about*. The news also tells us *how to to think about*

it. Both the selection of objects for attention and the selection of frames for thinking about these objects are powerful agenda-setting roles. (p. 62)

However, there is evidence that racial and ethnic differences influence audience reactions to media agenda-setting efforts. For example, Oscar Gandy and Larry Coleman (1986) concluded that Black college students rejected mainstream press criticism of the Rev. Jesse Jackson during his 1984 campaign for the Democratic presidential nomination. Similarly, in 1998, most Blacks maintained their support for President Bill Clinton despite the news media's critical coverage of his personal life.

Reception Analysis

This brings us to the various forms of reception analysis, which have examined the variability of learner responses to the media. This is particularly true when audiences come from different cultural positions (Korzenny, Ting-Toomey, & Schiff, 1992) or when the subject carries a heavy emotional load, such as racism and other forms of bigotry (Cooper & Jahoda, 1947). Scholars have adopted a variety of approaches to reception analysis in an effort to determine—or at least posit—how different audiences have or may have interpreted and drawn meaning from varieties of media (Bryant & Zillman, 1991; Jenkins, 1992). One approach has been the intensive study of audience reactions to specific important media products. Two major television phenomena, *All in the Family* and *Roots*, illustrate those multicultural learning variations.

Norman Lear's weekly television series, *All in the Family*, which burst onto the American television scene in 1971, became the launching pad for a series of empirical studies that revealed varying audience responses. This popular weekly series focused on antihero Archie Bunker. An equal-opportunity bigot, he embodied racism, sexism, and just about every other imaginable kind of "ism" or "phobia." The show sought to critique prejudice—particularly racial and ethnic prejudice—by making Bunker's expressions of bigotry appear to be comically absurd. By portraying bigotry as imbecilic and making Archie the target of audience laughter, Lear consciously tried to reduce prejudice—a clear case of a mediamaker using entertainment TV for multicultural pedagogical purposes.

Did he succeed? Maybe . . . but only for *some* viewers. Others agreed with Archie. As portrayed ingratiatingly by Carroll O'Connor, the laugh-provoking Archie emerged as a cuddly bigot, a lovable racist. This allowed viewers already predisposed to his views to latch onto his relentless, but comic, torrent of verbal bigotry as a confirmation of the validity of their own prejudices (Leckenby & Surlin, 1976).

Studies of *All in the Family* with American and Canadian audiences confirmed the operation of the "selective perception hypothesis." Viewers who were already highly prejudiced or dogmatic tended to admire Bunker, condone his racial and ethnic slurs, and identify with his beliefs (Brigham & Giesbrecht, 1976; Surlin & Tate, 1976; Vidmar & Rokeach, 1974). In contrast, a comparable study concluded that the selective perception hypothesis did not seem to operate with Dutch viewers (Wilhoit & de Bock, 1976). (I wonder what studies will show about the reception and impact on young viewers of the racist kid, Cartman, in Comedy Central's hit animated TV series, *South Park?*)

Roots, the widely watched January 1977, eight-night television miniseries tracing Alex Haley's family history from African origins to the post-Civil War United States, also drew a swarm of scholars. In a demonstration of the "third-person effect" of overestimating and misinterpreting the media's impact on others (Perloff, 1993), one study found that viewers believed the series would increase Black bitterness. However, these same respondents—both Black and White—stated that *their own* main reaction was sadness (Howard, Rothbart, & Sloan, 1978).

Stuart Surlin (1978) analyzed and compared the results of five studies conducted simultaneously with or immediately after the showing of *Roots.* While all of the studies focused on the topic of viewer "incidental learning," results varied. The studies generally concluded that a higher percentage of Blacks than Whites viewed *Roots.* Moreover, 60–80% of the viewers believed that the show had provided an accurate treatment of history. However, the studies split on the question of impact. While three of the studies concluded that the series seemed to have a pro-social effect on viewers, the other two provided support for the selective perception hypothesis—that viewers tended to react to it on the basis of their pre-existing perceptions and personal mental schema.

The *Roots* phenomenon also attracted retrospective scholarship. For example, one such study revealed that differences based on region, urbanicity, age, education, and income influenced the way Black viewers evaluated the miniseries in terms of both its significance and its role as evidence for Black historical progress (Fairchild, Stockard, & Bowman, 1986). Interestingly, this study also revealed little gender variation in responses to the importance of *Roots.*

This line of scholarship—addressing the role of the media in multicultural learning by analyzing media interaction by consumers from specific groups—has drawn still other researchers (Allen, 1981; Comstock & Cobbey, 1979). In general, these studies fall into two basic categories.

First are studies of the ramifications of media for different cultural groups. These include studies of such topics as the acculturation of Asian American immigrants (Yum, 1982); American Indian communication practices (Worth & Adair, 1972); the maintenance and decline of ethnic pluralism among U.S. Latinos (Subervi-Vélez, 1986); the response of persons of different Christian religious faiths to media entertainment and news (Stout & Buddenbaum, 1996); and self-esteem and group identification by various sectors of the African American community (Allen & Hatchett, 1986).

A second type of study addresses the media's role in fostering interracial, interethnic, and intercultural learning. For example, there have been studies about racial influences on the reception and interpretation of the 1992 Los Angeles riots following the court decision exonerating the police officers who beat Black motorist Rodney King (Hunt, 1997) and White college student perceptions of Black socioeconomic progress and decline (Armstrong, Neuendorf, & Brentar, 1992).

Some studies have focused on preschool and school-age children. Young people's intergroup learning has drawn scholarly attention (Berry & Asamen, 1993; Caron, 1979; Dates, 1980; Hartmann & Husband, 1972; Rapaczynski, Singer, & Singer, 1982). For instance, on the basis of his research, Bradley Greenberg (1972) concluded that White children often considered television depictions of Blacks to be more representative of reality than did Blacks whom they knew personally.

Others studies deal with media and the socialization of children of different racial and ethnic backgrounds (Berry & Mitchell-Kernan, 1982; Stroman, 1991). One study compared the reaction of students to Madonna's hit video, "Papa Don't Preach." A group of White suburban students viewed it as about problems resulting from pregnancy. In contrast, a group of young African Americans opined that it was an exploration of father-daughter relations (Christenson & Roberts, 1998).

Unobtrusive Empiricism

In contrast to the *obtrusive* empiricism of survey, pretest-posttest, and other forms of research in which audiences respond to specific scholarly queries, other scholars have drawn upon already existent evidence as the basis for *unobtrusive* empiricism. For example, Chon Noriega (1988–1990) used such an approach by examining film reviews in 30 publications to assess how Hispanic and non-Hispanic movie critics responded to Latino-made films about the U.S. Latino experience, like *La Bamba, Stand and Deliver,* and *Born in East L.A.* He discovered the operation of the selective perception phenomenon, in which ethnicity served as one determinant in predicting critic reactions. Nor did the ideology of non-Hispanic publications seem to be a factor. According to Noriega:

> Liberal non-Hispanic publications often relied on the same outsider's assumptions about the *barrio* that characterized the conservative publications. The *barrio* was a problem space, denied a history, culture and separate point of view, not to mention internal complexity. That assumption manifested itself first and foremost in the mistranslation of *barrio* as "slum," rather than as the more appropriate "neighborhood." As a result, the films were often discussed in the context of social problems, rather than in the context of cultural identity or even film history. (p. 23)

In short, burdened by their own media-learned expectations, Anglo critics berated the films because they failed to live up to their own internalized stereotypes of a Latino barrio.

Nor is this a unique case of group-based selective perceptions of media-disseminated multicultural content. Take the contrasting conclusions of the majority of Whites and Blacks concerning O.J. Simpson's guilt or innocence, based on evidence and commentary transmitted to them through television, radio, and the print media. Or the differential reaction of women and men on issues like sexual harassment, the Equal Rights Amendment, Anita Hill's testimony, and the Lorena Bobbitt trial.

Then there is the case of *Do the Right Thing*, African American Spike Lee's 1989 hit movie about interracial conflict, intraracial diversity, and urban pressures in the primarily Black Bedford-Stuyvesant section of Brooklyn. Again, as in Noriega's study of Latino films, critics provided unwitting evidence of how preexistent multicultural learning influenced reception.

Do the Right Thing received lavish praise from *some* White critics. However, others challenged its authenticity. One criticism was that Lee did not address the issue of drugs. And what's a movie about an African American community without drugs in the forefront? In other words, these White critics brought their media-massaged ghetto preconceptions to the theater, and when Lee failed to deliver, *he* was at fault.

That same criticism has descended upon other Black-made films, such as the 1990 African American teen comedy film, *House Party*, which also "failed" to deal with drugs. Certainly Black communities have a drug problem. But so do White communities—not only in the United States, but in other nations. Yet when was the last time that a White filmmaker received a critical roasting for making a drug-free movie about a White community?

Pulitzer Prize-winning columnist E. R. Shipp (1998), an African American, took two recent graduates of Columbia Graduate School of Journalism to see the 1997 film *Soul Food*. The event turned into an unexpected journey into race-influenced perceptions and reception as the two graduates, one Black, one White, reacted to the African American comedy-drama as if they had seen two different movies. The Black graduate joined the predominantly Black audience in verbally interacting with the movie, while the White graduate seemed disoriented by the shouting around him. Although their contrasting reactions do not reveal what each ultimately drew from the movie, Shipp commented, "That journalists of different racial or cultural backgrounds can view the same thing so differently only proves that they are like most people" (p. 5).

Some scholars have drawn upon a variety of sources as the basis for unobtrusively addressing multicultural impact and learning within specific intergroup and international contexts. For example, in his *War without Mercy: Race and Power in the Pacific War*, historian John Dower (1986) assessed racial pride and cross-cultural stereotypes of the enemy that developed in both Japan and the Allied nations prior to and during World War II. Casting a wide investigatory net that included media along with other forms of evidence, Dower explored multiple Japanese and Allied sources—from scholarly studies to propaganda tracts, from government reports to military training materials, and from popular periodicals to motion pictures.

But Dower took an additional step. He provided examples of how *both* sides made political and military decisions based on these stereotypes. In short, both Americans and Japanese internalized these stereotypes and transformed them into action, even when acting on those faulty media-reinforced perceptions led to military and diplomatic excesses and blunders.

Media-based Learning: A Projective Perspective

Alongside empirical scholarship—of both obtrusive and unobtrusive varieties—stands the second category of media impact scholarship—projective studies. Using this approach, scholars have attempted to assess and suggest how different audiences *may* or *are likely* to draw ideas and construct personal knowledge by drawing upon specific media.

Sam Keen's (1986) *Faces of the Enemy: Reflections of the Hostile Imagination* and Vamik Volkan's (1988) *The Need to Have Enemies and Allies: From Clinical Practice to International Relationships* argued that people *need* to hate. Stoked by media treatment, "the other"—the racial other, the ethnic other, the religious other, the cultural other, the foreign other—serves as a convenient outlet for that hate. Edward Said (1978) suggested the intercultural ramifications of both popular and scholarly treatments of "otherness" in his seminal *Orientalism.*

Some scholars have examined specific examples of the role of "otherness" in the media. For example, Blaine Lamb (1975) asserted that Mexican characters served that role as "other" for turn-of-the-century silent movie audiences. Because of the brevity of early silent movies, filmmakers needed a quickly identifiable, easily despisable foil. Mexicans, already stock villains in nineteenth-century dime novels, nicely served that purpose, along with American Indians.

Other projective studies have attempted to reconstruct historical learning. For example, some scholars have drawn upon autobiographies to suggest the impact of media learning on ethnic identity (Erben & Erben, 1991–1992). A few scholars have ventured into the challenging area of projectively assessing the ways that different audiences may have historically reacted to the media treatment of racial and ethnic groups (Staiger, 1992).

For example, in her article, *"The Scar of Shame*: Skin Color and Caste in Black Silent Melodrama," Jane Gaines (1987) based her analysis on the social and cultural characteristics of African American moviegoers during the 1920s. In that way she posited how such viewers probably "read" that film. She then went on to contrast this to latter-day reinterpretations of the movie, arguing that such reinterpretations tend to be burdened with distorting presentist assumptions.

The Cosby Show

In contrast to such projective analyses of past audiences, some scholars have used their own readings of specific media textbooks to suggest (or assert) what contemporary audiences are learning. They posit that others are probably reading the textbooks the way that they (the scholars) do. The smash hit TV series *The Cosby Show* has sparked numerous projective readings, resulting in nearly polaric conclusions concerning the show's potential impact on multicultural learning (Real, 1991).

Was *Cosby* the ideal positive-role-model minority show, featuring a well-educated, sophisticated, financially successful African American family? Or, by commission and omission, whether intentionally or unintentionally, did the series provide less salutary lessons, allowing or even inviting audiences to draw contrarian conclusions?

Analyzing 15 episodes of the *Cosby* series, media scholar John D. H.

Downing (1988) observed that racism was never mentioned. Yet Downing lauded the show for emphasizing the dignity of Black culture, for championing Black familial unity, for directly and continuously critiquing sexism, and for portraying Black-White relations in a manner that challenged racist thinking by transcending racism.

However, *The Cosby Show* has also drawn concerned reactions. For example, some analysts feared that the series' concentration on well-heeled African Americans and its failure to deal with the Black underclass might have unintentionally encouraged viewers to ignore the fact that the most American Blacks still face tremendous social and economic problems (Dyson, 1989; Jhally & Lewis, 1992). These criticisms echoed those leveled against the late 1960s TV series *Julia*, starring Diahann Carroll. As media scholar Paula Matabane (1988) wrote:

> "The Cosby Show," for example, epitomizes the Afro-American dream of full acceptance and assimilation into U.S. society. Both the series and Bill Cosby as an individual represent successful competitors in network television and in attaining a high status. Although this achievement is certainly not inherently negative, we should consider the role television plays in the cultivation of an overall picture of growing racial equality that conceals unequal social relationships and overestimates of how well blacks are integrating into white society (if at all). The illusion of well-being among the oppressed may lead to reduced political activity and less demand for social justice and equality. (p. 30)

The Godfather Disclaimer

Finally, the media industry and the media themselves sometimes provide grudging projective recognition of their potential for influencing multicultural learning. Possibly the iconic expression of that recognition was the "*Godfather* disclaimer." That bizarre phenomenon made its debut with the 1977 U.S. national network television showing of Francis Ford Coppola's *The Godfather Saga* (a revised, expanded, and chronologically structured version—sans flashbacks—of the two Academy Award-winning theatrical motion pictures, *The Godfather* and *The Godfather: Part II*). Prior to the showing of the TV film, the following words appeared on screen, simultaneously intoned by a solemn voice:

> *The Godfather* is a fictional account of the activities of a small group of ruthless criminals. It would be erroneous and unfair to suggest that they are representative of any ethnic group.

Forewarned that the characters were not "representative of any ethnic group," a nationwide audience watched the violent, multigenerational saga of the Corleone family and its criminal empire. The film began in Sicily, large segments were spoken in Italian with English subtitles, and most of the characters bore such names as Clemenza, Barzini, Tattaglia, and Fanucci.

Moreover, this gambit became the model for future movie and TV self-absolution. Other filmmakers copied and only slightly modified the "*Godfather* disclaimer." Subsequent controversial, often exploitive films that focused on specific ethnic groups engaging in widespread criminal violence, such as the 1983 *Scarface* (Cuban Americans) and the 1985 *Year of the Dragon* (Chinese Americans), copied and altered somewhat the "*Godfather* disclaimer."

Let's get serious. Does anyone really believe that such worthless words could significantly mitigate the teaching potential of these movie textbooks? In fact, howls of audience laughter during these and other disclaimers suggest that such warnings may do more harm than good by calling even more attention to the movies' linking of ethnicity and criminal acts. Yet the disclaimers did serve as projective mediamaker admissions that feature films do, in fact, teach and influence audience learning.

Media-based Learning: A Theoretical Perspective

Finally, alongside scholars who conduct empirical and projective analyses, some analysts have addressed the process of media-based learning by proposing and applying *theories* of audience reception—what meanings various audiences construct from different media products (Bryant & Zillmann, 1991; Jensen, 1987; Schwartz, 1973). Let's look briefly at a few of those theories.

Some analysts use schema theory (Fiske & Taylor, 1991). According to that theory, each learner (viewer/reader/listener) develops operational mental and emotional schema—sometimes referred to as "ideational scaffolding," "cognitive maps," or "anticipatory schemes." These schema are based on each individual's personal learning experiences in both school and society, including learning from the mass media. These personal schema then become the basis for making sense of the world. They provide reception frameworks through which learners extract, process, interpret, organize, integrate, and consolidate new information, ideas, and images, including those disseminated by the media (Candy, 1982; Gentner & Stevens, 1983; Graber, 1984).

Related to schema theorists are media analysts who draw upon Gestalt psychology. According to this approach, viewers and readers encounter a piece of communication and alter it by selectively remembering and omitting information and ideas, while supplementing or contextualizing that content based on their own beliefs and biases, thereby altering its meaning for them (Barry, 1997). In terms of learning about diversity, this Gestalt approach has numerous implications. For example, it suggests that if media textbooks challenge preexistent personal beliefs about specific groups, particularly strong beliefs with deep emotional roots, holders of such beliefs will consciously or unconsciously blunt the messages through selective omission, supplementation, and contextualization (Cooper & Jahoda, 1947). Moreover, media textbooks would more likely influence viewer beliefs about specific groups, intergroup relations, and other diversity-related topics if those media dealt with subjects about which viewers knew little, did not have firmly held beliefs, or did not harbor deep feelings.

Psychologist Leon Festinger (1957) went further with his theory of cognitive dissonance. According to this theory, once an individual's cognitive structure takes firm shape, it tends to repel those ideas that seem too dissonant. This would suggest that media or school frontal assaults on deeply rooted prejudices, particularly when those attacks lack subtlety, may well be rejected by those for whom they create too much dissonance.

Compare Festinger's formulation with a somewhat contrarian view, the "drench hypothesis" of Bradley Greenberg (1988). According to this formulation, learning will more likely occur when audiences watch programs that "drench" consumers with ideas and portrayals that are out of the ordinary. Greenberg, however, argued that most African American TV sitcoms "drip" rather than "drench" (as contrasted with *The Cosby Show*), eviscerating some of their teaching power and potential learning impact.

But none of us is *fully* aware of *every* aspect of our own reception schema, ideational scaffolding, cognitive structures, or prejudices, including those learned, reinforced, or shaped by the media. As part of his social learning theory, psychologist Albert Bandura (1977) described the "sleeper effect," which not only provides insights for understanding how media teaching/learning works but also has special implications for media-based learning about diversity. The "sleeper effect" suggests that ideas, often clothed as entertainment, can subconsciously enter and become part of a viewer's unrecognized cognitive or affective storehouse. Once they find a home, diversity-related beliefs or antigroup prejudices may lie dormant until provoked by some external stimulus, like a personal or mediated experience (Comstock, 1978). Remember how the question, What do you know about Gypsies?, provoked responses from fourth-grade students based on their "sleeping" knowledge!

Media consumers themselves provide evidence of the "sleeper effect." In the popular 1980 movie satire, *Airplane!*, the airline captain continually tries to seduce a little boy passenger, using subtle and not-so-subtle laughter-producing advances. At one point he asks the boy, "Have you ever stayed in a Turkish prison?", a line that provoked an uproarious audience response the night I saw the movie. Would that line have been as funny if it went, "Have you ever stayed in a prison?" Maybe. How about a "Swedish prison?" Nothing funny there. An "Argentine prison?" Probably not. But Turkish prison worked particularly well as humor. Why?

Because the movie's content—Have you ever stayed in a Turkish prison?—touched a sleeping chord. It connected with information, ideas, mental schema, and expectations of its audiences. It worked because the filmmakers had correctly predicted audience "sleeping" predispositions and cleverly manipulated them. The filmmakers presumed—and were proven correct—that audiences would respond to "Turkish prison" as a humorous trope for homosexuality.

But how could the filmmakers have predicted that response? Did they assume that most viewers had learned in school that Turkish prisons were hotbeds of homosexuality? Of course not. Few schools (at least American schools) teach *anything* about Turkey. Or that most viewers had read scholarly books about Turkey containing discussions of sex life in Turkish prisons? Dubious. Or that they had even read articles about Turkish prisons? A few viewers, maybe.

However, the makers of *Airplane!* must have known that millions of moviegoers had recently been exposed to the powerful imagery of Turkish prisons in the 1978 hit film, *Midnight Express*, adapted from American Billy Hayes's best-selling account of his imprisonment in Turkey. Simultaneously skillful in execution and sensationalistic in conception, the movie took Hayes's grueling narrative and reshaped it to further dehumanize Turks. (In contrast, while the book excoriated Turkish prison conditions, it also presented Turks in a far more human and diverse manner.) Moreover, the movie accentuated the themes of prison homosexuality and Turkish brutality.

With *Midnight Express* priming audiences, *Airplane!* merely had to present the "Turkish prison" line. Media-prepared audiences did the rest. Rapidly and reactively drawing upon their previous movie learning (or reinforcement) and their own preexistent internal "sleeping" images, audiences functioned as cocreators of the film's meaning by playing an active (if unconscious) role in constructing the Turkish image. (According to a Chinese proverb, "We see what is behind our eyes.")

Conclusion: Omnipresence of Media-based Learning

Serendipitously, I stumbled across another example of the "sleeper effect" in my own home. One morning in September 1986, while enjoying a cup of coffee and scanning the daily newspapers, I chanced to turn on the popular American daytime television game show, *The $25,000 Pyramid*. Competition involves two-person teams of total strangers. A series of words appears on a screen in front of one player, who then gives clues to guide the partner into correctly identifying the maximum number of words within the time limit. The team that gets the most correct words wins.

As I watched, the word "gangs" popped onto one cluer's screen. Without hesitation, she shouted, "They have lots of these in East L.A." (a heavily Mexican American section of Los Angeles). Responding immediately, the guest celebrity partner answered, "Gangs." Under competitive pressure, two strangers had instantly achieved mental communion through their coinciding visions of a Chicano community as being synonymous with gangs. Moreover, they had also served as media teachers by transmitting this ethnic stereotype to a national television audience.

Unfortunately, East Los Angeles does have Chicano gangs. But it also has a multitude of far more prevalent features, like families, schools, businesses, churches, and socially contributing organizations. Yet gangs, not such other aspects of East L. A. life, had rapidly and reflexively linked these total strangers. Why?

The answer lies with the "sleeper effect" and the media, which have demonstrated a fixation with Latino gangs. From news reports and documentaries to TV series and feature films, the media have selected, elevated, and reinforced gangs as *the* quintessential popular vision of East L.A. (and many other Latino communities). *Pyramid* both dramatized this media learning and added to the bombardment of media teaching. The media, in short, have created a gang-featuring public curriculum on Latinos.

The *Pyramid* and *Airplane!* examples further illustrate the multicultural teaching power of the media and their capacity to influence public perceptions of groups, nations, and cultures. Media multicultural textbooks—both news and entertainment—provide myriad, continuous opportunities for consumers to extract, construct, or reinforce knowledge, beliefs, and attitudes about diversity. We can never know precisely what each individual—including each student—has learned multiculturally from the media. Yet we can be virtually certain that media-based learning about diversity is occurring.

PART III

Media and Education in Contemporary Perspective

CHAPTER 6

October 1997:
A Multicultural Media Journal

Now that we have explored the broad topics of mediamakers, media content, and media learning, let us focus on the *contemporary* media multicultural curriculum, the context in which schools currently operate. We cannot determine *precisely* what the current media curriculum is teaching. There are simply too many newspapers, magazines, television programs, radio shows, and movies for anyone to be able to identify and describe the *entire* curricular content. Nor can we specify the precise nature of each person's media consumption or create an all-inclusive, up-to-date picture of an individual's media-based multicultural learning.

We all, however, can gain insight by examining our own *personal* media multicultural curricula, which we each create through choice, accident, and habit. This allows us to contemplate the contemporary media curriculum's potential for teaching and learning. In this chapter I will provide a multicultural media journal model, which can be used by anyone—student, teacher, or parent—to develop greater self-awareness of personal media multicultural curricular exposure and learning patterns. In Chapter 7 I will demonstrate how to use such personal journal evidence to draw broader conclusions about the media multicultural curriculum. In Chapter 8 I will suggest pedagogical strategies, including the use of such a journal, to help students more effectively and analytically grapple with their own media multicultural learning.

When I give long-range multicultural education training, I sometimes ask participants to keep personal media curriculum journals—records of and reactions to the multicultural teaching that they encounter during their *normal* media consuming. I emphasize *normal*. If you specifically search for such media, you reduce the validity of your analysis by skewing that natural curriculum. Just pursue your usual media habits, but with one additional dimension. Make note of and think about its multicultural content. In this way you can assess the media multicultural context in which you normally operate, the teaching that this curriculum offers, and what you may be learning.

To begin, write a brief description of your general media consumption habits. When I am home, I read two newspapers every day—my hometown Riverside (California) *Press-Enterprise* and the nearby *Los Angeles Times*, usually in that order. I regularly read *Newsweek* and *Sports Illustrated*, as well as myriad special-interest magazines. Besides movies (in theater or on TV), my television viewing mainly includes news (occasionally in Spanish), sports, police series (*Law & Order* and *Homicide: Life on the Street*), British mysteries (*Morse* and *Silent Witness*), and an occasional comedy. While driving, I usually surf talk radio. When I'm on the road giving lectures and workshops, I consume *U.S.A. Today,* local daily newspapers, and local newscasts, which help me get a quick fix on the community's diversity scene.

After doing this general self-assessment, keep an annotated record of the multicultural dimensions of one month's (or one week's) media consumption. To illustrate, I will share mine. For no particular reason, except that it coincided with writing this book, I chose October 1997. While continuing my normal media consumption habits, I also kept a journal of media multicultural content. The following day-by-day journal synthesis suggests the extensiveness, variety, and unpredictability of that curriculum. It also demonstrates how, over time, this approach can be used to reassess constantly the continuities and changes in the media multicultural curriculum.

Let the Media Curriculum Begin

Wednesday, October 1. "Love gay kids, bishops say," read the lead story headline of the *Press-Enterprise*. That story dealt with the document, "Always Our Children," issued the previous day by the Administrative Board of the National Conference of Catholic Bishops. Even more multiculturally, the article stated the varying positions on homosexuality taken by the Union of Hebrew Congregations, the Southern Baptist Church, and the Episcopal Church. Welcome to the media-disseminated multireligious values debate.

Page one of the *Los Angeles Times* carried a story about the release of a federal commission report on immigration. It called for an overhaul of the Immigration and Naturalization Service, the naturalization process, the education of immigrant children, the oath of allegiance, and legal immigration. To provide multiple perspectives on the report and help organize that information for readers, the paper rounded up the usual spokespeople, representatives of such organizations as the Federation for American Immigration Reform and the National Council of La Raza.

In both newspapers, the treatment of diversity ran throughout. This included what would emerge as an ongoing curricular strand: discrimination (in this case, age—a class action suit by 70-and-over professors against the California State University system); and harassment (sexual—a feature article on Anita Hill of Clarence Thomas confirmation hearings fame and her new book, *Speaking Truth to Power*).

Of particular interest to me was a story entitled "Hispanic Marrow Donors Sought." Bone marrow transplants can only take place between people with similar genetic makeup. Because of the underrepresentation of minority groups in the National Marrow Donor Program, fewer than 5% of minorities find donors, compared to 84% of non-Hispanic Whites. To the degree that ethnicity influences genetic matches, vital for successful transplants, this makes a compelling public health argument *against* the oft-heard suggestion to drop "race" as a government record category.

Talk Radio Weighs In

Thursday, October 2. The newspaper textbooks continued some of the previous day's multicultural themes. More on immigration, including a news story that Sierra Club members would vote on a proposal to support immigration reduction to restrain population growth, as well as Alexander Cockburn's (1997) lacerating column, which began, "One of the dirty semisecrets of American environmentalism has been its century-long obsession with population control and racial eugenics. Today, the obsession is alive and malign as ever" (p. B-9). More on sexual harassment—news that a Dallas law firm had won the heavy competition to handle Paula Jones's lawsuit against President Clinton.

Today's media curriculum also introduced a new multicultural theme, the October 4 million-Christian-man march organized by the Promise Keepers. The *Press-Enterprise* carried hers-and-his columns by Ellen Goodman (a White woman) and Clarence Page (a Black man). I mention race and gender because the paper regularly prints pictures of its columnists, thereby transmitting multicultural messages to those who only glance at the headlines (not necessarily written by the columnists). "Women, back to the cheerleading section" above her picture; "Promise Keepers echo Million Man March" above his.

I also made my first October foray into talk radio. Dr. Laura Schlessinger's show opened with the announcement that this was a prerecorded program due to her observance of Rosh Hashanah, the Jewish New Year—a reminder that the United States is not a purely Christian nation, but rather a multireligious country with a majoritarian Christian religious tradition. Dr. Laura discussed a new study demonstrating that immigrant children tend to do worse in school as they become more Americanized. This served as a (probably unintentional) critique of the immigration commission's report calling for the more rapid Americanization of immigrant children.

Then there was Rush Limbaugh, replaying a previous day's extended conversation with a caller from South Dakota. After talking at length about such topics as income taxes, the caller shifted the conversation to Mexicans. It turned out that he had moved (escaped) to South Dakota from Hidalgo County in south Texas, lamenting that the United States had already *lost* south Texas and southern California to Mexico. As evidence of this territorial "loss," he stated that there were now eight *Mexican* congressmen from south Texas. Wrong! There are *no* Mexican congressmen from south Texas, but rather a number of *American* congressmen who *also* happen to be of Mexican ancestry, a distinction that Limbaugh chose not to point out. Let's hope that listeners used their analytical thinking skills to correct this misinformation and keep it from becoming part of their mental schema.

It's Just Entertainment

Friday, October 3. Dr. Laura still observing Rosh Hashanah (as mediated by her radio program). Christian men still gathering in D.C. (as mediated by television and print).

While multicultural newspaper articles abounded, the day's major curricular action occurred in the *Times* entertainment section. First came the debut of two new movies: *The Matchmaker,* about the search for an Irish American politician; and *Kiss the Girls,* a "buddy" movie in which a Black male forensic psychologist and a White female surgeon team up to search for a serial killer/kidnapper. Then there was a brief note that MGM had reluctantly accepted a tough NC–17 rating for *Bent,* the film adaptation of the award-winning play about homosexuals in a Nazi concentration camp. This led to a protest by the Gay & Lesbian Alliance Against Defamation, arguing that a similar display of hetero sex would have received a softer R rating.

Most intriguing was an essay by *Times* TV critic Howard Rosenberg on that evening's PBS documentary, *Redefining Racism: Fresh Voices from Black America.* The program featured Larry Elder, an articulate, engaging, Los Angeles African American radio talk show host, whose multicultural curriculum belabors the obvious point that White racism is not the *only* problem that Black Americans face. I decided to give the Elder documentary a try, but halfway through it my wife and I switched to a movie due to the tiresome repetition of the familiar Elder theme.

Moreover, the TV textbook's title was disingenuous, maybe even hypocritical. Fresh Voices? Elder has his own radio show. Walter Williams, one of his guests, appears on television, is quoted regularly in the press, and sometimes sits in for Rush Limbaugh. Julius Lester has been a regular media presence for years. In fact, Elder's guest list became an unintentional parody of the program's title.

Game Day

Saturday, October 4. The morning newspapers brought a multicultural curricular bonanza of articles, columns, and letters on immigration, affirmative action, Hispanic business, Black library resources, race relations study circles, the Promise Keepers, and varying responses to the Catholic bishops' position on homosexuals. On the entertainment front, a feature story on the new African American hit movie, *Soul Food*, included a discussion of whether or not White audiences would patronize it, while another article addressed the heated pro-and-con debate among Catholic organizations concerning the new TV series *Nothing Sacred*, about an independent young Catholic priest. To those engaged in the debate, the series was not just entertainment.

Later, I took a brief break from writing to watch part of the Mississippi-Tennessee football game. Instead I found the CBS announcers teaching multiculturally. Mississippi coach Tom Tuberville had appealed to Ole Miss students *not* to wave Confederate battle flags—a school tradition—because it detracted from the team, which has many Black players. In addition, as one announcer pointed out, it also made it more difficult for him to recruit Black players. Nonetheless, Confederate battle flags swayed in the stands.

Promises, Promises

Sunday, October 5. The big Sunday news was the previous day's gathering of the Promise Keepers in Washington, a story involving religion, race, and gender. I should say stories, because television and newspaper textbooks provided different—and revealing—emphases, illustrating the media's five types of multicultural teaching/learning functions.

From what I had previously learned—mainly through media textbooks—the Promise Keepers were a Christian, mainly White movement.

Those were my *expectations*. Yet starting on Saturday, TV news emphasized racial brotherhood and gender conflict. Close-ups featured Black
faces or White and Black hands intertwined, while interviews with participants almost invariably included a Black man. I assume this *information*
was accurate. However, the reporting, shot selection, and editing *organized* that information to portray the event as a celebration of racial unity,
transmitting the *value* of interracial brotherhood and *modeling* positive
interracial contact. Then came women, usually a shot of a National Organization for Women leader (more of the media-anointed usual sus-
pects) expressing the fear that the Promise Keepers might lead to relegat-
ing women to the back of the familial bus.

Sunday's papers confirmed my revised media-alerted expectations.
Stories and photos emphasized the event's multiracial dimensions, accompanied by now-predictable Black and White clasped hands and a list
of the Keepers' seven promises, with number six reading, "Reach beyond
any racial and denominational barrier." (The October 13 *Newsweek* coverage would also feature a close-up of Black and White men, with the cap-
tion, "'Racial reconciliation' is yet another subject of controversy.") However, these newspaper stories also reported the numerical predominance
of White men, something not conveyed by television coverage. Finally,
they added another dimension—the presence of Messianic Jews and Jews
for Jesus.

My media learning raised three important multicultural questions.
Will these men actually walk the walk of racial brotherhood in their daily
lives? Will the Promise Keepers actually implement the laudatory goal of
reaching across denominational barriers, or will the movement's effort to
"take back our country for Christ" increase inhospitability for non-
Christian religions? While fostering greater male responsibility, will the
movement confirm or belie the female protesters' fears? Only time . . .
and the media . . . will tell.

Monday, October 6. Today talk radio weighed in. Dennis Prager
lauded the Promise Keepers, while John Kobylt and Ken Chiampou reacted with their usual cynicism. From a newspaper report I learned that
movement founder Bill McCartney had appeared on NBC's *Meet the Press*.
To the degree that the Associated Press story was accurate, it supported
the legitimacy of the women protesters' fears. Addressing the issue of
familial decision-making, McCartney reportedly stated, "Somebody has
to break the tie" and the man should take the authority, "tenderly and
gently." I know how my wife would react if I came home and informed
her that henceforth, on disagreements, I would "break the tie" . . . even if
it were "tenderly and gently."

Yet the day's newspaper multicultural curriculum went well beyond the Promise Keepers. Previews of the upcoming Supreme Court session, with cases involving affirmative action, sexual harassment, and Indian territorial rights. The impact of California's successful antiaffirmative action initiative on UCLA law school. A controversy over the federal government's building of a Continental Divide recreational trail through northern New Mexico. Rerouted around the Jicarilla Apache reservation due to tribal opposition, the trail now encountered challenges from Rio Arriba County Hispanos, because it would disrupt their livestock grazing in Carson National Forest.

But the crown jewel of that day's multicultural curriculum was the *Press-Enterprise* two-page editorial section . . . a rainbow coalition of pictured columnists. One Black male (Clarence Page), one Brown male (Richard Estrada), one White male (George Will), and one White female (Joan Beck)—each organizing information, providing interpretations, disseminating values, and building expectations about a different multicultural topic. In order of page placement: Will in support of a multiracial census category; Estrada on the importance of multiethnic role models; Beck on the implications of a national reading and math test for women and minorities; and Page questioning the value of college entrance examinations, including their tendency to *underpredict* the performance of Blacks and Latinos.

And, despite reading those two newspapers, someone that day probably voiced that nonsensical notion that if teachers simply discussed similarities and refrained from talking about human differences, students wouldn't notice them. That is, if we could also prevent students from ever reading newspapers or listening to talk radio or watching television or going to the movies.

Tuesday, October 7. More stories and commentary on immigration, affirmative action, and, of course, the Promise Keepers, with pro and con letters, as well as newspaper columnist spin doctors. Moreover, columnist Cal Thomas ventured into the multicultural educational dimensions of fictional TV, comparing the treatment of God in two series, *Touched by an Angel*, which he liked, and *Nothing Sacred*, which he didn't like.

The *Press-Enterprise* covered the week-long National Coming Out Day activities at my school, the University of California, Riverside. I learned that Maggie Hawkins, director of UCR's Lesbian, Gay, Bisexual, and Transgender Resource Center (LGBT), credited *Ellen's* coming-out episode and the current hit movie, *In & Out*, with providing visibility for the conference.

Thomas and Hawkins illustrate two pervasive elements of media multicultural education. First, relentless media *intertextuality*—media drawing from and commenting on other media. Second, the power of entertainment media. Both Christian conservative Thomas and LGBT activist Hawkins recognized the multicultural teaching power and learning potential emanating from the entertainment media.

We're Off to See the Wizard

Wednesday, October 8. Travel day from Riverside to Washington for a couple of professional engagements. During my drive to the airport, talk radio focused on some byzantine El Paso story about a highly effective Mexican American undercover narcotics agent, who apparently became exposed, partly due to racism and jealousy of DEA and FBI rivals. Crime and race were still on my mind when I arrived at the airport, only to discover that they were also in the day's newspapers ... and in the airport waiting area.

First the preliminaries. The morning papers continued with ongoing multicultural themes: affirmative action, immigration, bilingual education, language (controversies over language usage in the workplace), and sports (the influence of culture on a Samoan running back at the University of Southern California and the achievements of an African American quarterback at the University of Toledo, who overcame being born with severe club feet and still has to run on the edges of his feet).

But the day's major multicultural media event began with a *Times* opinion piece, "Bias in Hiring Is a Bigger Problem Among Smaller Companies." This included a statement by a local entrepreneur that, "The media portrayal of African Americans as violent and involved in crime and drugs works against them, especially in small-business hiring." (Ironically, the paper also carried reviews of the new Tupac Shakur film, *Gang Related,* in which the late rap singer played a corrupt cop.)

Sitting across from me in the airport, a White couple loudly berated Mike Hernandez, a Los Angeles City Councilman who had been arrested for buying cocaine and had admitted his addiction. But rather than simply—and legitimately—criticizing Hernandez for his betrayal of public trust, they turned it into an "ethnic" thing, ranting about how awful it was now that Latinos and Blacks were in positions of power.

Then their remarks *really* turned ugly, with derogatory comments about Hernandez's physical appearance. In truth, he doesn't exactly look like Andy Garcia. Unfortunately, neither do I. Yet this couple had reframed the media bombardment of stories and pictures about this wayward elected official into an indictment of an entire ethnic group. I can't recall media coverage of Watergate, Iran-Contra, or the Monica Lewinsky affair becoming an indictment of Whiteness.

But the plot thickens. That very same *Times* also carried an article, "Genuine Apology or Sorry Excuse," using Hernandez as the launching pad for analyzing apology strategies used by public figures, augmented by a catchy photo of a dark-skinned young man holding the letters, "I'm Sorry." As I put down the paper, I recalled the entrepreneur's statement about bias in hiring.

Thursday, October 9. Consulting in D.C., followed by a long walk and casual reading. Because I subscribe to lots of publications, which invariably stack up, I use road time to catch up. Today my goal included back issues of *Sports Illustrated.* A reprieve from media multicultural education? Hardly.

I began with the September 1 special issue on the National Football League, featuring a story entitled "Party of Five," about emerging stars of the five American Football Conference Central Division teams. The core of the story was the fact that three of them were "young, mobile, strong-armed, African-American quarterbacks" (Silver, 1997, p. 190). The story highlighted their struggle to overcome the long-standing presumption that quarterback was not a natural position for African Americans.

Ensuing issues continued *Sports Illustrated*'s multicultural curriculum. September 8: A story about the Continental Basketball Association's attempt to become a minor league alternative to college for (mainly Black) newly graduated high schoolers à la professional baseball's minor leagues. September 15: A cover photo of young African American tennis sensation Venus Williams, with the lead story focusing on her achievements and racially tinged clashes at the U.S. Open Tournament; and a story on temperamental Chicago Bears linebacker Bryan Cox, once again featuring the topic of racism.

Then the day's news. *USA Today* carried articles on affirmative action, the treatment of Catholicism and abortion on that evening's episode of *Nothing Sacred,* and that day's *Ellen* story (her anger over ABC's plan to place an "adult content" warning before one of her episodes). CNN reported that numerous advertisers had withdrawn from *Nothing Sacred* and that advertiser pressure had led *Esquire* to pull a story about a gay man. Both *USA Today* and local D.C. television teemed with ethnic crime stories, most significantly the court martial of Army Sergeant Major Gene McKinney (an African American) for sexual misconduct. By the time I actually watched *Nothing Sacred* that night, it was multiculturally almost anticlimactic.

Friday, October 10. A day spent walking around the National Mall, ending with the Vietnam War Memorial. As I gazed at the gut-wrenching list of Americans who had died in Vietnam, the enormous number of Spanish surnames provided eloquent silent testimony of the thousands of Latinos who had given their lives in war to protect the right of Rush Limbaugh's South Dakota caller to air his vitriolic radio textbook about Mexico taking over south Texas. (I also wonder what he thought when the April 12, 1999 *Newsweek* carried a cover photo of the first three U.S. soldiers captured in the NATO conflict with Serbia and two of them were Mexican Americans . . . one from Texas?)

After more than six hours of walking, I dove into five back issues of *Newsweek*. All contained myriad multicultural stories, most prominently a special report on the 40th anniversary of the federally enforced desegregation of Little Rock's Central High School. The "My Turn" section, which each week features a full-page guest column, caught my eye. Two of the five columns were written by African Americans—Thomas Sowell (September 8) and James Meredith (October 6)—both conservatives, both champions of color blindness, yet both of whom wrote about (what else?) race. Larry Elder would probably include them among his "fresh voices from Black America," although both are quoted continually by the mainstream media and Sowell has his own syndicated newspaper column.

Saturday, October 11. After a day-long meeting to plan an upcoming school district multicultural workshop, I used my flight home to peruse miscellaneous magazines. First came various ethnic magazines. These demonstrated the critical role of group niche media, which apply alternative lenses to stories that have been covered quite differently by the general interest media.

For example, *Hispanic Business* carried an article on the year 2000 census. The mainstream media had been focusing on the debate over census treatment of the growing number of multiracial Americans. *Hispanic Business,* on the other hand, examined a facet I had not previously encountered. A federal task force had recommended that the question, "Are you of Hispanic origin?" be moved *ahead* of the race question, because sample surveys revealed less confusion among respondents than in the 1990 census format, which placed the Hispanic question *after* race.

I then turned to other periodicals, which further added to my media multicultural curriculum. Take the September 1997 *Phi Delta Kappan*, which carried an interview with E. D. Hirsch Jr., best known for his 1987 book, *Cultural Literacy*. Hirsch pointed out that he had expanded his original cultural literacy concept by forming a multicultural advisory committee in 1988. Even my late-night drive home was accompanied by a talk radio discussion of sexual harassment. My trip had turned into nearly wall-to-wall media multicultural education.

Meanwhile, Back in Riverside

Sunday, October 12. I declared today a media-free zone. Time for family, including jigsaw puzzles with Holly and Melissa. Oh, yes, I did give a talk on diversity and intergroup relations at a local Presbyterian church.

Monday, October 13. The morning papers and talk radio revisited some of the standard multicultural themes, but also broached some new diversity-related topics: the largest Reform Jewish congregation to appoint an openly gay rabbi (it happened to be in southern California), a talk radio attack on diversity training, and radio talk show host Ronn Owens defending the inclusion of "nigger" (designated a pejorative term) in the *Miriam Webster Dictionary*.

But the main media multicultural topic was Nation of Islam leader Louis Farrakhan's call for Blacks to transform Thursday, October 16, the first anniversary of the Million Man March, into a national day of atonement to remind White Americans of the importance of Blacks. How? By staying home from work and school. Launched by the media-savvy Farrakhan on Sunday via NBC's *Meet the Press*, by Monday the story had traveled intertextually to newspapers and talk radio—I only heard the negative reactions of Ronn Owens and Larry Elder.

Tuesday, October 14. And the multicultural beat went on. Dan Walters's column on immigration: because of the federal government's crackdown on the U.S.-Mexican border, more illegal immigrants are remaining permanently in the United States rather than returning annually to Mexico. (Larry Elder argued on radio that illegal immigration was not a problem.) Cal Thomas's column on gender and employment. The resilient ethnic press: a fascinating article on *Bien*, the nation's only Danish-language weekly newspaper, published since 1882. But maybe the most striking, symbolic multicultural entry was a color photo of the seven newly chosen members of the Tournament of Roses Royal Court—a multiracial, multiethnic rainbow of sisterhood. Today's media had transmitted the values of both intragroupness (Farrakhan and *Bien*) and intergroupness (the Royal Court)!

That night, after watching a movie on HBO, I was slow to flip off the set. On came a stand-up comedy special. How did the comic bill himself? Richard Jeni: A Good Catholic Boy. Welcome to the America of self-hyphenation.

Wednesday, October 15. On my flight to the San Francisco Bay Area to speak at a community college, I read my two daily newspapers, abounding as usual with diversity-related articles. Ditto during my return flight with the October 10 *Chronicle of Higher Education*, including the experiences of a White professor in a traditionally Black college and the interracial dimensions of the career of one of my favorite jazz musicians, pianist Dave Brubeck. To top it off, during my homeward drive, talk radio weighed in with a discussion of protests against Native American sports mascots.

Thursday, October 16. The day began with the normal media multicultural curriculum as both daily newspapers carried stories and commentary on diversity, including California's upcoming antibilingual education initiative and a scathing retrospective on *The Bell Curve*. For the first time in days I watched a national newscast, in this case ABC. Stories included the continuing economic gender cap and a White family's crusade to carve an enormous mountain monument to Chief Crazy Horse.

Time out for entertainment. Tonight I chose *Cracker*, ABC's adaptation of the popular English TV mystery series about a misanthropic forensic psychologist. Since it turned out to be the second segment of a two-part show, "Hell Hath No Fury" (I had missed the first part), I was about to turn it off, but the introduction so mesmerized me that I had to watch it.

The complex story dealt with a Latino transsexual. Raised by his Mexican immigrant parents as a boy, Luis wants to be a girl, a fact he can confide only to his sister, Ana. Rejected for a sex-change operation, he begins taking estrogen. Desperate to be a mother, the grown Luis kidnaps a Latino infant and then telephones his sister to tell her that the baby is God's gift for his lifetime of suffering. Called in on the case, Cracker works on Ana's Latina guilt to extract this information and then finds Luis, who is about to jump with the baby off a cliff into the ocean. Cracker successfully appeals to the woman inside Luis to hand him the baby before leaping to his death.

While this synthesis does not do justice to the complexity and nuances of the story, I relate it because it reveals how far the entertainment media have come in embracing multicultural themes. No, they're not just entertainment.

Back on the Road Again

Friday, October 17. Off again, to Miami for another national conference, this time on higher education. The drive to the airport brought an extended radio discussion of religious diversity in the United States, while the day's papers provided more variations on continuing, now expected, multicultural themes: Indian gambling, affirmative action, bilingual education, Louis Farrakhan, and a sexual harassment suit.

The papers also introduced what would become a new, ongoing, controversial media curriculum topic, a Beverly Hills speech by Vice President Al Gore in which he lauded Hollywood for one of its media textbooks, *Ellen*. Going beyond content to learning impact, Gore opined that the show had caused Americans to "look at sexual orientation in a more open light."

Saturday, October 18. Today was almost completely devoid of the media . . . except that I gave a conference workshop on Race and the Media. Yet during one of my few spare moments I caught a local TV newsbreak with a Latina and a Black man as coanchors. That image jogged my thinking about media silent visual messages—in this case, opportunity and integration. The coanchors symbolized both ethnic upward mobility (you, too, can make it) and intergroup teamwork (strength through diversity).

Sunday, October 19. I devoted my cross-country flight home to working on this book manuscript. But as soon as I began my drive from the airport, the talk radio curriculum took over in full multicultural force, with discussions of sexual harassment and gays in the military.

The Sunday papers turned out to be a multicultural curricular jamboree. Race and ethnicity: Indian reservation newspapers; the troubled economic condition of U.S. Latinos; White flight from the suburbs to rural areas; the 25th anniversary of Jackie Robinson's death; and, most intriguing, the significance of "Whiteness" in the United States. Immigration: tougher financial standards for sponsoring foreign relatives to live in the United States. Language: a column by Ron Unz, head of California's antibilingual education initiative. Sexual orientation: the 30th anniversary edition of *The Advocate*, a national gay and lesbian news magazine, in which 30 prominent homosexuals predicted their situation 30 years hence.

Monday, October 20. Off to northern California for tomorrow's K–12 workshop on limited-English-speaking students. As fate would have it, that day's newspaper curriculum included various articles on language and cultural diversity. Growing multilingualism on the Internet. A review of Anne Fadiman's new book, *The Spirit Catches You and You Fall Down*, about the linguistic and cultural clash between medical personnel and the Hmong parents of a young girl with severe epilepsy in California's San Joaquin Valley. And a thought-provoking column on bilingual education. Thanks to the media multicultural curriculum, I had new ideas to ponder for the workshop.

Tuesday, October 21. Getting dressed for my workshop, I flipped on *The Today Show* and received a nonstop gender multicultural lesson. First came an interview with Daphne Scholinski, author of *The Last Time I Wore a Dress*. Born with female sexual parts but wanting to be a boy, Daphne was ultimately placed in an institution because of her "gender identity crisis." Today Scholinski is comfortable being a man. Next came a discussion of *The Rules II*, lifestyle guidelines for a woman to get the man she wants.

During my flight home, *USA Today* provided lengthy letters to the editor concerning civil rights for gays and the ABC series, *Nothing Sacred*, as well as a feature story about life within America's Mormon community and that church's relations with other Christian religions. Back home, my newspapers added to the day's media curriculum: a new postage stamp honoring Kwanzaa (an African American celebration), an Orange County experiment with single-gender academies, and the paucity of Asian Americans in higher levels of government. The little time I had spent with the media that day had provided a curriculum on race, religion, gender, and sexual orientation.

Red-eye Time

Wednesday, October 22. Off to the east via an overnight red-eye flight to Charlottesville, Virginia. I read my day's papers before I tried to sleep. Lots of multicultural stories, including a cornucopia of episodes about who's suing whom about what type of discrimination.

Thursday, October 23. A crazy day of travel. Landed at six A.M. at Washington Dulles, took a short hop to Charlottesville to give a Federal Executive Institute faculty seminar on integrating diversity into the curriculum, returned to Dulles, and then flew on to Cleveland.

The CNN Airport Network carried a Larry King interview with the media-omnipresent Anita Hill and a story on job disparities of minority women within corporate management (also covered in the *Cleveland Plain-Dealer*). *USA Today* served up a full-scale multicultural textbook, with stories on middle-class Black families reinvigorating older urban neighborhoods, the continuing controversy over Confederate battle flags at Ole Miss football games, and a New Jersey court decision approving the adoption of a little boy by a gay male couple. And Peter Johnson's "Inside TV" column focused on NBC's ongoing series, *The Sex War: The Tension Between Men and Women*, including the controversy that all of the series executive producers were men.

Finally, as I unpacked in my Cleveland hotel room, I turned to Showtime for some late-night escapism. Instead I stumbled into the conclusion of a 1996 movie called *Bullet*, an ultraviolent flick about an urban gang feud, whose main antagonists were Jewish (Ben) and Black (Tank). I watched it only in passing, so I can't vouch for the details, but I think Tank shot and killed Ben, after which Ben's brother cut Tank's throat. Oh, well, it's just entertainment.

Friday, October 24. The morning TV news brought more multicultural stories, including the upcoming Million (Black) Woman March and the University of Toledo's African American quarterback, who had succeeded despite his deformed feet (previously in the newspapers). After a stimulating diversity conference at Cleveland State University, where I gave the luncheon address, I relaxed with *USA Today*. It provided yet another range of multicultural stories and columns, from the Million Woman March to women in the military to growing success of the gay rights movement, rebutted by a story that a federal appeals court had upheld a Cincinnati initiative forbidding the city from adopting protections based on sexual orientation.

Saturday, October 25. A quiet day in Cleveland, good for museum visiting, manuscript editing, and reading. Of course, diversity was present, including a *Phi Delta Kappan* article on a precedent-setting sexual harassment case at Canada's University of Victoria, a reminder that the United States doesn't have a monopoly on multiculturalism . . . or discrimination.

Predictably, *Sports Illustrated* carried stories about racism, including an ironic pair about two Penn State athletes: Black running back Curtis Enis, who had been the *object* of racial slurs in high school; and White quarterback Kerry Collins (then a Carolina Panther) who had *used* racial slurs. *Newsweek* also proved predictable with its myriad articles on diversity, including yet another *Ellen*-based story, albeit expanded into a discussion of new frontiers in the TV treatment of homosexuality. More personal for me, however, was an article on disability—Bill Clinton's hearing loss—since I belong to that generally ignored "minority" group of tinnitus sufferers, who live with constant ringing in our ears and have to endure a wrap-around environment of noise pollution.

The Home Stretch

Sunday, October 26. Returning home, I found diversity-laden Sunday papers. Nationally: Black women gathering en masse in Philadelphia; immigrants and refugees facing cultural, linguistic, and economic barriers, as well as undocumented workers moving into the Midwest because of job opportunities; and the first of many stories about religious protests against celebrating Halloween. Locally: in Riverside, study circles on race relations; and, in Los Angeles, the blossoming of Koreatown.

Maybe most striking was a *Parade* article about the Police Officer of the Year selected by the International Association of Chiefs of Police. It was accompanied by vignettes and photos of the ten officers who received honorable mention, a rainbow coalition of Latinos, Anglos, and African Americans . . . a vivid values message of multicultural institutional integration and contributions to American society.

Monday, October 27. Today's multicultural curriculum spread throughout the media. Newspaper stories on various dimensions of diversity. Talk radio's Larry Elder critiquing the Million Black Woman March in Philadelphia, as well as discussing a *Jet Magazine* article about the large number of Black women marrying White men. Local TV news with stories about Los Angeles City Councilman Mike Hernandez pleading guilty to cocaine possession and Jesse Jackson leading a protest march in Sacramento.

Then came a multicultural bonanza, the October 27 *Newsweek*. Letters in response to James Meredith's "My Turn" column. Feature stories on Roberto Goizueta, the legendary deceased Cuban American CEO of Coca-Cola, and Allen Iverson, the controversial African American guard for the NBA Philadelphia 76ers.

But the multicultural mother lode was the magazine's follow-up to Vice President Gore's Hollywood speech lauding *Ellen*'s positive depiction of lesbians—a full-scale multiperspective teaching unit. First was an interview with the vice president. Then came "Al's Hollywood Shuffle," a critical response by former vice president Dan Quayle. Finally there was "Gore's Gay Gambit" by *Newsweek* regular Jonathan Alter.

Although Gore and Quayle certainly didn't see eye to eye when it came to *Ellen*, they *both* lined up *with me* about the media's critical teaching role—as information spreader, idea organizer, values disseminator, expectation builder, and behavior modeler. Having hit the jackpot with two vice presidents, I wished this could have ended the month. But there were still four days to go. Media, don't fail me now.

Tuesday, October 28. They didn't. Newspapers overflowed with multicultural teaching: a protest march against Proposition 209 (California's antiaffirmative action initiative); the guilty plea of a local Nazi Low Rider who had assaulted two Black men; and the publication of Salvadoran immigrant Sandra Benitez's second novel, *Bitter Grounds*. Then there were columns by Thomas Sowell attacking the use of race as a factor in college admissions and Dan Walters analyzing the Sierra Club's upcoming vote on the reduction of immigration.

Most interesting was a feature story about Arcadia High School, whose student council was pondering whether or not to eliminate the school's Apache warrior mascot. The apparent care with which the students approached the issue, including open forums and extensive reading, seemed to exemplify the *best* in multicultural education. And the media provided the public textbook on those laudable efforts, as the students prepared to vote on their recommendation to the school board.

Wednesday, October 29. Everywhere I turned there was media multicultural education, from newspapers to talk radio, where Larry Elder discussed women referees in the National Basketball Association and Dennis Prager spoke about accent discrimination. I also watched more television than usual.

While reading the morning papers, I turned on *Tap,* a 1989 film about an African American ex-con torn between resuming his former life as a burglar and pursuing his desire to become a dancer, the latter which he did. Message—putting a life of crime behind you pays. *Law and Order* that night featured a story about three Dominicans suspected of killing a woman in a street shooting. The papers carried stories on Mike Hernandez (including an editorial cartoon) and Nushawn Williams (an African American in upstate New York accused of infecting numerous women with the AIDS virus). Then came the late-evening NBC local news, with the nightly Mike Hernandez update and a story about conflict, including fighting, between Somali and other Black students at a San Diego high school. I guess this was the day for the media curriculum to catch up on ethnic violence and criminality.

But the newspapers featured far more. Sports? A column on the enormous Latino role in the recently completed World Series, as well as stories and photos of the first two NBA women referees, one Black, one White—good ethnic balance. Education? The California Teachers Association's announcement of opposition to the state's upcoming antibilingual education initiative, as well as an interview with Chancellor Robert Berdahl about how the University of California, Berkeley, was coping with Proposition 209, which eliminated race and gender as admissions factors. Religion? A racial discrimination lawsuit involving an African American girl who was suspended from a Seventh-Day Adventist School for supposedly violating its dress code, as well as the decision of Mormon-owned Brigham Young University to remove four nudes from the traveling exhibition of French sculptor Auguste Rodin, including his classic "The Kiss." Today's curriculum nearly created multicultural overload.

Thursday, October 30. Overload marches on. Today's newspapers were cover-to-cover multicultural textbooks, with the *Times* front page alone carrying *four* diversity-theme stories! That day's entries covered immigration, NBA women referees, diversity training, the boom in cosmetics targeted at Asian American women, discrimination law suits (including the California Supreme Court upholding the right of employers to save money by replacing older workers), political implications of Indian reservation gambling, a Latino protest against the continued congressional investigation into the 1996 election of Loretta Sanchez, and, of course, the Mike Hernandez affair. Finally, based on task force recommendations, the Clinton administration had issued new guidelines which meant that, for the first time, Americans could check off more than one racial category in the year 2000 census.

Multicultural stories dominated talk radio. Larry Elder, who regularly criticizes others for talking too much about race, talked, as usual, about race . . . in this case, the new census guidelines. This came on the heels of Dennis Prager blasting the Indiana University administration for punishing a fraternity that had held a scavenger hunt with presumably racist and sexist overtones. The more I listen to talk radio, the more I realize that it has become a mainstay of media multicultural education.

Friday, October 31. My last day. Would the media let me down? Not to worry. Diversity stories ran from national (the increased deportation of illegal immigrants) to state (reactions to the court decision approving the firing of older workers) to local (a city council election in which representation for ethnic communities had become a major issue). A pair of stories highlighted the two-way flow of culture across national boundaries: one about Halloween's impact on the Mexican border city of Tijuana; the other on the impact of Mexico's Day of the Dead on southern California.

It was also a big day for the entertainment curriculum, as refracted by the news media. The ongoing letters to the editor regarding the culture war about *Ellen*. The mixed success of efforts to make the Los Angeles theater scene more multicultural. Reviews of two new movies with multicultural themes: *I Love You, I Love You Not*, about anti-Semitism in a New York City prep school; and *Switchback*, concerning an African American serial killer.

As it was Halloween night, the long parade of ghosts and goblins to our front door restricted my TV viewing to the concluding episode of "Blood Ties," a *Homicide: Life on the Street* three-parter. Once again, the killer turned out to be an African American. But the case was solved by a tenacious Black detective, supported by his equally dedicated Black chief—the standard bad-ethnic/good-ethnic balancing act values message of 1990s' crime shows. In an unusual twist, the killer's millionaire father used his wealth to protect his son from the law, thereby adding the message that rich Blacks can mimic rich Whites in using their resources to avoid justice. Trick or treat!

To top off the day, *Times* television critic Howard Rosenberg previewed the upcoming TV revival of Rodgers and Hammerstein's *Cinderella*. But this time it was a multiracial *Cinderella*, a perfect ending for a week in which the federal government had decided that the census should recognize the United States not only as a multiracial nation, but also as a nation of an increasing number of multiracial individuals.

Coexecutive produced by Whitney Houston (who also played the fairy godmother), it featured Brandy as the Black Cinderella and Paolo Montalban (Filipino, according to Rosenberg) as the prince, the offspring of a White king and Black queen (Whoopi Goldberg). As Rosenberg quipped, "You have to suspend belief to buy the notion that the prince, while trying to trace the black Cinderella through her tootsies, wouldn't notice that most of the females participating in the big try-on are white," followed by his summation of the show as "a fat social message squeezed into a dainty, glass slipper of a fable" (p. F-31).

Although *Cinderella* doesn't rank as one of my favorite musicals, I watched it. I have never seen a more color-conscious effort to portray a color-blind society, especially the prince's ball—a Ku Klux Klansman's nightmare, with every imaginable combination of interracial dancing couples. Holly and Melissa loved it . . . and never mentioned race.

Postscript

A final ironic note. On October 1, the day I began keeping my media multicultural education journal, the *Press-Enterprise* carried the the annual Field poll of the confidence that adult Californians felt about 34 major American institutions. High technology companies ranked at the top of the list, with insurance companies (34) and the legal profession (33) bringing up the rear. While higher education ranked near the top (4), organized religion (18) received more negatives than positives. The U.S. Supreme Court (9) barely edged out the presidency (12), although both had positive ratings, while Congress trailed badly (20), receiving a negative rating.

How about the media? Way down the list, at number 25, stood television and radio news. Two notches below those media, at number 27, sat the public school system.

CHAPTER 7

The Contemporary Media Curriculum as School Context

As my October 1997 curriculum journal demonstrates, unless you boycott media entirely, you cannot avoid media teaching about diversity. It surrounds, informs, and influences all of us—preschool children and K–12 students, teachers and administrators, parents and school board members.

Using my journal as an illustration, I will suggest the characteristics of the contemporary media multicultural curriculum, which in turn creates the context for school education. Moreover, drawing on this analysis, I will then present a Potential Impact Paradigm for hypothesizing the likely effects of the mass media on public learning about diversity.

Even while recognizing that each month's media curriculum has its own special features, that each person has unique media selection habits, and that each consumer filters the media in a personal if often subconscious manner, we can nonetheless tease out certain basic curricular dimensions of the media. I will address these by means of five analytical categories: pervasiveness, themes, patterns, perspectives, and ideology.

Pervasiveness

To be exposed to mass media is to experience multicultural education. Media provide constant, relentless, often surprising multicultural teaching. When we consume media, multicultural teaching and learning will likely occur.

Teaching about diversity pervades all forms of media—information and entertainment, general interest and niche, from every constellation in the galaxy of ideologies, interests, and groups. Sometimes consumers choose media textbooks *because* they contain multicultural content. But multicultural education is also likely to occur unexpectedly in media we choose *without realizing* that they contain information, ideas, or images concerning diversity.

When tuning into talk radio, listeners are not usually aware whether or not they will be encountering discussions of immigration, religion, language, or gender relations. Before reading articles in *Sports Illustrated* or on newspaper sports pages, consumers usually do not know when they will encounter discussions of race relations or overcoming physical handicaps. Media coverage of the last month of the stirring 1998 Mark McGwire-Sammy Sosa home run derby became, in many respects, a course in cultural identity, intergroup perceptions, cross-cultural relations, and even media treatment of diversity.

Moviegoers may encounter unexpected scenes that treat or comment upon race, ethnicity, gender, or religion. Before watching the 1996 Jack Lemmon-James Garner comedy *My Fellow Americans*, Laurel and I had no idea that two ex-presidents would accidentally participate in a Gay Pride Parade while fleeing from assassins, leading to a concluding shootout in which a closeted gay Secret Service agent becomes the hero.

Themes

With mediamaker gatekeepers and spin doctors coming from different directions and espousing different positions, it should come as no surprise that the media multicultural curriculum sends mixed, sometimes conflicting messages about diversity. Yet diversity themes in the media tend to fall into four categories: ongoing, recurring, transitory, and single-shot.

Ongoing. Certain diversity-related themes seem to appear with almost predictable regularity. Few journal days would pass without my encountering some media treatment of certain themes: immigration; homosexuality; language (including controversies over the workplace and bilingual education); intergroup differences and inequities (from education to career advancement, from cultural incompatibilities to access to transplants); and lawsuits involving various types of discrimination based on gender, age, religion, language, accent, sexual orientation, and, of course, race, including so-called reverse discrimination.

The major surprise (to me) was that month's relatively modest news media attention to ethnic involvement in crime, with the major exception of the omnipresent story of Councilman Mike Hernandez. A possible contributing factor for my "crime-lite" month was that I spent considerable time on the road, and, therefore, watched relatively little local TV news. Movies and TV series, however, picked up some of the ethnic crime slack.

Recurring. Certain individuals, groups, and multicultural themes seem capable of capturing media attention on a recurring, although not continuous, basis. Such is the case of the Reverend Louis Farrakhan, head of the Nation of Islam. When Farrakhan speaks, the media listen, report, and comment. In October 1997, he gained brief but widespread access to the media multicultural curriculum with his call for a one-day Black work boycott.

Numerous curricular themes recur, even if intermittently. Diversity and the census often receive media attention: data released; responses to and interpretations of that data; and debates over census content, categories, and procedures. Protests over Indian sports mascots and team names appear episodically (Pewewardy, 1999), as do discussions of the special status of Indian reservations—currently focusing on gambling casinos. Even Cinderella visits periodically, although never before as uniquely and consciously multiracial as in the 1997 Whitney Houston production. That show also provided a fortuitous, entertainment-packaged embodiment of the same week's news announcement that, in the year 2000 census, Americans will be able to check off more than one racial category. Personal multiracialism should become an increasingly recurring, possibly ongoing, theme in the media curriculum—maybe even in schools—given the rapidly growing number of multiracial children, who defy traditional American categorization (Chiong, 1998).

Transitory. Certain multicultural textbook themes enjoy their moment on the media main stage and then recede, as if they had built-in term limits, like school materials consigned to the rear shelves of district depositories. The Promise Keepers came, flourished, and went . . . mediawise, of course. The Million (Black) Woman March came, drew lesser media attention, and also went. The Ole Miss Confederate flag controversy garnered a few weeks of attention. Mike Hernandez ultimately and mercifully sank into virtual media oblivion.

Ellen (even with a boost from Vice President Gore), Paula Jones (until upstaged by Monica Lewinsky), and *Nothing Sacred* (until buried by poor ratings) earned intensive but "term-limited" media attention. Some of these topics may attain recurring curricular status, but they have yet to prove their media longevity.

Single-shot. Finally, the media curriculum teems with multicultural stories that earn only single-shot (or single-day) media treatment. In curricular terms, these can be viewed as comparable to textbook inserts of photos or minibiographies of "famous women"—present but marginal. Yet cumulatively they provided variety to the media curriculum.

Patterns

Beyond types of themes, certain media structural patterns, in themselves, influence the nature of the curriculum. Take two of these: the combination gatekeeper-spin doctor role; and the tendency to generate ongoing multi-day curricula about selected diversity-related topics, with each type of media spinning that topic according to a temporal pecking order.

By selecting which topics, information, and ideas will and will not be made accessible to the consumer, mediamakers serve as curricular gatekeepers. In this way they influence—at times even determine—what voices do and do not gain access to media dissemination. At the same time mediamakers often put a spin on those topics and voices, such as through commentary or framing (for example, headlines, teasers for ensuing TV news stories or talk radio topics, and marketing of movies and television programs). These frames succinctly suggest to consumers what they should expect and extract from the media textbook.

For example, take Rush Limbaugh's October 2 gatekeeping decision to replay, in its entirety, a previous caller's diatribe about the so-called Mexican takeover of South Texas. In this case Limbaugh also provided a spin by deciding *not* to correct the caller's assertion about eight Mexican congressmen from Texas (actually, all were *Americans,* of Mexican descent).

Then there is the media temporal pecking order, illustrated by the treatment of the Promise Keepers gathering in Washington. First, pre-event anticipatory stories and commentary framed the event and primed consumer expectations. Second, radio and TV provided on-the-spot coverage via highly abbreviated segments. This was followed by phase three—newspapers—which also used headlines and photos (for example, the visual *overrepresentation* of minority participation) to frame or reframe the event's meanings. Fourth, by providing their various spins, pundits tried to influence how media consumers interpreted, drew values from, and maybe even changed behavior as a result of the mediated event. Fifth, gatekeepers allowed selected letters to the editor or talk-show callers to add their voices to that media curriculum. Finally, magazines weighed in with postmortems. And, if we wait long enough, we may even get a TV docudrama or feature film, comparable to Spike Lee's 1996 *Get on the Bus,* which concerned the Million Man March.

Perspectives

One of the most intriguing aspects of that month's media multicultural curriculum was the variety of ways in which multiple perspectives on diversity-related themes made their appearance. Take four of these processes: internal multiple perspectives, external dueling perspectives, mainstream versus niche media, and media intertextuality.

Internal Multiple Perspectives. Individual media textbooks often provide—or make the pretense of providing—multiple perspectives on diversity-related issues. Sometimes perspectivism (or pseudo-perspectivism) is the very format of the textbooks. For example, TV talk shows like *Crossfire* ("From the left, from the right"), *Both Sides*, and *Politically Incorrect* often deal with diversity-related topics.

When newspeople want to provide multiple perspectives on a multicultural topic—or at least give that appearance—they often round up the usual voices. Typically this means oft-quoted spokespersons for prominent organizations. As a result, what passes for media-disseminated multiple perspectives often turns out to be predictable reiterations of organizational creeds.

Multiperspective patterns have also become entertainment media staples, such as Hollywood's hoary good-ethnic/bad-ethnic tradition. Taking root in 1930s movies, that form traditionally involved two members of the same ethnic group (usually Irish Americans or Italian Americans), sometimes brothers, one choosing the criminal low road, the other choosing the socially constructive high road, occasionally even law enforcement. This intraethnic balance trope has become nearly standard on television. (In fall 1998, NBC offered *Trinity*, a series involving three Irish American brothers—a policeman, a priest, and a criminal.) In other shows, such as *Homicide: Life on the Street* and *Law and Order*, this balance has been reconfigured as multiracial as well as multiethnic. This allows for plenty of criminals of different backgrounds, balanced by the racial and gender diversity of crime fighters.

External Dueling Perspectives. Alongside multiple perspectives *within* a single story or show stand dueling perspectives in different media textbooks or chapters. Occasionally this occurs within the same product. In addressing the purported impact of *Ellen* on American thinking and mores, the October 27 *Newsweek* ran three separate contrasting perspectives: an interview with vice president Al Gore, an opinion piece by former vice president Dan Quayle, and an essay by *Newsweek* regular Jonathan Alter.

Sometimes *different* media textbooks accidentally and incidentally offer alternative perspectives on diversity-related topics, sometimes with unintended irony. This struck me when October 1 newspapers reported the federal immigration commission's call for the more rapid Americanization of immigrant children. But in the next day's Dr. Laura rebroadcast, she discussed a new study indicating that Americanization, in fact, was contributing to the *decline* of immigrant educational achievement. However, those specific dueling perspectives became part of the media curricula of only those people who both read that article and heard that particular Dr. Laura segment.

Whether or not the individual consumer becomes exposed to multiple media perspectives depends greatly upon personal habits. Casting a wide media net—varieties of print media and talk-show hosts of differing ideological persuasions—brings greater likelihood of encountering contrasting visions of diversity and multiple interpretations of diversity-related issues. Conversely, the narrower a consumer's media habits—relying on a single hometown newspaper, the same daily newscast, or the same radio talk show host to filter the wide world of diversity—the more likely the consumer will fall under the potential tyranny of a small number of curricular gatekeepers and spin doctors.

Mainstream versus Niche Media. Niche media offer a variation of this process. The mainstream press, general interest television, and even national talk radio provide a different set of frames than, for example, the ethnic print press, non-English-speaking television, and religious radio stations or networks (Kaniss, 1991). As of 1998, there were 1,600 Protestant evangelical radio outlets, while the Spanish-language Univisión ranked as the fifth largest U.S. TV network.

A word of caution lest this discussion seem too celebratory of media multicultural curricular diversity. The *power* factor cannot be ignored. Niche media generally do not reach the wide range of consumers touched by mainstream media. Ethnic and religious publications are usually read by their adherents or others with a special interest in those topics. But because most do not enjoy widespread dissemination to a diverse audience, they generally lack the broad teaching potential of major national magazines like *Time* or *Newsweek.* Spanish-language radio stations have now grabbed the number one listenership spots in certain cities, such as Miami and Los Angeles, but this does not give them the extensive teaching power of a Rush Limbaugh or Dr. Laura, disseminated nationally through the mainstream media. Power still counts. As sociologist Todd Gitlin (1980) argued:

> Those who rule the dominant institutions secure their power in large measure directly and indirectly, by impressing their definitions of the situation upon those they rule and, if not usurping the whole ideological space, still significantly limiting what is thought throughout society. (p. 10)

The presence of mediated multiple perspectives in no way suggests an equality of access to audiences. Nor, for that matter, do educational catalogues or supplementary reading lists featuring materials about women and different ethnic groups demonstrate an equality of access to classrooms. States, districts, schools, and teachers greatly influence student exposure to diverse ideas by their gatekeeping of educational materials.

Intertextuality. Finally, the month of October 1997 illustrated the role of media intertextuality in the multicultural curriculum. Newspapers discuss television shows. Magazines expand upon newspaper stories. Radio and TV talk show hosts draw ideas from print media, even while criticizing those very media for their biases (meaning, of course, that their biases diverged from those of the commentator). TV and print movie critics discuss . . . well . . . TV and movies. Films and television series draw upon stories that have been unearthed, disseminated, and publicized by the news media.

For example, NBC presented a series, *The Sex War: The Tension Between Men and Women*, which drew on a variety of sources, including information and ideas disseminated by the print media. Conversely, that series received criticism, some of it appearing in the print media, because all of the series' executive producers were men.

Outside forces, too, use media intertextually to comment on media textbooks. The United States abounds with organizations that devote themselves to monitoring, expressing concern about, and protesting against the media curriculum for fear of its pedagogical influence. When mediamakers create textbooks that transmit values or model behavior considered by some to be demeaning or antisocial, protests will likely erupt, both by other mediamakers and by outsiders who disseminate their ideas through the media. Most commonly, this means print media and talk radio airing external criticisms of the entertainment media. The two most significant October 1997 multicultural curricular protests were directed at entertainment television—*Ellen* and *Nothing Sacred*. Presumably this had to do with concerns over teaching—and potential learning—about homosexuality and religion.

Ideology

Discussions of diversity-related ideology within the American media often boil down to two basic either/or framed arguments. Are the media conservative or liberal? Are they or are they not biased against and therefore provide negative treatment of Group X (conversely, are they too "politically correct")? Yet the tunnel-vision nature of these questions actually impedes the consideration of ideological complexities.

First, conservative versus liberal. My October 1997 odyssey buttressed my belief that this dichotomy is worse than useless when it comes to analyzing the nuances of the media's multicultural curriculum, and even multiculturalism itself. Yet it dominates because it taps into a consumer comfort zone, the American lust for simplistic, clear-cut dualisms or at least straight-line continua rather than the complex multiperspective contemplation of issues.

Equally simplistic are analyses that frame the issue in yes/no terms of political correctness or media bias against a group. Is media treatment of Topic W good or bad? Is the media's portrayal of members of Group X positive or negative? Do the media stereotype or not stereotype Group Y? Are the media politically correct when it comes to Group Z? The issues of treatment, portrayal, and stereotyping are important, but far too complex for such either/or approaches.

Rather ideology operates in a more subtle fashion in the contemporary media multicultural curriculum. October 1997 exemplified three kinds of current curricular ideologies—maybe better yet, ideological battlegrounds. I would describe these as multiculturalist, desegregationist, and Americanist. These three ideological arenas should be viewed as intersecting and overlapping, rather than as parallel and discrete.

Multiculturalist. The media seem to confirm Nathan Glazer's book title, *We Are All Multiculturalists Now* (1997). However, when I suggest that the media generally subscribe to a multicultural ideology, I am not arguing that they always adopt a "celebrating diversity" cheerleading position. Rather, I would call the reigning media ideology one of "recognitional multiculturalism"—the implicit, often begrudging, recognition of the growing societal pervasiveness and tenacity of diversity.

Emanating from this basic recognitional multicultural ideology is a media curriculum that reverberates with competing (although not necessarily equally disseminated) voices (Gray, 1995; Simon & Alexander, 1993). Sometimes these voices extol diversity, emphasize its positive benefits, suggest how to improve mutual adaptation to increasingly pluralistic settings, or analyze continuing short falls in equity, justice, and intergroup understanding. For example, the *Los Angeles Times* periodically carries a column called "Multicultural Manners" by Norine Dresser (1996), author of a book with the same title.

In contrast, other media voices express their recognitional position in oppositional terms, ranging from angst to anger, from concern to calumny. The major target appears to be multicultural tenacity—the refusal of some groups to "melt" fully into the proverbial pot. Such groups maintain and even more publicly display their differences from the traditional norm, whether these differences involve language, cultural practices, ethnic pride, non-Judeo-Christian religious beliefs, or gay identity.

One curricular irony is that, in explicitly criticizing multiculturalism, mediamakers actively add to that curriculum by dwelling on diversity-related issues. Even as they insistently denounce multiculturalism, they simultaneously call attention to diversity and reinforce expectations that multiculturalism has indeed become an indelible part of the nation's fabric. For example, while vigorously proclaiming that our nation should *stop* focusing on race, some of those very same mediamakers argue their positions by writing myriad columns or spending hours of broadcast time *focusing* on race.

But increasingly more common than either celebration or condemnation are those recognitional voices that present and ponder the inevitable dilemmas of a multicultural society. What should be the limits, if any, on immigration? How should we address the mutual adaptation of immigrants to American society and American society to immigrants? To what degree should people of diverse ethnic backgrounds be pressured to surrender, permitted to preserve, or encouraged to strengthen their languages or cultural practices? In what respects should diversity be a private matter or a consideration in public celebrations, school education, and the workplace? In what respects should the norms of American institutions be modified in response to the growing presence of women in nontraditional settings? What is the relationship between diversity and equity?

A vivid October 1997 illustration of recognitional multiculturalism appeared in the editorial section of the October 6 Riverside *Press-Enterprise*. It featured four columnists—a Black man, a Latino man, an Anglo man, and an Anglo woman—whom some might try to place neatly in dualistic conservative or liberal boxes or on a liberal-conservative straight-line continuum. Yet in their columns on different diversity-related topics, *all four* demonstrated their recognition of multiculturalism even as they diverged *in four directions* in their responses to it.

Desegregationist. The media curriculum as a whole operates from a moderately desegregationist, Rodney King-type "Can't We All Just Get Along" ideology. For the most part the media curriculum disseminates generally noncontroversial, sometimes platitudinous desegregationist positions (Campbell, 1995).

Barriers to access should be removed (often expressed without fervor for full integration). We need better intergroup understanding (or at least peaceful coexistence). Intergroup contact is good (even if limited). We should foster intergroup cooperation (particularly if conflict seems to threaten community comfort zones). We believe in equity, justice, and fairness (but defined in widely divergent ways, with media combatants trying to seize, claim, and define the diversity high moral ground on issues like immigration, affirmative action, bilingual education, or antidiscrimination laws).

These moderate desegregationist leanings also flourish in the entertainment media in shows ranging from *Star Trek* to myriad interracial buddy movies (Bernardi, 1998; Carby, 1993; Fuchs, 1993; Golumbia, 1995–1996). However, most such shows lack the interracial pith of the TV series, *Spenser: For Hire*, where race provided continuous subtext, pervaded dialogue, often became central to the plots, and provided density to the tense core relationship between White private detective Spenser and his enigmatic Black ally and sometimes antagonist, Hawk.

Occasionally such shows implicitly champion *functional* color blindness—that color, even if noticed, doesn't or shouldn't matter. At other times they extol *true* color blindness—not even recognizing physical differences. For example, the conclusion of the 1997 disaster flick *Volcano* proclaimed such a platitude. Staring at the multiracial team of victorious volcano fighters, now covered with gray ash, a little boy remarks, "Look at their faces. They all look the same."

Yet while the media curriculum emphasizes desegregation, it simultaneously disseminates messages about the existence and sometimes the value of a degree of group aggregation (although most media and media-disseminated external voices oppose total self-segregation) (Dyson, 1993; Noriega, 1992). Although news media applaud desegregation, they also cover, often in laudatory terms, group aggregationist aspects of American life: Black investment clubs, Hispanic businesses, Jewish private schools, Native American and Danish newspapers, and the flourishing of Los Angeles's Koreatown.

Group-focused aggregationist filmmaking about diverse racial and ethnic experiences shares the entertainment media curriculum with desegregationist cross-racial and gay-straight friendship movies. Audiences can choose aggregationist movies like *Down in the Delta* and *Mi Familia* as well as desegregationist flicks like *Lethal Weapon* and *In & Out*. Aggregationist all-Black and all-White situation comedies coexist with the desegregationist hospital staffs of *ER* and *Chicago Hope*.

Americanist. This may be the most subtle and contested ideological space, simultaneously a battleground and a common ground. Today most media voices champion America and Americanism, while also providing their own spin on Americanism, the meaning of America, and the nature of being or becoming American. Most ominously, it emerges in prescriptions of who is (and who isn't) deemed to be a "real American," implying that those who diverge must be unreal, surreal, or lesser kinds of Americans.

The media resound with claims, counterclaims, and competing definitions of Americanism in the context of growing societal diversity and recognitional multiculturalism. The nature of America has become a major thread of media-disseminated debates over or dramatizations of multiple language use (in education or in the workplace), immigration (legalization of residency or the education of immigrant children), attempts to redress inequities (sexual harassment or different types of discrimination), the tensions between ethnic cultural practices and American institutions, and the relationship between cultural maintenance and the process of Americanization.

Diversity, in short, has become a prism through which mediamakers, from columnists to moviemakers to radio talk show callers, vie for America. Whether implicitly or explicitly, the media multicultural curriculum has become a site where diverse individuals, groups, organizations, and institutions jockey to define and redefine being American, a process paralleled in schools (Apple & Christian-Smith, 1991; Cornbleth, 1998).

Media and Learning

By continuously inspecting and reinspecting the media curriculum, we can gain a better understanding of the contemporary public learning environment in which school educators, students, parents, and other societal curriculum forces operate. This can also help us better engage the school opportunities and challenges created by the media multicultural curriculum.

As curricular gatekeepers, the media, to an immense degree, provide and restrict access to the "stuff" from which we learn multiculturally. And as spin doctors, the media frame, organize, and attempt to influence what we learn and how we think multiculturally. Yet while scholarship has demonstrated that media contribute to (not determine) multicultural learning, the *precise* assessment of that influence remains a perplexing scholarly challenge. Two major problems stand out.

First, multiple teaching forces operate simultaneously. Not only do schools teach, but, in addition to the media, so do other dimensions of the societal curriculum—for example, family, peers, religious institutions, and social organizations, including hate groups (McLeod & Reeves, 1981). This makes it extremely difficult to separate clearly media influence from other societal and school influences or to isolate consistently media-derived learning from learning based on other sources.

This leads to the second dilemma. No matter how rigorously scholars may try to assess media content—the *balance* (or bias) of news stories, the *frequency* (or absence) of different categories of news or entertainment depictions of selected groups, the *group representativeness* (or unrepresentativeness) of particular movie or TV characters, or the *factual accuracy* (or inaccuracy) of docudramas—analysts face a confounding dilemma. While content and reception (teaching and learning) overlap, they do not coincide. One scholar's content analysis does not necessarily mirror another consumer's learning from that same content.

Limits of Content Analysis

Particularly in the case of the entertainment media, casual audiences do not normally concern themselves with the cerebral issues of analyzing content for accuracy or representativeness. Movie and TV entertainment depictions of different groups, treatment of various aspects of diversity, and dissemination of ideas *incidentally* teach consumers. Conversely, audience learning varies because of consumers' diverse, if unconscious, readings of the same media textbooks, based greatly on the knowledge and attitudes that each brings to the media experience. One of the inevitable generalizing limitations of content analyses is that casual consumers do not necessarily view, read, or listen the way content analysts analyze.

As a result, the attempted categorical precision of content analysis may unwittingly misrepresent the messiness of media multicultural teaching and learning. For example, in content analysis it makes sense to separate media images of Cuban Americans from other U.S. Latinos and from Cubans in Cuba. However, when it comes to learning, audience perceptions of Cuban Americans may be influenced by—at times may merge with—reactions to media treatment of other Hispanics and of Cuba itself.

Content analysts may differentiate ethnic backgrounds (for example, Polish Americans, Slovakian Americans, and Hungarian Americans). Yet media depictions of various ethnic groups of Eastern European origin have contributed to a generalized perception of Americans of Eastern European ancestry, leaving in their wake both selected images of specific national-origin White ethnic groups and an undifferentiated image of people with "odd" surnames, heavy accents, boisterous weddings, factory coveralls, bowling bags, and torn T-shirts (Golab, 1980).

Content analysts may distinguish between Japanese Americans and Japanese. Yet we need to consider them together when assessing potential audience impact (Hamamoto, 1994). World War II movies and emotionally narrated 1930s and World War II newsreels (Higashi, 1998; Nornes & Yukio, 1994) involving Japanese military atrocities have become a continuously recycled staple of television for more than a half-century since they were produced. They have influenced media consumer attitudes not only toward Japanese, but also toward Japanese Americans, as expressed to the present, for example, in anti-Japanese American letters to the editor. For example, the December 10, 1991 edition of my hometown newspaper, the Riverside *Press-Enterprise*, ran the following letter to the editor.

> I simply cannot understand the reasoning of President Bush for thinking he or the United States government should apologize for the Internment of 120,000 Americans of Japanese ancestry during World War II. Reverse that picture. Do you think for one minute, the Japanese government would not have put all Americans in their nation in internment? (No apology warranted, 1991, Sec. F, p. 7)

Overlooked, of course, was the fact that Americans of Japanese ancestry are Americans, not Japanese. Or take the case of Marvin Okumura, a third-generation American preparing to become a United Airlines pilot, who received the following interoffice letter: "Dear Jap Okamura. All you Japs think you can buy or get anything you want. . . . Now a Jap pilot at United Airlines makes me puke. . . . Go fly at Nip Air where you belong" (Efron, 1991, sec. A, p. 1).

The gap between categorical content analysis distinctions and potential media learning becomes even more problematic with regard to American Indians. When including Native American characters, some movies or TV shows identify specific Indian nations. But casual viewers do not mentally file away years of media depictions of Indians in separate, pure, unsullied tribal categories . . . even assuming that they noticed those precise identities upon first viewing a particular media textbook. As a result, media Indians have contributed to viewers' generic perceptions of Native Americans as a whole.

Then there is the age gap. Most content analysts are adults. What about young people? Certainly children differ from adults in how and what they learn about diversity from their media experiences—particularly from movies, television, and videotapes (Liebert & Sprafkin, 1988).

The Children Now Report

Take one study, Children Now's 1998 *A Different World: Children's Perceptions of Race and Class in the Media* (Children Now, 1998). Interviews were conducted in early March 1998 with 1,200 children ages 10–17 (300 Blacks, 300 Anglos, 300 Latinos, and 300 Asian Americans). The results provided a single, time-restricted, but revealing glimpse into the reaction of school-age children to the media treatment of diversity. Following were five conclusions:

1. Asian American children felt the news media treated Asian Americans more fairly than did the entertainment media. In contrast, African Americans found entertainment media treatment fairer than news media treatment when it came to Blacks.
2. Asian American, Latino, and Black children listed Black television figures as their most admired, while White children preferred White TV figures. No Latino or Asian American TV figures were selected.
3. More than 90% of those interviewed said there were enough White main characters on TV and a slight majority said there were enough Blacks, but only about one-fifth said there were enough Latino or Asian American main characters. Yet a majority of each group felt it important for young people to see those of their racial or ethnic background on television.
4. Going beyond the issue of frequency to the quality of characters on entertainment TV, a strong majority of each group felt that White characters were portrayed most positively. Likewise, all four groups concurred that Latinos were portrayed most negatively. According to these young consumers, the greatest disparity in favor of White characters was that they were more likely to be portrayed as wealthy, well-educated, and having leadership qualities, while the greatest disparity toward "minority" characters was that they were more likely to be depicted as breaking the law or having financial difficulty. In particular, nearly 60% of respondents opined that Black actors were most likely to be cast as criminals.
5. These perceptions also tended to hold up when it came to the news media. All four groups of respondents felt that Whites were more likely to be shown doing good things and that Blacks and Latinos were more likely to be shown doing bad things, with Asian Americans falling in the middle. When it came to the news

media treatment of teenagers, respondents found these ethnic disparities to be even greater.

Like all inevitably obtrusive surveys, this one raises some questions. For example, did these elicited perceptions of media imbalances demonstrate that these students were truly critical media consumers? The mere identification of distortions does not guarantee that those very distortions did not influence respondent learning. What about the more surreptitious impact of the media, such as possible "sleeper effects" or other influences on subconscious student learning about diversity?

A Potential Impact Paradigm

Given the impossibility of continuously ascertaining and monitoring media-based learning, how do we move beyond the limitations of stating that some people are influenced by some media at some time? Let me suggest a prism that can be used by attentive, conscientious educators—school and otherwise—not just by academic scholars. After considering the research literature, particularly concerning media reception and media-based learning, and assessing the nature of the media curriculum, I have developed the following interpretive framework for hypothesizing the *potential* multicultural learning impact of the mass media. According to this paradigm, viewers *tend* to react to media textbooks about diverse groups and other diversity-related themes according to four basic teaching-learning scenarios: coincidence, conflict, marginalism, and novelty.

Coincidence. If a media textbook's treatment of a social group, culture, nation, or some other diversity-related theme coincides with a media consumer's existent beliefs, it will tend to reinforce them. Because that media textbook's truth mirrors the consumer's truth, they share the same comfort zone of teaching and learning. In such situations, there is unlikely to be any consumer oppositional response or even critical consideration.

This occurs when consumers hold the same beliefs as a newspaper column on immigration or a talk show host's commentary on affirmative action. It occurs when viewers share the values modeled by intergroup cooperation on *Law and Order* or interracial love in Whitney Houston's *Cinderella*. It occurs when viewers support media-disseminated messages, such as a TV interview in which the head of the Promise Keepers defines the role of women in the family or when lesbian role modeling takes place on *Ellen.*

Conflict. Let's assume, however, that the messages in the above media textbooks conflict with some consumers' views about those same topics. Particularly when those beliefs are deeply held, if a media textbook directly challenges them or presents multicultural themes in a manner jarringly dissonant to a consumer's emotionally cemented personal vision, then those messages will tend to be consciously or unconsciously rejected, modified, or otherwise muted. This occurred for me when I heard the Limbaugh caller's statements about Mexican congressmen from Texas.

What if a movie, TV show, magazine story, newspaper column, or radio talk show presents information that contradicts or calls into question a consumer's *strong* beliefs about ethnic group traits, gender roles, a diversity-related government policy, or some aspect of intergroup relations. In that case, the consumer would tend to reject or minimize the importance of that information.

A consumer might contextualize a discordant film situation, news story, or talk show commentary as being inaccurate, unrepresentative, limited in application, or a rare exception to the consumer's thoughts about that theme rather than broadly generalizable and therefore a threat to the consumer's belief system. Rebecca Ann Lind (1996) found that White viewers, as compared to Blacks, reduced the importance of a specific media textbook when both groups watched a television news story on Minneapolis realtors who used race as a factor when deciding which neighborhoods to show to diverse prospective buyers. African Americans saw the story as reflective of the essence of being Black in the United States. White viewers recognized the discrimination, but limited the story's importance by viewing it as merely a local problem.

The bombardment of stories about Mike Hernandez's cocaine problem did not modify my perceptions of Latinos *as a group* because it conflicted with my deeply held belief system. In contrast, that bombardment tended to be consonant with and therefore confirmed, hardened, and apparently raised the emotional level of the belief system of the couple I overheard at Ontario Airport, where they used Hernandez as a launching pad to attack Latinos in general.

Marginalism. Now suppose that the news media present ideas falling marginally outside of but not in direct conflict with a particular consumer's set of beliefs. These media messages are not coincident with, but they are compatible with that consumer's visions or values. This could be through the media treatment of a person identified as belonging to a particular group, dissemination of a pundit's argument about a diversity-related topic, or presentation of information about some government civil rights policy.

If it does not directly challenge or conflict with the consumer's beliefs, such media content would have a greater potential for adding to the consumer's knowledge base, maybe becoming incorporated into the knowledge pool, and possibly influencing personal organizational schema. In fact, it might even bring about some behavioral change, possibly more so than media textbooks that either reinforce or directly challenge that belief system.

This probably occurred with me while engaging the media treatment of the Promise Keepers. I knew something about the organization before the October 1997 Washington gathering and the accompanying media barrage, but I had no strong feelings about it. The media enlarged my exposure through treatment that did not challenge my previous beliefs. Rather, they added to my knowledge base, while raising additional questions and expectations about the Promise Keepers.

Nothing Sacred is a bit more problematic. I know much more about Catholicism than about the Promise Keepers. Moreover, I did not approach the series as a source of information. However, I do not know—cannot possibly know—whether or not the show, and, more importantly, the intradenominational conflict about it may have had some "sleeper effect" on my vision of American Catholics.

Novelty. But what if a media presentation deals with a group, nation, or diversity-related topic about which the consumer knows little or nothing? Then the media's message, if remembered, would have the potential for becoming an unchallenged part of the viewer's knowledge pool and belief system, because it encountered little competition from previous learning. In that case this media presentation could well become *the* main source of knowledge on the subject. Before my encounter with the article on *Bien,* I knew absolutely nothing about the Danish-language press in the United States. Gordon Berry and Claudia Mitchell-Kernan (1982) argued that television's most powerful socializing effect occurs when "the viewer is not already supplied with a set of values which would provide a standard against which to assess the views offered by television" (p. 4). In fact, this applies to all media.

Think of newspaper or magazine stories you may have read concerning a religion or culture about which you had limited or no knowledge. Such stories probably encountered little learning competition. Imagine the number of movie viewers for whom *Witness* became a major source of knowledge about the Amish, for whom *Midnight Express* became a major source of knowledge about Turkey, for whom *Missing* became a major source of knowledge about South America, for whom *Gandhi* became a major source of knowledge about India, for whom *The Year of Living Dangerously* became a major source of knowledge about Indonesia, or for whom pre-*Dances with Wolves* Westerns had been major sources of knowledge about nineteenth-century American Indians.

This also applies to diversity-related topics, not just groups or nations. Shortly after Mexico granted the right of dual nationality to Mexicans—meaning, for example, that Mexicans could become naturalized U.S. citizens and still maintain Mexican nationality (although not the right to vote in Mexico)—participants in my workshops began raising this issue. It turned out that many had little prior knowledge about the broader topic of dual nationality or citizenship, whether regarding the United States or globally. Virtually *all* of their knowledge about this topic had come from media news and commentary about Mexico.

Conclusion

This, then, is the media context within which schools operate. A powerful, pervasive media multicultural curriculum, with ongoing, recurring, transitory, and one-shot themes, whose presentation is influenced by media structural patterns, and with multiple perspectives on diversity, muted by severe imbalances in the power to disseminate ideas. A series of intersecting, overlapping ideological battlegrounds, among which are three I have presented as multiculturalist, desegregationist, and Americanist.

There is abundant evidence that learning occurs from both nonfictional and entertainment media textbooks. Yet it is impossible to determine precisely and continuously what consumers—including students—are learning from that curriculum. Now add a consideration of my paradigm for hypothesizing potential multicultural learning from the media by considering the teaching-learning scenarios of coincidence, conflict, marginalism, and novelty.

With these ideas in mind, we will turn our attention to schools. How can they operate more effectively within this complex mediated multicultural context? Better yet, how can they build from that context to make school multicultural education more effective, constructive, and transformative?

PART IV

Schooling in a Multiculturally Mediated World

CHAPTER 8

Mass Media, Multiculturalism, and Schools

Schools operate in the context of an enveloping, immersing societal multicultural curriculum, featuring a cascade of mass media textbooks that contribute to learning about diversity. This means, of course, that school educators simply do not have the power to decide *whether or not* multicultural education will occur. It will. Along with schools, the mass media *are* education . . . both the news media and the entertainment media, as well as those increasingly popular hybrids known by such names as "infotainment."

Given this world of mediated education about diversity, school educators face two major decisions. First, they must decide *if* they will participate *consciously* in the inevitable process of multicultural education. Second, if they choose to participate consciously, they must decide *how* they will respond to, deal with, and build from that media curriculum, other than simply complaining about it (Farber, Provenzo, & Holm, 1994). In being proactive, they need to consider the world of scholarship.

Scholarly Relationships

Given the parallel growth of scholarship on diversity in the media and on school multicultural education, it would be reasonable to expect a rich literature that explicitly explores this intersection. Unfortunately, such is not the case. When it comes to diversity, with a few notable exceptions (for example, Giroux, 1997; Stein, 1979), media scholars and education scholars have tended to operate in separate universes. When they do cross disciplinary boundaries, education scholars tend to critique the media without comprehensively addressing the issue of what schools can do about it, while media scholars tend to deal with such topics as how to use movies in the classroom (Carson & Friedman, 1995; Summerfield, 1993). Yet an examination of these two generally isolated scholarly fiefdoms reveals certain similarities in approach, albeit with variations in focus.

Media scholars examine decision-making and actions by media-making institutions and individuals, while education scholars dissect decision-making and actions by the textbook industry, school systems, teachers, and administrators. Media scholars analyze ownership structures, while education scholars look at such issues as school governance and financing. Media scholars inspect the influence of advertisers, while education scholars examine corporate influence on public schools, including the distribution of "free" supplementary classroom materials and advertising through Channel One (Fox, 1996).

Media scholars analyze media content, while education scholars analyze textbooks and curricula. Media scholars examine pressure groups and censorship efforts, while education scholars look at protest movements against textbook content, classroom materials, library holdings, and even school names. Media scholars attempt to assess reader, viewer, and listener responses and learning, while education scholars assess student responses and learning. And the comparisons could go on. Yet seldom do these scholarly efforts intersect.

Gerald Michael Greenfield and I carried out a small-scale pilot study to test the potential for linking media and education multicultural scholarship, resulting in an article, "Harmony and Conflict of Intercultural Images: The Treatment of Mexico in U.S. Feature Films and K–12 Textbooks" (Greenfield & Cortés, 1991). We restricted our examination to two teaching dimensions—textbooks and feature films—and to one foreign nation rather than diversity within the United States. Yet the methodology suggests one avenue for assessing confluence and conflict involving media-based and school-based multicultural education.

In comparing and contrasting the treatment of Mexico in U.S. social studies textbooks and feature films, we looked both at Mexico in general and at a series of critical themes in Mexican history, such as the emigration of undocumented workers to the United States. On the basis of our content analysis, we identified three types of textbook-feature film teaching relationships. On some themes textbooks and feature films tended to reinforce each others' intercultural messages. On other topics they tended to challenge each other. In still other places, by omission, one sector permitted the other to be more dominant and influential as an educational force.

Despite the paucity of research on the multicultural dimensions of the media-school relationship, I will draw upon the separate fields of media and school multicultural education scholarship to propose a new, integrated paradigm for media-related multicultural education. It consists of three dimensions: premises, school educator responses, and areas of school engagement.

Premises

Three basic research-based premises serve as the common ground for creating this new educational paradigm.

Exposure. Virtually all students, parents, and school educators are exposed to the mass media multicultural curriculum. For most people, avoiding that curriculum entirely would require a major conscious effort—for example, *never* reading a newspaper or magazine, turning on the radio or television, or going to a movie. While each person's media multicultural curriculum will be to some extent unique, in other respects it will overlap others' patterns of consumption.

Influence. As a result of consuming media, students, parents, and school educators will learn something—probably a considerable amount—about diversity. While we will never be able to specify precisely what each individual learns, we can sometimes discern patterns of learning or, through content analysis, hypothesize potential learning.

Interaction. Such media-based multicultural learning will inevitably affect schools. Neither students nor teachers, parents nor administrators park their nonschool learning—including diversity-related learning, laden with unrecognized "sleeper effects"—at the schoolhouse door. Laura Angélica Simón's poignant 1997 documentary film, *Fear and Learning at Hoover Elementary,* dramatically revealed how both students and school personnel were influenced by, reacted to, and brought to school the bitter 1994 media-disseminated debate over California's Proposition 187, which sought, among many things, to bar illegal immigrant children from public schools.

School Educator Responses

Working from these three premises, we can identify and assess at least four basic patterns of school educator responses to the presence of the media multicultural curriculum: recognition, attention, exploration, and action-oriented investigation. These four patterns can be conceived in hierarchical order of intensity of engagement with the media, from passive to transformative.

Level One—Recognition. At minimum, all educators—school as well as nonschool—must admit that media-based multicultural education, both teaching and learning, is taking place. Even educators who want nothing to do with the media— don't watch TV, go to the movies, read newspapers or magazines, or listen to the radio or recorded music, and wouldn't be caught dead consorting with *Beavis and Butthead*—need to recognize that most students are consuming media.

Beyond this, they should realize that students will bring some of their media multicultural learning to school, maybe even into the classroom (Christenson & Roberts, 1998). In turn, this may influence student reactions to classroom teaching efforts and other school interactions. Viewing such movies as *Amistad* or *Gone with the Wind* could influence the classroom study of slavery (Beck, 1998). Following, even in a casual manner, the TV and radio coverage of the O. J. Simpson or the Rodney King beating trials could influence how students respond to textbook treatments of race relations. Reading press reports of sexual harassment cases or viewing *Ally McBeal* could influence reactions to the topic of gender. Watching *The Crucible* or newscasts on various religions' position statements on male-female relations could influence how students react to the study of religion in history.

Certainly some 1980 editors of the *Senior Weekly Reader* recognized the likelihood of media-based multicultural learning. The social context was the era's global oil crisis, with gasoline shortages, ballooning oil prices, and long lines at the gas pump. On a daily basis, the American news media pointed the finger of blame at the oil-supplying Arab nations, while TV and moviemakers churned out fictional depictions of greedy, manipulative Arab moguls (Shaheen, 1984). American citizens, including parents, retransmitted their media-stoked, anti-Arab ire through conversations, sometimes within earshot of their children.

Then came the March 5, 1980 *Senior Weekly Reader.* On the cover appeared an American Indian, wearing a tie, wrapped in a blanket, and adorned by the omnipresent headdress so rooted in American mediated popular culture (Bird, 1996; Stedman, 1982). But instead of riding a horse, he sat astride a camel laden with containers labeled Gas, Oil, and Coal. Next to the camel appeared the words, "U.S. Indians—New Energy Sheikhs?", which also headlined the related article inside the publication (*Senior Weekly Reader,* 1980).

What media-derived and reinforced knowledge, attitudes, and expectations were the editors assuming? That students knew about the oil crisis and blamed it on Arab leaders? That students could identify an Indian simply by a headdress? (Even Holly and Melissa can do that, thanks to *Pocahontas*.) That placing an Indian on a camel would draw upon their media-based personal schemas to create an interpretive framework for the article, would reinforce their fears and expectations of a continued oil shortage, and would influence their values (maybe prejudices) concerning Indians and their perceptions of reservation resources? That the word *sheikh* would generate the "sleeper effect" and awaken media-honed Arab images already lodged deeply in students' minds? (The Teaching Tips page even included a question, "What picture comes to your mind when you read the word *sheikh*?") That referring to Indians as "new energy sheikhs" would encourage them to transfer their media-massaged sheikh image to Indians? All of the above? And all of this *before* the students ever opened the publication to *read* the story . . . or even if they *never read* the story!

Senior Weekly Reader editors recognized previous media-based multicultural learning. They understood it, drew upon it, and manipulated it. As part of the media—a youth-targeted part of the media—they also reinforced the negative image of Arabs, while simultaneously using "Arabness" to frame—better yet, taint—Native Americans.

Level Two—Attention. Beyond mere recognition, school educators should pay attention to *what* the mass media are teaching about diversity. Certainly we all have other things to do with our lives besides dealing with the media. But without expanding or modifying their normal media selection patterns, school educators can consume a bit differently.

They can pay attention to what multicultural images are being transmitted, what multicultural messages are being disseminated, and what multicultural lessons are being taught. How do movies portray gender roles and relations? What do newspaper columnists and magazine writers, including headline writers and photo editors, transmit about intergroup relations? How do radio talk show hosts and TV newscasters frame, interpret, or comment upon diversity-related stories or issues? By paying more attention to the media curriculum, particularly those elements that students are likely to consume, educators can gain insight into potential media-based multicultural learning.

It is important to remember, however, what media research has shown about differential impact. The same media textbook's messages and images will be filtered, modified, and even recalled in diverse ways. Among other factors, developmental age combined with generation gaps influence variations in media reception and learning. Teachers and students may well have differing responses to and interpretations of the same TV sitcom, newspaper story, song lyrics, talk show commentary, or Disney movies.

Therefore, assessment of *actual* student learning requires a different kind of attention. It requires attention in school to when students use media—including entertainment media— as information or as bases for arguments, even when they do not *explicitly* cite such sources. For example, if they have not yet studied it in school, they may have learned about twentieth-century race relations from TNT's 1997 miniseries *George Wallace,* from the 1988 feature film, *Mississippi Burning,* or from Showtime's 1996 *Mr. and Mrs. Loving.* If not in school, where would they have learned about the battle over the admission of female students into The Citadel or about ongoing controversies over immigration, affirmative action, domestic partnership benefits, or official English? For many students, knowledge of these topics comes primarily from newscasts, published journalistic accounts, radio commentary, or docudramas, even though that media-generated learning may come second-hand from parents or peers as informants and spin doctors according to Lazarsfeld's two-step flow model.

Level Three—Exploration. Rather than simply recognizing or paying attention to the media's multicultural teaching dimensions through normal consumption patterns, school educators may look for media sources that serve as multicultural textbooks. This could mean being certain to read and assess stories or columns when headlines suggest diversity-related content. It could mean selecting movies or TV programs whose titles, reviews, synopses, or word of mouth indicate multicultural content. It could mean surfing talk radio to find discussions of diversity-related issues.

I seldom read articles about drug busts. They happen, but I'm usually not interested in the details. Yet a headline in the June 25, 1998 *Los Angeles Times*—"With Drug Arrests, Urban Grit Smudges Amish Life"— drew me in (Fritz, 1998). I've become particularly fascinated with the Amish since giving a media lecture at Millersville University in Pennsylvania Amish country, and, I must admit it, since seeing Peter Weir's haunting 1985 film, *Witness.* So the article, which explored the impact of population congestion and modernity on Amish life and culture, joined *Witness* as part of my personal multicultural curriculum.

The exploratory teacher can also make special efforts to discover what students have learned multiculturally from the media. This can occur by direct questioning, by initiating discussions about a widely disseminated current media multicultural topic, or by giving assignments that specifically tap such learning. It can also come through careful observation, as at the attention level.

Level Four—Investigation. For educators more deeply concerned with the transformative possibilities of media multicultural education, opportunities for investigation and classroom implementation abound. Beyond the abundant scholarship about the diversity-related content of the mass media, the media themselves often address that content issue. As with all media textbooks, these need to be analyzed, not just absorbed.

For example, I generally read the columns of Karen Grigsby Bates, who writes regularly about diversity for the *Los Angeles Times*. While I don't always agree with her, these columns generally contain thoughtful, nuanced analyses of diversity. In the September 19, 1997 *Times*, Bates argued that prime-time network television had created its own type of social segregation. She suggested that while two types of network entertainment series—medical and lawyer/police shows—had become desegregated, the TV world of situation comedy remained segregated. In particular, she pointed to the suffusing whiteness of such popular comedy series as *Frasier, Friends, Mad about You, Caroline in the City,* and *Seinfeld.* According to Bates, these shows send the implicit message "that an ethnically homogeneous life is a desirable life" (Bates, 1997, p. B–9).

But investigatory educators should not view their quest for knowledge merely for knowledge's sake. They should continually use their new insights to transform their pedagogy and to become more effective in other areas of school-media multicultural engagement.

Areas of School Engagement

This brings us to the third dimension of my media multicultural education paradigm—areas where individual school educators, schools, districts, or states can become involved in explicitly integrating the mass media into policies and practices. Following are eight such areas:

1. Assessing one's own media multicultural learning.
2. Dealing with student multicultural learning.
3. Using the mass media as a curricular resource.
4. Developing student analytical thinking about media.
5. Professional development concerning the media.
6. Working with parents as multicultural coteachers with the mass media curriculum.

7. Working directly with the media.
8. Combatting stereotypes and stereotyping.

Educator Self-assessment. School educators should periodically conduct their own October 1997-style self-assessments. Special attention should be paid to how the media address two topics: racial, ethnic, religious, or other groups from which a school's or district's students derive; and diversity-related topics that are addressed—or should be addressed—in the curriculum.

While conducting this self-assessment, school educators should consider how that media teaching may have been influencing their perceptions and interactions with students, families, and communities. (In a 1996 *Newsweek* "My Turn" column, an Arab American young lady recalled telling her high school chemistry teacher that she had to leave school a few days before Christmas vacation in order to visit her sick grandmother in the Middle East. The teacher reportedly responded, "Don't come back in a body bag," provoking classroom laughter [Asfahani, 1996].)

Concerning curriculum, as teachers prepare to approach any diversity-related topic, they should take stock of their own media exposure to that or related topics. This applies whether a teacher is preparing to have students discuss an elementary school story on Native Americans, a middle school literary selection dealing with gender relations, a high school government unit on desegregation, or a U.S. history textbook treatment of westward expansion.

Nobody is immune to media multicultural teaching. But all school educators can become more alert to that curriculum, more self-analytical about incidental personal learning, and more conscious of how that learning may be influencing their personal interactions, classroom treatment of various topics, and other educational decision-making.

Student Multicultural Learning. Teachers should develop the habit of incorporating student media learning into the classroom. As in the case of the Gypsies described in the Prologue, before starting a unit on some diversity-related topic, students can be asked to discuss or write brief essays about what they already know about the subject. To the degree possible, they should also indicate the sources of their knowledge and ideas.

This strategy can suggest the student schemas with which teachers are working, including preexistent misinformation, misconceptions, and possibly even stereotypes. It may also reveal that, for some topics, students may truly have blank slates. Finally, it helps students recognize the presence of media multicultural teaching, become more aware of its potential impact on their own thinking, and maybe even become more analytical media consumers.

Mass Media as Curricular Resource. The past two decades have witnessed a sharp growth of interest in the topic of media literacy (Media Literacy Symposium, 1998). This has included both scholarship and curriculum materials aimed at helping teachers draw upon media at various grade levels (Brown, 1991; Schwoch, White, & Reilly, 1992).

Mediamakers have long produced or marketed media for school use. *The Weekly Reader.* Educational documentary films. Capsulized versions of feature films adapted for schools. General interest national magazines marketed to schools, sometimes accompanied by teachers' guides. Channel One, a national television "network" that creates daily newscasts, complete with advertisements, for showing in schools. Teachers, schools, and districts that adopt or accept such materials are already involved in using media as teaching resources, although they may do so without carefully assessing their multicultural implications.

Then there is that much larger universe of media resources, those designed for public consumers, not for the classroom. Teachers can—and many do—incorporate those materials within their multicultural teaching frameworks, usually using three basic approaches—external, internal, or historical.

First is the pedagogical incorporation of the mass media as they operate *outside* of school. Discussions of current events should include a consideration of the media treatment of such events. Homework assignments can involve students noting and assessing how different media coincide, vary, or even conflict in their treatment of a selected diversity topic. Students should also be encouraged to use the media as *one* source—used critically, of course— in preparing research papers or class presentations.

Students can also be asked to keep analytical journals of the mass media treatment of a diversity-related topic a week or so *prior* to the introduction of that topic in the classroom. For example, students can assess media treatment of current immigration issues for two weeks prior to studying the topic of nineteenth-century immigration in a U.S. history class. They can assess media treatment of relations among groups—for example, racial or religious—prior to reading a novel that deals with contact among people of different backgrounds. They can assess media treatment of physical disabilities prior to reading a story in which a character's disability is a major factor.

The second basic approach is the classroom use of commercial media. Dudley Barlow (1997), an English teacher at Plymouth Canton High School in Canton, Michigan, described the following strategy. He structured one of his courses around the question, what happens when an individual's values conflict with those of the group? As the major piece of literature, Barlow used Mark Twain's *The Adventures of Huckleberry Finn*. To focus students on that central question before they read the book, Barlow used the 1967 movie, *In the Heat of the Night*. He then concluded by having them examine the 1993 film, *Schindler's List*. In this way he used two feature films to illuminate Huck's dilemmas concerning Jim, by placing those dilemmas in the comparative context of Oskar Schindler and of Police Chief Bill Gillespie in *Heat*.

Third, mass media history can be incorporated into various types of courses or units. Included should be a consideration of the media's relationship to diversity-related issues. For example, in the study of World War II, attention should be paid to the ways that different nations used media to demonize the enemy and to galvanize public support, such as by eulogizing Rosie the Riveter and by consciously creating movie military units with obvious multiethnic representation.

Student Analytical Thinking. In the pedagogical use of the mass media, students should be continuously encouraged and assisted in thinking analytically about media as sources for the personal construction of multicultural knowledge. Critical thinking has been widely trumpeted in the litany of state and district educational goals. (It has also encountered fierce opposition from those who prefer inculcation—meaning *their preferred inculcation*, of course—as contrasted to helping students become more independent, insightful thinkers.)

Critical thinking exercises and questions appear in most history, social studies, literature, and language arts textbooks, as well as in media literacy and prejudice-reduction materials (Derman-Sparks & Philips, 1997; McLaughlin & Brilliant, 1997; Potter, 1998; Teaching Tolerance, 1997). Yet most critical thinking materials focus on reproduced print sources, such as literature, historical documents, newspaper stories, photographs, and cartoons, as well as stills from movies or television programs. Only sparingly do those materials incorporate the exploration of the mass media as they currently operate *outside* of school. While media literacy materials do deal with the contemporary media, they only tangentially or incidentally touch upon questions of diversity. Conversely, prejudice-reduction and other multicultural materials sometimes deal with the media, but they generally take a relatively simplistic approach, seldom addressing the vital nuances raised in this book.

Moreover, there is a disturbing tendency among many students, and, for that matter, some teachers to conflate critical thinking with criticism. They are not the same. For that reason, I prefer the term *analytical thinking* to critical thinking, because it mutes the unintended (I hope) invitation for students to engage in wall-to-wall media bashing.

Teachers and students can easily fall into the trap of transforming the constructive process of media-oriented analytical thinking into semimindless games of nonstop criticism, pin the tail on the stereotype, or "proving" how awful the media are through a parade of examples. Certainly students should be encouraged to be critical if their evidence-based analysis leads them to thoughtful conclusions that certain media have distorted a diversity-related topic or demeaned a particular group. However, they should not be encouraged or instructed to begin with the predisposition to find fault with the media or to assume group stereotyping.

Professional Development. There is no substitute for ongoing, effective professional development (Lewis, 1997). Enhancing media literacy, including an understanding of the multicultural dimensions of the media, should be part of all educators' professional development. It should begin in preservice teacher education and should continue throughout each educator's career.

The media curriculum surrounds and immerses us. It teaches, and students learn from it. Later, as adults, students will rely on the media for much of their knowledge of the world, including diversity within that world. If school educators want to enhance thinking stills and transform student ways of addressing the media, particularly the media multicultural curriculum, they themselves need to become continually more adept at this process. While educators can do much on their own, there is no substitute for the inclusion of media literacy education, including media multicultural education, with any district's staff development program.

Working with Parents. But why stop with teachers? The media multicultural curriculum provides an opportunity, albeit a challenging one, for parental involvement in school education. As gatekeepers, parents and extended families influence—although they are seldom able to control—their children's media consumption. As sometimes-unaware spin doctors, they become incidental media-based multicultural teachers.

Even as I write this chapter, I think about the roles Laurel and I have played and the choices we have made in helping shape the media curriculum for Holly and Melissa—through selection, permission, restriction, encouragement, and interaction with them. I also think about the diversity-related children's books that we have read to them: Susan Lowell's *The Three Little Javelinas* (who get help from a Native American woman and a Mexican American man in their efforts to build a house that will thwart their nemesis, the coyote); Barbara Joosse's *Mama, Do You Love Me?* (the conversations of a little Eskimo girl and her mother); Janell Cannon's *Stellaluna* (a cross-cultural allegory about the opportunities and challenges of building intergroup friendships, involving a lost baby bat who is raised by birds); and Tynia Thomassie's *Feliciana Feydra LeRoux* (a brave little Cajun girl who helps the men of her family capture a huge alligator).

What can schools do to address family-based media multicultural education? At parent meetings, school educators can discuss that process, provide media illustrations, and even suggest the roles parents can play in helping to constructively influence their children's media-related multicultural learning. Parent workshops can address such topics as media literacy, the multicultural dimensions of the mass media, and strategies for constructive parent involvement in processing these topics (Axelrod, 1997; DeGaetano & Bander, 1996). My own experiences in conducting parent and community workshops on media literacy and home-based media multicultural education have demonstrated what others have argued—that many parents would like to become more involved in their children's education and are eager for ideas on how to become more effective, including in the area of intergroup understanding (Bullard, 1996).

Working with the Media. Educational institutions constantly deal with the media, an unavoidable area of engagement (Maeroff, 1998; Watson, 1998). Some districts have public relations departments to represent the district to the media. Their efforts include attempting to get media support, usually translated into positive coverage. Sometimes this involves "damage control" after some diversity-related district incident, as this may quickly become a sensationalized part of the community's media multicultural curriculum.

When achievement test scores vary among ethnic groups, when discrimination or sexual harassment suits are filed, when campus fighting with perceived racial overtones breaks out, or when there is an occurrence that someone considers religiously offensive, school districts look for ways to frame the story for the media. When districts, schools, or teachers take potentially controversial diversity-related actions, they carefully need to prepare media relations plans. This is vital, whether establishing or eliminating bilingual education programs, developing courses on women or ethnic groups, adopting multicultural guidelines for the selection of literature, or such major steps as taking a position on Ebonics or creating the Portland (Oregon) Baseline Essays on diverse ethnic groups.

Students, too, can become involved in working with the media. For example, if student analysis of local newspapers or television reveals inequities or fallacies in media treatment of certain groups or diversity-related topics, classes can communicate that analysis to the mediamakers. Conversely, mediamakers can be invited to schools to discuss the decision-making process behind such treatment. In such ways students can be encouraged to move beyond using analytical thinking merely for classroom or personal exercises and to become active in constructively contributing to the media multicultural curriculum.

Conclusion and Preview

The mass media multicultural curriculum is omnipresent and influential, inevitably affecting schools. Educators can respond to those inevitabilities in ways ranging from passive recognition to transformative investigation and action. Finally, schools can and sometimes must engage the media in a variety of arenas. The integration of these three dimensions of the school-media relationship provides a paradigm for a comprehensive media-responsive approach to multicultural education.

But you may have noticed that I have not yet discussed a final, specific area of school engagement with the mass media—stereotypes and stereotyping. How can schools help students learn to deal with that critical subject? Because this topic involves thorny, perplexing issues, both in schools and in society at large, it will be treated separately in the next chapter.

CHAPTER 9

Struggling with Stereotypes: Uses and Abuses of a Critical Concept

To this point I have made sparing use of the term, "stereotype" . . . on purpose. Stereotyping is a critical social issue and is certainly fundamental to understanding media multicultural education. This also makes it a vital concept for schools.

"Stereotype" and "stereotyping" are powerful, evocative terms. When used carefully and selectively, they communicate important ideas. Yet, like other oft-appearing words in discussions of diversity, like "racism," "sexism," and "homophobia" (or, for that matter, "discourse" and "hegemony"), they can lose their power through overuse. When employed repeatedly and indiscriminately, such words become little more than wearying rhetoric or stultifying jargon.

So let's take a closer look at stereotypes. But rather than beginning with a definition, I want to tease out the characteristics of stereotypes and stereotyping by distinguishing them from and exploring their relationship to other basic concepts. Three relationships can be particularly troublesome: generalizations, labels, and depictions.

Generalizations

"We need to stop categorizing and generalizing about people."

Wrong. We all generalize. We all need to generalize. We create categories of items, actions, or ideas, and then develop generalizations about common (although not necessarily identical or universal) characteristics of those categorized items. We need, use, and draw upon generalizations to make sense of the world around us and to communicate with others.

Take the item, light switch. Once I know that there is a category of items known as light switches and have learned how a few of them work, I can walk into most rooms for the first time and illuminate them, even though I have never previously used that particular light switch . . . thanks to the ability to generalize.

Or take automobiles, which offer a bit more variety than light switches. Once I have learned to drive, I can apply my "car" generalizations to new (for me) automobiles. This allows me, for example, to rent a car, get in it for the first time, and drive away. Admittedly, I may have to make minor adaptations, such as ascertaining the location and operation of certain controls. But that is much better than having to learn about each automobile from scratch. So three cheers for generalizations. On the other hand, if I were burdened with a stereotype of an automobile—for example, that the controls must always be in a certain place and all car radios must operate the same way—I would soon become a basket case trying to drive any car but my own.

Let's turn to multiculturalism. When Laurel and I decide to go out for dinner, we sometimes discuss categories of restaurants—Thai, Peruvian, Italian, or Pakistani—because we share generalizations about those different types of cuisines and the kinds of items we are likely to find. On the other hand, because we have not stereotyped these cuisines, if we select a Chinese restaurant, we will be neither dismayed if one of the expected items is missing from the menu nor nonplussed if it lists a previously unencountered item. Evidence-based generalizations, good; stereotypes, bad.

Generalizations may develop on the basis of personal observation and experience—how light switches work, how to drive different types of automobiles, what food is likely to be found in different types of restaurants. But schools and the mass media are also sources of generalizations.

Media as Generalizers and Stereotypers

Newspapers report the results of scholarly studies comparing the attitudes, experiences, and behavior of women and men. Magazines discuss the results of studies about differential disease rates: whether men or women are more likely to contract a particular type of cancer or suffer heart attacks; that African Americans are more likely to have sickle-cell anemia than are Whites; that HIV strikes a higher proportion of the national population based on sexual orientation, race, ethnicity, or gender. TV newscasts disseminate reports on comparative educational attainment or college admission for different social groups. Radio talk show hosts and their callers discuss and elaborate upon these and other kinds of reports, such as comparative group crime rates. In their reportorial function, the mass media serve as major curricular sources for generalizations about diversity.

But are they also, then, a source of stereotypes? The answer is yes (Lester, 1996). But here we need to separate the noun from the verb. A particular news report can contribute to a group stereotype (the noun) even if that report itself does not stereotype (the verb). By selecting and continually repeating news stories of a particular type about a social group—including reports of scholarly studies—news media can increase the likelihood that consumers will develop stereotypes about that group. The issue of creating stereotypes, then, is more a function of selectivity and frequency than of accuracy.

The issues of frequency and selectivity also apply to news stories about *individual* members of a social group, as contrasted to generalized reports about that group. If news mediamakers adopt, however unconsciously, a pattern of news treatment that regularly shows members of a particular social group in a limited range of activities—for example, crime or welfare—while simultaneously ignoring other types of activities, they set the table for the development of public stereotypes. This occurs even though individual mediamakers might take umbrage at being accused of stereotyping. The vital issue is not whether these mediamakers are stereotypers—that is, whether they hold and choose to disseminate stereotypical beliefs about certain groups. More important is whether or not they use their positions to disseminate information, images, and commentary that *contribute* to group stereotypes . . . whatever the beliefs or pedagogical intentions of the mediamakers.

Changes in media production patterns sometimes contribute to the formulation of group generalizations and stereotypes. For example, over the course of the twentieth century, newspapers have moved from emphasizing focused descriptions of individual events to additionally providing social or comparative context for those events. Two factors have accelerated that trend.

First, radio and television, particularly with round-the-clock news coverage, have usurped newspapers' nineteenth-century role of being the first media to report an event, a fact which has forced newspapers to assume expanded follow-up roles as interpreters and context-providers. Second, computer-generated graphics allow newspapers to provide visually dramatic statistical profiles (involving use of categories) as context (Barnhurst & Mutz, 1997). Many of these profiles are based on attitude surveys that categorize respondents by gender, race, or religion.

In other words, the very nature of contemporary media news dissemination, interpretation, contextualization, and commentary inevitably becomes multicultural education by contributing to group generalizations.

That process can also contribute to the formation or reinforcement of group stereotypes, even though individual mediamakers may not think of themselves as stereotypers.

Schools, Generalizations, and Stereotypes

A comparable process occurs in schools. Teachers constantly disseminate or contribute to student construction of group generalizations. In fact, one central role of schools is to help students learn what a generalization is, how to develop generalizations on the basis of evidence, and how to apply them in new situations.

One and one usually add up to two. Chemistry, physics, biology, and other sciences are based on the development of generalizations through observation and experimentation. When students address such subjects as history, cultural geography, anthropology, sociology, and comparative religions, they inevitably use group generalizations (for example, about nations, various world cultures, and different groups *within* the United States).

This, of course, raises the same thorny issue as the media multicultural curriculum. When it comes to social diversity, how can schools best help students learn to develop and sensitively use group generalizations, while mitigating the possibility that these generalizations will harden into stereotypes? How can students learn about gender differences, the basic beliefs of various religions, and the core threads of diverse ethnic experiences without developing group stereotypes?

Two strategies seem most obvious. First, schools need to help students develop an understanding of the nature, similarities, and often-subtle distinctions between *generalizations* and *stereotypes*. Second, students need to learn to apply and test these distinctions, with the mass media serving as a valuable and critical source of examination.

So what, precisely, differentiates a generalization from a stereotype? Sorry, no easy answers, no hard-and-fast rules, no clear lines of demarcation. In my multicultural education and media workshops, we often devote considerable time to brainstorming this issue and applying it to media examples, with the inevitable conclusion that there are fuzzy areas where the two categories overlap. However, three basic differences usually emerge: flexibility versus inflexibility; intragroup heterogeneity versus homogeneity; and subtlety versus unsubtlety in their application to individual group members. These and other distinctions should be explored in schools. (For various interpretations of stereotyping, see, for example, Bar-Tal, 1997; Devine, 1989; Dyer, 1994; Gilman, 1985; Lalonde &

Gardner, 1989; Leyens, Yzerbyt, & Schadron, 1994; Macrae, Stangor, & Hewstone, 1996; Oakes, Haslam, & Turner, 1994; Perkins, 1979; Seiter, 1986.)

First, group generalizations must be flexible and permeable. Group knowledge should be contingent—that is, it should always be open to change upon the discovery of new information, ideas, and interpretations that might challenge current beliefs. Group generalizations, based on contingent knowledge, exist to be used but also to be modified in the face of compelling new evidence. Group stereotypes, on the other hand, tend to be fixed, rigid, and resistant to new knowledge, particularly if it contradicts or questions those beliefs. Where generalizations are permeable to new ideas, stereotypes tend to remain impermeable to challenging evidence, including information or ideas encountered in schools or in the media.

Second, where generalizations incorporate the notion of intragroup heterogeneity, stereotypes tend to foster notions of intragroup homogeneity. When dealing with social groups, generalizers are willing to expand their visions of diversity *within* groups, based on personal, school, or media encounters. Moreover, this process may also influence the basic generalizations themselves. In contrast, stereotypers tend to treat such contrarian individuals as "exceptions," so deviant from the bulk of the group that they do not challenge or alter the basic content of the stereotype, as in "oh, but you're different" or "but you're not *really* a _____." That's why a stereotyping bigot can honestly say that "one of my best friends is a _____," while still maintaining the stereotype about others in the group.

Third, generalizations provide *clues* to individuals who belong to different social groupings, but in stereotypes those clues tend to become assumptions. For example, there is nothing wrong with developing generalizations about different groups—men or women, Cuban Americans or Korean Americans, Muslims or Seventh-Day Adventists. Such generalizations provide useful *clues* about how individuals who belong to those groups are *likely* to believe or even act in some circumstances. After all, isn't this one of the reasons for teacher workshops about different cultures—to be able to use that group knowledge as clues for working more effectively with individual students and families of those backgrounds? However, such clues should never harden into assumptions that *all* individuals who belong to that group must think, feel, or behave a certain way. At that point generalizations have rigidified into stereotypes.

In speaking about members of a group, generalizers tend to use or imply such words as "some," "many," and, occasionally, "most." In contrast, stereotypers tend to use or imply "all" or "almost all" when dealing with or talking about certain groups or members of those groups. More-over, by speaking or writing in this sweeping manner, stereotypers en-courage others to internalize those perceptions and apply them broadly to "all" or "almost all" of a group's members.

The mass media contribute to both group generalizations and group stereotypes. For that reason they also provide a rich source for analysis. How do different print or broadcast news media differ in their story se-lection patterns about various groups or group members? In what ways do they provide (or fail to provide) context for a more balanced under-standing of reports involving groups? When do news disseminators use (or imply) such words as "some," "many," "most," or "all"? In what ways do headlines or newscast lead-ins try to preshape organizational schema of consumers, thereby creating more fertile conditions for generalizing and possibly stereotype-building? In what ways do visuals add to or chal-lenge group generalizations, as well as stereotypes?

We all generalize. According to contemporary brain research, we all also have the propensity to develop stereotypes and draw on them. Ste-reotypes develop easily, rigidify surreptitiously, and operate reflexively, providing simple, comfortable, and convenient bases for making personal sense of the world. Because generalizations require greater attention, con-tent flexibility, and nuance in application, they do not provide a stereo-type's security blanket of permanent, inviolate, all-encompassing, per-fectly reliable group knowledge. Schools need to face this challenge by helping students learn to understand and use, not abuse, generalizations.

Labels

"We ought to teach students not to use group labels."

Wrong again. Like generalizations, labels are inevitable. Without them, we could not communicate.

I use the label "lights"—as in, "Please turn on the lights"—without having to explain what a light and a switch are. I converse using the label "car" without having to describe what it is. In choosing a restaurant, my wife and I use ethnic labels to discuss our decision.

We all use—we need to use—labels for groups of people. Without them we wouldn't be able to communicate about social issues, interna-tional relations, or historical events. Try explaining Massachusetts Bay Colony, westward expansion, immigration, or the nineteenth amendment without them. Labels enable us to talk about ethnicity and religion, gen-der and age, regions and cultures, nations and continents. In fact, groups themselves create and employ labels—the National Association for the

Advancement of Colored People; the Christian Coalition; the National Organization for Women; the Jewish Federation; the Gay, Lesbian, Bisexual, and Transgender Resource Center; the League of United Latin American Citizens; the Council for Exceptional Children; and the Japanese American Citizens League. For that matter, how about Republicans and Democrats?

But, as with generalizations, labels can have their downside. They can be used as group slurs (Allen, 1990). They can offend or be construed as offensive. They can also become a war zone of sometimes polarizing and stultifying argumentation. Should we use the term Latino or Hispanic, Native American or American Indian, Black or African American or Afro-American or Colored, hyphens or no hyphens?

But even without these problems, by their very nature, group labels tend to elicit generalizations, often stereotypes. They can serve as possibly unintended invitations to draw too many conclusions about the group being named. In other words, it is easy to read too much into labels and their use. Moreover, communicators sometimes use group labels to imply stereotypes, while group labels may trigger stereotypes in the minds of consumers.

Once again, the mass media play a role. The next time you read a magazine or newspaper, watch a newscast, or listen to a talk show, notice how frequently group labels are used—racial, ethnic, religious, national, regional, sexual orientation, and, most unavoidably, gender.

As source material for the school study of group labeling, the mass media provide immense pedagogical possibilities. Which labels are chosen, how are they used, and in what context are they presented? Are there patterns of adjectives that tend to be used in conjunction with certain group labels? Do particular mediamakers use group labels in a manner that demeans or contributes to stereotypes of that group? Like the study of generalizations and stereotypes, the examination of mass media labels and labeling should be an essential part of school multicultural education.

Depictions

"Why are the media *always* depicting or stereotyping us (or them) as _____?"

They probably aren't. Depictions *can* reflect or contribute to stereotyping. But depictions do not automatically qualify as stereotypes, although some critics of the media conflate and thereby confuse these categories. Assessing the complex nature of those relationships requires careful analysis.

As generalizations can harden into stereotypes and labels can be used in a stereotypical manner, depictions can contribute to group stereotypes, both through the entertainment media and through fictional educational materials. A movie or television show depicts characters, each of whom belongs to various social categories—gender, age, physical characteristics, and perceived racial identity, to name a few of the more obvious. They may also speak with accents; carry distinctive surnames; have explicit ethnic, national, or religious identities; communicate in languages other than English; or demonstrate sexual orientation through words or actions.

Some critics of the media treat just about every *individual* depiction as an example of *group* stereotyping. If a movie shows a woman in the kitchen, it is guilty of stereotyping women as belonging in the kitchen. If a sitcom includes a Hispanic maid, it is guilty of stereotyping Hispanic women as maids. If a film portrays an African American committing a crime, it is guilty of stereotyping African Americans as criminals. If a TV show portrays a Christian as religiously intolerant, it is guilty of stereotyping Christians as intolerant. If a story portrays a Jew as avaricious, it is guilty of stereotyping Jews as avaricious. Leave aside the fact that some women cook, some Hispanic women are maids, some Blacks commit crimes, some Christians are religiously intolerant, and some Jews are avaricious.

In fact, stereotyping *may* be occurring. Mediamakers often draw upon or manipulate group stereotypes, particularly if they believe that this will resonate with perceived preexistent audience stereotypes. But simply because a single movie or TV show depicts a character who belongs to a group—any group—in a negative way, does not create a prima facie case for stereotyping. Yet some critics—professional and amateur, particularly knee-jerk interest group spokespeople (often self-proclaimed) —automatically react if a particular media presentation depicts *any* individuals of their group in a manner that they dislike, accusing those media of stereotyping. Sometimes those very protests kindle stereotypes.

This occurs even *within* groups. In 1998, a plenary session of the Association for Asian American Studies overruled the executive board's decision to award its best fiction prize to Japanese American Lois-Ann Yamanaka's critically acclaimed novel, *Blu's Hanging*. The grounds were her depiction of a minor Filipino character as a rapist and child molester. According to press reports, protesters claimed that the character perpetuated the stereotype of Filipino men as sexual predators (James, 1999). I have not read the book. There may have been other very good reasons for voting against the award. But the stereotype argument simply doesn't hold. For a social stereotype to exist, it must be widely held. Not only have I never considered Filipino men to be sexual predators, but in 30 years of studying stereotyping, I have never even come across that so-called stereotype. Maybe such a stereotype exists in Hawaii, but it certainly has little national reverberation. Or at least it didn't until the protest.

However, even though not *all* media (or fictional or educational material) depictions constitute group stereotyping, even nonstereotype-driven depictions may well *contribute* to stereotypes. The issues are frequency and variety. Are members of a particular group depicted in a certain way with great frequency? And is this frequency of depiction accompanied by a lack of variety of group members in other endeavors or with other characteristics? Are these depictions part of a consistent bombardment of similar disseminated images of other members of the group, regardless of the maker's intent (or its absence)?

Now suppose that this limited range of movie and TV characters coincides with patterns of news coverage, buttressed by infographics, while news coverage simultaneously ignores or downplays other aspects of the lives of members of that social group. This may well result in the development or reinforcement of media stereotypes . . . even if no characters were merely stereotypes, each story were accurate, and every editor simply deemed each selected story to be important.

But sometimes media actually do stereotype. That is, they select news stories because they "typify" a group, or they create characters or plot lines that draw upon what mediamakers perceive as group characteristics . . . or at least characteristics that they believe fall within audience expectations or comfort zones.

Mass Media and Stereotypes

So how do we draw the line between stereotypes and legitimate generalizations, distinguish stereotypical from nonstereotypical labeling, or determine that entertainment depictions are stereotypical or nonstereotypical? When does the mass media treatment of a group and its members become the embodiment of a group stereotype? I would like to suggest a four-stage general model (not rigid or deterministic), based on three premises:

1. Although some may deny it, mediamakers recognize that consumers learn multiculturally from the media.

2. Although they may proclaim their innocence, mediamakers realize that some of this media-based multicultural learning takes the form of internalizing stereotypes.
3. Although they may not always recognize it, mediamakers sometimes draw upon those stereotypes in order to meet what they feel are consumer expectations, and in some cases (as common in advertising) they manipulate those stereotypes to provoke desired reactions.

As an illustration of this model, take the common media image of Italian Americans as often involved in criminal, particularly mob, activity. Few other groups' criminality has been so regularly trumpeted in the mass media. Although this does not mean that all media depictions of Italian Americans committing crimes should be considered stereotyping, even nonstereotypical treatment may *contribute* to stereotype reinforcement.

Stage One: Reality. Media treatments of societal groups and their individual members usually have *some* basis in reality, even though that treatment may not reflect the vast majority of that group. Some Jews are skilled in business. Some Muslims are fanatical terrorists. Some Christians are anti-Semitic. Some Hispanics speak broken English. Some Indians suffer from alcoholism or follow traditional tribal ways. Some Asian Americans are good in mathematics, while some maintain exotic (to most Americans) cultural practices. Some Blacks are on welfare or are good athletes. Some White men can't dunk a basketball.

And some Italian Americans have been involved in crime, as have some Americans of most backgrounds. Therefore, the mere making of a *few* movies or television shows about Italian American criminals or offering news coverage of Italian Americans involved in crime does not in itself provide compelling evidence of media stereotyping (any more than a few depictions of the other types of individuals just listed).

Stage Two: Seminal Treatment. Second comes the creation of a seminal, trend-setting, highly influential media depiction of members of a social group, drawing on selected aspects of that group's reality. This might be a major motion picture. It might be a widely watched and broadly discussed TV program or series. It might be widespread news coverage of a single event or a major story from a single media source, later picked up for broader media dissemination and intertextual commentary.

Such seminal media depictions either *establish a model* for future media textbook depictions of that group, *reinvigorate a long-established* (possibly dormant) *pattern* of depictions, or *provide a new variation* to the media treatment of that group. Such occurred with *The Godfather*, first as a novel, later as a series of motion pictures (Lebo, 1997). It was certainly not the first media treatment—not even the first movie—about Italian American organized crime. The Cosa Nostra and other Italian American mob hearings and trials have long fascinated the news media, while movies incorporating Italian American organized crime have been around since the silent era.

But *The Godfather* reinvigorated the theme. Not only did it give renewed impetus to the genre by demonstrating its immense commercial appeal, but it also became a model that has remained popular to the present. It added to the American popular lexicon, injecting "an offer you can't refuse" into long-term conversational repartee. Even the film's director, Francis Ford Coppola, became concerned that his runaway hit movie had overly glamorized the young mob don, Michael Corleone. So in *The Godfather: Part II*, Coppola emphasized the degeneracy of the new mob leader (Pechter, 1975).

Stage Three: Widespread Imitation. In this stage, other media sources imitate the seminal depiction, repeating it with variations. Movies incorporate a repeated pattern of plots, characterizations, and behaviors by members of the target group. Television series become imitative. Other media play up and embellish the seminal story. Why? Because some mediamakers recognize that audience expectations have been raised, creating a fertile ground to be tilled. With each addition to the media bombardment, the potential grows that media learning will occur as the stereotype becomes reified.

The aftermath of *The Godfather* illustrated that pattern. After *The Godfather* came other major films and TV docudramas about Italian American organized crime, as well as a slew of minor flicks (in the old days, these might be called "B movies") about or including Italian American gangs (Casillo, 1991). News stories about Italian American crime took on an added flourish. Italian surnames of public figures "gained" an added dimension . . . somewhat guilty until proven innocent. This momentum has carried to the present. In May 1998, when CBS hit audiences with four hours of *The Last Don II*, NBC countered the following week with four hours of *Witness to the Mob*.

Moreover, the post-*Godfather* era also witnessed a proliferation of individual Italian American movie and television criminals. In some cases their ethnicity was integral to the plot. In other cases, however, their ethnicity had no significance for their screen actions, yet mediamakers saddled generic villains with Italian surnames. Taking advantage of pre-sumed media-based learning, mediamakers drew upon and manipulated these media-conditioned stereotypes of Italian American criminality.

Stage Four: Humor, Parody, and Caricature. Once mediamakers assume that audience learning has occurred, including the internalizing or reinvigorating of stereotypes, the stage is set for media to derive hu-mor based on that learning. Much of humor, particularly parody and caricature, depends upon the establishment of predictable patterns of consumer thinking and reacting to labeled social categories. For that rea-son media humor provides a useful litmus test for the perceived existence and pervasiveness of stereotypes. Moreover, such humor demonstrates a willingness to draw upon and manipulate those receiver schemas of group knowledge and stereotypes. Those mediamaker insights into what stereotypes already lurk within consumers enable them to predict how audiences will react to parodies, caricature, or other types of group-based humor (Schwartz, 1973).

The release of the mob parody *Prizzi's Honor* (1985) demonstrated the teaching effectiveness of *The Godfather* and its clones. A hit both with critics and at the box office, *Prizzi's Honor* relied heavily on mediamaker assumptions about media-honed viewer schemas on Italian Americans and criminality. It illustrated their conviction that audiences already had such abundant stereotypes about Italian Americans as criminals and that these could be effectively tweaked. In the past decade, Italian American mob parodies have become a movie and TV staple, notably in HBO's 1999 hit series, *The Sopranos.*

Mediamaker awareness of the tenacity of multiple ethnic stereotypes became a basis for the hilariously touching 1991 film, *Only the Lonely.* A shy Irish American policeman (John Candy) falls in love with an equally shy Italian American girl (Ally Sheedy), which horrifies his passionately ethnic mother (Maureen O'Hara). To save face, O'Hara accommodates to the new reality by telling her son that this is okay as long as she isn't Sicilian, only to be told that she is. Then, when the two women meet over dinner, Sheedy adds to O'Hara's consternation when she mentions that she is also half Polish. No discussion of ethnic characteristics was neces-sary. Already possessed of stereotypes, the audience supplied the ethnic meaning of these interactions.

Let's put it another way. Seminal media presentations create, strengthen, or legitimize depiction patterns for different social groups. Because such seminal textbooks usually attempt carefully (if not always delicately) to achieve some aspect of group authenticity, they may not actually be guilty of stereotyping (although they may draw upon or contribute to stereotype formation or reinforcement). More important, they establish a model. By relentlessly copying that model, ensuing mediamakers harden the stereotypical nature of that image, often through mindless, careless, or exploitive repetition.

Evidence of mediamaker recognition of the reification of such consumer stereotypes can be observed when minor media products continually repeat certain types of group characterizations, whether in entertainment media or through news dissemination. Often such products lazily draw upon media-legitimized patterns of depiction and deliver what mediamakers think stereotype-conditioned audiences expect or will react to in a predictable, media-taught manner. In some cases mediamakers commercialize stereotypes by using them as a source for humor.

Depictions versus Stereotypes

Major or seminal depictions alone do not demonstrate the existence of group stereotypes. To determine that individual depictions have actually evolved into a stereotype requires an examination of a broad and continous array of media treatments—minor films, parodies, TV situation comedies, newspaper stories, documentaries, and talk radio. Put another way, a wide selection of media—not just a few important examples—are necessary to ascertain whether so-called trend-setting media have really set trends. An interethnic comparison further illustrates this process.

The Godfather reinvigorated a long tradition of Italian American organized crime movies. To a lesser extent, the 1983 *Scarface* helped to reify a pattern for the treatment of Cuban, Colombian, and other Latino drug dealers, which soon became movie and television status quo (*Miami Vice*, for example), as Latino gangs vied with Italian Americans for the media crime crown.

Yet *Year of the Dragon* (1985) did not set off a comparable splurge of media textbooks on Chinese American crime. Nor did *Once Upon a Time in America* (1984) launch a string of Jewish American organized crime films. While *Year of the Dragon*'s depiction of ethnic crime rightfully concerned Chinese Americans, provoking a protest, it did not have the long-range media multicultural curriculum stereotyping influence of *The Godfather* and *Scarface*.

Or take the comparative media curricular influence of *Superfly* (1972) and *Gordon's War* (1973), two films of the so-called blaxploitation genre so popular in the 1970s. *Superfly* legitimized and popularized the movie and television depiction of African American drug dealers, who have since become entertainment media regulars, arguably achieving stereotypical status. In contrast, *Gordon's War,* which celebrated African Americans who fought against drug dealing, failed to establish that as a widespread movie theme. (One major exception has been when Blacks are paired with White crime fighters, as in such interracial buddy movies as the *Lethal Weapon* series and in many current TV police shows.)

Depictions, in short, are not synonymous with stereotypes. Yet media stereotyping does occur, and such stereotyping influences perceptions and attitudes, including those of both students and school educators.

Schools versus Stereotypes

Schools, then, cannot avoid the issue of stereotypes and stereotyping. The universal need for generalizations and labels, the inevitability of media depictions, and the human propensity for stereotyping intersect to raise a series of critical pedagogical questions. How can teacher education programs help prepare teachers to deal with stereotypes—their own, those held by their students, and the subject itself (Tran, Young & DiLella, 1994)? How can school educators best help students understand the stereotyping process (Stephan, 1999)? How can they help students learn to generalize without stereotyping, use labels with nuance, and determine when depictions become stereotypes?

First, let me suggest what not to do, something I have often seen in educational materials. Do not—repeat, *do not*—simply ask students to go out and look for media stereotypes. What are they supposed to look for? What media evidence are they supposed to use, how are they supposed to gather it, and how are they supposed to evaluate it? How are they to determine when media generalizations or depictions attain stereotype status? If Holly or Melissa came home with such an assignment, I would immediately go to the teacher and ask what she or he meant by stereotypes and if the students had learned how to use evidence to decide whether or not media depictions, images, or generalizations were, in fact, stereotypes.

Without a careful, structured, cumulative, step-by-step process, lessons or assignments on stereotyping can become facile exercises in futility. Go find an advertising image and label it a stereotype. Watch a TV show and call a character stereotypical. Read a news story that treats some individual negatively and accuse it of stereotyping. Easy but misleading. Media-based assignments or projects should not begin with the *assumption* of stereotyping. In approaching the issue of media stereotyping, school educators should develop a clear, coherent plan that actually builds long-range understanding.

Schools should begin by helping students learn the differences between generalizations and stereotypes. They should then progress to simple exercises that help them learn to identify image patterns, including patterns of group treatment in the mass media. From there they should gain experience in discussing—and maybe disagreeing about—whether or not particular patterns of media treatment do, in fact, add up to stereotypes. Finally, and only after completing these preliminary steps, older students should engage in projects in which they attempt to analyze and assess the mass media in an attempt to determine *if* stereotyping is occurring, *what* media-based stereotypes currently exist, and *how* they are being disseminated.

Yet few students will have the time or resources to carry out a broad-scale examination of media stereotyping. Rather, they should conduct carefully constructed assignments or narrowly focused, well-conceived research projects. Consider the following possibilities.

1. Select *one* radio talk show host and listen to the program regularly over a two-week period to determine if the host uses a *pattern* of treatment when discussing a particular ethnic group or even individual members of that group.
2. Collect *all* articles about women in one (or maybe two) daily newspapers over a two-week period to determine if there is a *pattern* of topic selection.
3. Over a period of time, watch TV network national news shows to see if there is a *pattern* of treatment of religion.
4. Read and collect movie reviews for one month to determine if there is a *pattern* of movies about ethnicity, a specific ethnic group, or a specific diversity-related topic.
5. Look at a wide range of magazines to see if there is a *pattern* of adjectives being used when referring to or discussing a particular nation, culture, region, or religion.

Conclusion

As part of the process of preparing students to take their places as constructive participants in a multicultural society, schools should help them learn to work analytically with evidence, including that evidence emanating from the media. This should include the determination and assessment of mass media *patterns.*

Such pedagogy must avoid imposing on students the assumption that engaging the media automatically leads to detecting media stereotypes. Students should not be sent on simplistic search-and-destroy missions with guaranteed results, such as encouraging them to collect examples to "prove" that a predetermined stereotype exists or to use a single movie or television program as the basis for accusing the media of stereotyping. To do so is to "stereotype" the media themselves.

The issues of mass media stereotyping, as well as the broader goal of helping students learn to generalize without stereotyping, are too important to be dealt with in a facile manner. They are also too important for schools to avoid.

CHAPTER 10

Multicultural Education in the Cyberspace Era

Now we're moving deeper into the brave new world of cyberspace. This raises a fundamental question. In what respects has cyberspace become a dimension of the mass media?

Cyberspace provides a means—actually various means—of communication. Much of it closely resembles good old-fashioned person-to-person narrowcasting. Person-to-person E-mail, for example, falls somewhere between the telephone and what is now disparagingly referred to as "snail mail." Temporally more flexible but not nearly as personal as the telephone (I still prefer hearing a voice rather reading one). Quicker but less readable than *real* mail (give me a piece of paper, even if carted laboriously by the little guy in the shell, rather than eye-straining words on a monitor).

But much of cyberspace has the basic mass media characteristic—one source transmitting and many sources receiving. Traditional media organizations—newspapers, magazines, TV networks, and individual radio and television stations and programs—have their own websites. Then there are the new cyberspace media like the WebTV Network and on-line magazines and newspapers. According to some estimates, by the end of 1998 Netcasting had generated more than 500,000 radio and TV "channels."

Following the introduction of commercial radio, 38 years passed before it had entered 50 million American homes. It took television only 13 years to reach that same level, but the Internet is estimated to achieve this within five years. According to a Pew Research Center for the People and the Press survey, while in 1995 only 4% of Americans obtained news through the Internet, by 1998 this had risen to 20% (Samuelson, 1998).

But, unlike with most of traditional media, in cyberspace the receivers constantly talk back. They do so through chat rooms, Usenet groups, electronic bulletin boards, multiaddressed E-mail, and their ilk (Borden & Harvey, 1998; Harper, 1998). We can dispense with such clichés as "crossing the bridge into the twenty-first century," entering the "information age" (this also could have been said about the immediate post-Gutenberg world), or living in a "virtual world." Whatever your way of conceiving, describing, or labeling it, we are inexorably moving into a new era, in which the computer and other new communications technologies are adding to and in some respects fundamentally changing the process of the dissemination and exchange of information, images, and ideas, including those related to diversity.

Some have argued that the Internet actually came of age as a part of the mass media in January 1998, with the beginning of the media circus concerning sexual relations between President Bill Clinton and White House intern Monica Lewinsky. According to Michael Kinsley, editor of the online *Slate Magazine*, "This story has done for the Internet what the Gulf War did for CNN, and what the Kennedy assassination did for television in general" (Cimons, 1998, p. A–5). *Newsweek*, the first member of the traditional mass media to learn of the allegations, held off publishing them. So cyberspace, in the person of Matt Drudge and his "Drudge Report," beat *Newsweek* and the other traditional media to the punch by reporting on *Newsweek's* decision. This included, of course, releasing the story itself.

Once launched into cyberspace, the story took on a life of its own. Led by cyberspace, the rest of the mass media followed intertextually. TV reporters, radio broadcasters, talk show hosts, newspaper columnists, magazine writers—soon thousands of mediamakers joined the "feeding frenzy." In the first seven months of 1998, the Center for Media and Public Affairs counted 1,172 jokes about President Clinton and sex by four leading TV comics—David Letterman, Jay Leno, Bill Maher, and Conan O'Brien. One radio talk show host whom I admire presented a passionate, well-argued denunciation of the media for their fixation on the affair . . . yet from that point on, often when I turned on his program, *he*, too, was fixating on it.

Cyberspace not only beat the other media to the punch; it also continued to be a major source for Lewinsky affair junkies. Unable to get enough "news" from the traditional media, including the incessant "analysis" on talk radio, junkies continued to seek the latest rumors, revelations, and speculations on cyberspace. According to some reports, cyberspace sites dealing with the affair recorded a record number of "hits."

But does cyberspace differ in any major respects from other forms of mass media? Let me suggest two kinds of differences, each with serious multicultural and educational implications. First, cyberspace *can* be more democratic. Second, cyberspace *can* be more effective than other media in fostering both intergroup and intragroup dialogue. Let's examine these two propositions.

Cyberspace as Mass Media Democracy

Cyberspace as democracy has less to do with content and learning than with the process of creation (Katz, 1997). Cyberspace has facilitated an enormous expansion of mediamakers . . . or at least people who can add to media content. The traditional mass media inevitably limit the number of content creators, particularly because of the enormous cost of participation, as in A. J. Liebling's oft-repeated quip, "Freedom of the press is reserved for those who own one."

While cyberspace does not equalize the power to communicate ideas widely, at least anybody with access to an online computer and knowledge of how to use it can join some cyberspace conversation, contribute ideas, and be read by who knows how many others (Trend, 1997). For example, as of 1997, amateur movie critics had created some 200 websites. Unfortunately, cyberspace access and skills have not developed in a multiculturally equitable manner (Berdayes & Berdayes, 1998). According to a 1998 study, a huge Black-White access gap exists both in home computer ownership and World Wide Web usage (Kiernan, 1998). Some have gone so far as to call it the "World White Web" (Shaw, 1997).

Not all cyberspace messages reach the large audiences of television or newspapers (of course, print media, particularly those of a specialty or niche nature, also face distribution problems). But, more and more, individuals can have their cyberspace say, including creating multicultural minitextbooks, with the realization that somebody, somewhere, may read them. According to Howard Mehlinger (1996):

> In the past, schools have been places where people in authority decided what would be taught (and possibly learned), at what age, and in what sequence. They also decided what would *not* be taught—what would not be approved knowledge. The new technologies provide students access to information that was once under the control of teachers. (p. 402)

Certainly Mehlinger overstates the case for previous school control over knowledge, as my discussion of the media multicultural education has demonstrated. Yet he is correct about the power of the new technologies—particularly cyberspace and VCRs—to alter the relationship between nonschool and school education.

This leads us back to the traditional mass media formulation: *Who* says *what* to *whom* through *which channel* with *what effect?* Through its multiple channels, cyberspace provides the opportunity for more who's to express their what's to varieties of whom's. The mass media multicultural curriculum operates through myriad cyberspace textbooks—specific chat rooms, Web pages, on-line magazines, and other sources where ideas about diversity and diverse groups are exchanged or at least put out for others to read. With *what effect?* At this point, your guess is as good as mine. While a growing number of scholars are examining cyberspace, to date relatively few of them have approached it from a mass media perspective (Morris & Ogan, 1996).

Empirical research on the multicultural ramifications of cyberspace is likely to be far more complex than with traditional mass media. It will be far more difficult to specify the group identities of invisible cyberspace mediamakers—according to some scholars, they exist only as text (Gerlander & Takala, 1997)—than to assess those characteristics of actors, magazine editors, TV anchorpersons, and movie directors. In fact, some scholars worry that cyberspace may render real life social divisions invisible, thereby encouraging cyberspace participants to ignore the existence of such societal issues (Porter, 1997). It will be far more difficult to analyze cyberspace media multicultural content—to filter out diversity-related content from the zillions of cyberspace messages and images—than it has been when dealing with the extensive but comparatively limited universe of movies, magazines, and TV shows. It will be far more difficult to analyze media impact—to determine and examine a valid sample of consumers in order to assess the multicultural learning that results from the Internet.

But we can be certain that cyberspace multicultural education is taking place. The more young people become involved in seeking information on the Internet, exposing themselves to cyberspace ideas and images and making their own contributions to cyberspace content, the more likely they will both learn and teach about diversity-related topics as simultaneous multicultural consumers and creators.

Intergroup and Intragroup Communication

Mass media history has involved the struggle between general interest media—those that try to reach a broad audience with multifaceted content—and niche media—those that seek a specific target audience with a focused type of content. NBC, ABC, and CBS versus ESPN, Turner Classic Movies, and Comedy Central. *Time* and *Newsweek* versus *Essence, Hispanic, Ms.,* and *Out.* Hollywood movies versus women's "alternative films." Citywide daily newspapers versus the ethnic and religious press. General interest and niche media compete and coexist, with the general interest media currently holding the consumership upper hand, even if it is a declining one.

In cyberspace, however, niches dominate. You don't usually enter cyberspace by casting a casual net as you do when you flip through the daily newspaper, leaf through a general interest magazine, or channel surf on cable TV. Most Internet users (57% according to a 1997 *Business Week*/Harris Poll) repeatedly head for specific sites, while most others seek out certain topics (Shaw, 1997). Cyberspace comes as close to "designer mass media" as anything we have yet experienced, the closest we have yet come to creating the opportunity for the total fulfillment of media "uses and gratifications" (Rafaeli, 1986).

Therefore, the old media question demands a cyberspace reformulation more along the lines suggested by media reception scholars—who goes to what sites to talk to whom about which topics with what results? The answers to that broad question may hold the key to dissecting the potential implications of cyberspace for mass media multicultural education.

First, an optimistic view. People, including students, of widely varying backgrounds will use cyberspace to communicate across national, ethnic, cultural, and religious lines. They will share common interests, build common ground, and seriously explore complex, sometimes controversial, topics relating to diversity. Indeed, anecdotal evidence, much of it coming from teachers, suggests that many young people can and do use the Internet to converse, strike up friendships, and learn about others who are culturally different. Take, for example, the CyberPeace project created by Santa Monica, California high school student Andrew Friedman to foster ongoing dialogue involving Jewish Israeli, Arab Israeli, Palestinian, and Jordanian students (McAllister, 1997).

Those adopting that optimistic position, including many teachers, wax eloquent about the multicultural—or better, intercultural—potential of the Internet. The Internet becomes an avenue for continuous cross-cultural conversations and for building multicultural and global common ground (Association of American Colleges and Universities, 1998; Cairncross, 1998; Davis & Wendelyn, 1998). Such *intergroup* conversations will serve to foster an inclusivist national Unum, although maybe not the identity-blind world envisioned in the MCI commercial, "The Internet knows no age, gender, race, or nationality. What a great time to be alive" (Deetz, 1997, p. 125).

While fostering Unum, the Internet also enriches Pluribus. The proliferation of niches has also meant the proliferation of *intragroup* conversations, people drawn into websites and chat rooms with people like themselves, or at least with whom they share powerful cultural, religious, and ideological commonalities (Goldstein, 1998; Holmes, 1998).

Internet sites based on racial or ethnic identity, religious beliefs, sexual orientation, gender, and language expand on the affinity-building roles played by face-to-face intragroup gatherings and traditional niche media targeted at America's diverse communities, including communities that communicate in languages other than English. These interactions can foster a greater sense of group commonality, heritage, identity, and pride. They can also serve to explore intragroup differences, clarify issues of special interest to members of the group, and even mobilize group action (Jones, 1997).

But there is a more pessimistic perspective (Ebo, 1998). Intragroup cyberspace communication can also contribute to polarization and foster bigotry (Kaplan & Bjorgo, 1998). Hate-based and conspiracy websites that attack, demean, and maybe incite violence against target groups, as well as recruit new adherents to their organizations. (According to the Simon Wiesenthal Center, the number of hate-based Internet Web pages tripled in 1997 [Oldham, 1997].) Chat rooms in which like-minded folks reinforce each other's animus toward and stereotypes about other groups. The opportunity for people to seek out ideological compatriots to confirm their own prejudices and arm themselves with better arguments for justifying discrimination and the maintenance of inequities.

In these ways, self-selected "cybertribes" can contribute to real-life segregation, societal fragmentation, and intergroup violence (Shenk, 1997). Add to this the outcry over the potential influence of violence-laden video games, particularly in the aftermath of the April 1999 massacre carried out by two game-fascinated students at Columbine High School in Littleton, Colorado. *Los Angeles Times* writer David Shaw (1997) posed the dilemma in the following manner:

> Will people's ability to narrowly tailor all the information they receive isolate them from opposing viewpoints, thus undermining political dialogue and furthering polarizing the body politic? . . . What will happen to our already fragmented sense of community if everyone is reading different stories on different subjects . . . and, in essence, communicating by e-mail and in online chat rooms only with people who share their own interests? The many flaws of the traditional news media notwithstanding, these media—daily newspapers and network television in particular—have long served as both a reality check and a kind of social glue, a common cultural reference point in our polyglot, increasingly multicultural society. (p. A–26)

While many people from various ideological and interest group positions may hold a less sanguine view of the traditional news media, their decline as "social glue" and "common cultural reference point" is a concern. Through cyberspace, intragroup mass communication can facilitate a polarizing circle-the-wagons Pluribus, champion Unum as an exclusivist idea (an America in which there is only room for "real Americans," meaning Americans just like "us"), and jeopardize the creation of a fully inclusivist Unum. The triumph of isolationist, hate-based ethnocentric intragroup solidarity based on the exclusion and oppression of others could turn cyberspace into a multicultural education nightmare.

Schools, Cyberspace, and Diversity

The addition of cyberspace to the mass media multicultural curriculum hypertrophies old challenges and opportunities while creating new ones for school educators. Consider some of the following multicultural questions.

If cyberspace is going to become a more democratic medium, how can schools improve access for students of all backgrounds and empower them to use it effectively (Gandy, 1998)?

How can schools foster constructive intergroup cyberspace communication, including the honest discussion of serious diversity-related topics?

How can schools encourage the constructive use of intragroup cyberspace conversations while mitigating their polarizing possibilities?

In what respects should schools function as cyberspace gatekeepers, such as by restricting access to hate-based sites?

How should schools deal with the burgeoning world of cyberspace underground student newspapers, including those laced with bigotry?

Given the extent that entertainment and information media have become conflated in terms of multicultural teaching and learning, how might cyberspace further influence students' visions of reality (Morse, 1998; Reeves & Nass, 1996)?

Conclusion

Functioning as a dimension of the mass media, cyberspace operates like an ever-growing zoo of niches. As an anarchically democratic arena, cyberspace provides opportunities for people to cross intercultural bridges. Conversely, it can draw them into narrow, constricting perceptual and attitudinal tunnels.

Cyberspace does not alter the basic nature of media multicultural education. Individuals and institutions will continue to create media, including cyberspace media. Those media will continue to teach, generating and providing multicultural content, from which media consumers will learn. The teaching-learning dimension of media multicultural education remains. Yet cyberspace expands the mass media spectrum, just as did each of the previous innovators, going back to Gutenberg. And in doing so, it enlarges the media multicultural curriculum.

Multicultural education will happen. The mass media, operating as multicultural educators, guarantee that. Can school educators more effectively and constructively deal with the reality and inevitability of media multicultural teaching and learning? Can they challenge it and build on it, comprehend it and grapple with it, help students use it and not be used by it? Can schools draw upon the media as rich sources of educational transformation, an ever-widening source of pedagogical possibilities?

The mass media as multicultural education are with us for the duration. How schools and school educators deal with that reality may well be one of their greatest challenges during the twenty-first century.

She's Black, I'm White

One day, out of nowhere, around the end of her kindergarten year, Holly offhandedly mentioned that she was going swimming that afternoon with her friend, Tyisha. Just as offhandedly, Holly added, "She's Black, I'm White." At that moment I wished that psychologist Beverly Tatum (1997) (author of *"Why Are All the Black Kids Sitting Together in the Cafeteria?" And Other Conversations About Race*) were standing next to me, suggesting the perfect response. No such luck.

Holly and Melissa had grown up amidst racial and ethnic diversity. Holly's first main squeeze—when she was three—was a Black five-year-old a few houses down from us. She and Melissa have watched plenty of movies and TV shows with racially diverse characters. Yet, except for *Pocahontas,* I had never heard either of them use skin color or ethnic designations to categorize characters or any people they knew. And it was the first time that I had ever heard one of the girls place *herself* within a racial category.

We had consciously avoided exposing them to racial labeling in our conversations, deciding that we would address that issue at the appropriate developmental time . . . or when it inevitably arose through the normal course of events. Now it had.

Somehow, somewhere, sometime during her kindergarten year, Holly had learned to employ racial categorizing and labeling. Where and when she learned about Black and White, I'm not sure. In her cryptic five-year-old manner, she gave me various explanations at different times. She had learned it from some of the kids in her (thoroughly desegregated) school. She had learned it from one of the teachers (reportedly while discussing ethnic food). She had heard it from Tyisha herself. And once she said that it had come from something she had seen on TV, although she couldn't remember the show.

We weren't upset. In a society suffused by racial thinking, ethnic labeling, and a thoroughly multicultural media curriculum, it was bound to happen. Holly (at five) and Melissa (at four) had merely taken that inevitable step from perceiving physical differences to discussing them within the historically developed, socially imbedded, media-disseminated American cultural tradition of racial categorization.

Equipped with their new American racial vernacular, Holly and Melissa had entered a new phase of their multicultural education. We are going to try to make that education a constructive one. We can only hope that the mass media and the schools do their part, too.

One day, shortly after the swimming announcement, I found one of Holly's many blue-pen drawings on the den table. It showed two little girls, one colored blue, the other without color except for the blue outlines of her face and body. Above the blue girl was the name Tyisha. Above the other girl was the name Holly. Beneath Tyisha's figure was the word *Black*. Beneath Holly's figure was *White*.

I looked away momentarily, pondering the implications of Holly's new use of racial vocabulary. But when I looked back at the drawing, I noticed something else. Holly's two little girls—one Blue, one White—were holding hands.

References

Abercrombie, N., & Longhurst, B. (1998). *Audiences: A sociological theory of performance and imagination.* London: Sage.

Aboud, F. (1988). *Children and prejudice.* Oxford, England: Basil Blackwell.

Abt, V., & Seesholtz, M. (1998). Talking us down: "The shameless world" revisited. *Journal of Popular Film & Television, 26*(1), 42–48.

Adoni, H., & Mane, S. (1984). Media and the social construction of reality: Toward an integration of theory and research. *Communication Theory, 11,* 323–340.

Allen, I. L. (1990). *Unkind words: Ethnic labeling from Redskin to WASP.* New York: Bergin & Garvey.

Allen, R. L. (1981). Communication research on Black Americans. In H. A. Myrick & C. Keegan (Eds.), *In search of diversity, symposium on minority audiences and programming research: Approaches and applications* (pp. 47–63). Washington, DC: Corporation for Public Broadcasting.

Allen, R. L., & Hatchett, S. (1986). The media and social effects: Self and system orientations of Blacks. *Communication Research, 13*(1), 97–123.

Alvarez, M., Huston, A. C., Wright, J. C., & Kerkman, D. (1988). Gender differences in visual attention to television form and content. *Journal of Applied Developmental Psychology, 9,* 459–476.

Alwood, E. (1996). *Straight news: Gays, lesbians, and the news media.* New York: Columbia University Press.

Anyon, J. (1979). Ideology and United States history textbooks. *Harvard Educational Review, 49*(3), 361–386.

Apple, M. W., & Christian-Smith, L. (1991). *The politics of the textbook.* New York: Routledge.

Armstrong, G. B., Neuendorf, K. A., & Brentar, J. E. (1992). TV entertainment, news, and racial perceptions of college students. *Journal of Communication, 42*(3), 153–176.

Asfahani, M. (1996, December 2). Time to look and listen. *Newsweek,* p. 18.

Association of American Colleges and Universities. (1998). *DiversityWeb: Where diversity and learning are linked through the Web.* Washington, DC: Association of American Colleges and Universities.

Atkin, C., Greenberg, B., & McDermott, S. (1978). Race and social role learning from television. In H. S. Dordick (Ed.), *Proceedings of the sixth annual telecommunications policy research conference* (pp. 7–20). Lexington, MA: D.C. Heath.

August, D., & Hakuta, K. (Eds.). (1998). *Educating language minority children.* Washington, DC: National Academy Press.

Axelrod, L. (1997). *TV-Proof your kids: A parent's guide to safe and healthy viewing.* Secaucus, NJ: Citadel Press.

Bagdikian, B. (1983). *The media monopoly.* Boston: Beacon Press.

Bandura, A. (1977). *Social learning theory.* Englewood Cliffs, NJ: Prentice-Hall.

Banks, J. A. (1993). Multicultural education for young children: Racial and ethnic attitudes and their modification. In D. Spodek (Ed.), *Handbook of research on the education of young children* (pp. 236–250). New York: Macmillan.

Banks, J. A. (1991). Multicultural education: Its effects on students' racial and gender role attitudes. In J. P. Shaver (Ed.), *Handbook of research on social studies teaching and learning* (pp. 459–469). New York: Macmillan.

Bannon, L. (1998, May 15). The publisher plans new type faces for the L. A. Times. *The Wall Street Journal,* pp. A1, A6.

Barlow, D. (1997). Schindler: Huck in a major key. *Education Digest, 63*(4), 40–43.

Barnhurst, K. G., & Mutz, D. (1997). American journalism and the decline in event-centered reporting. *Journal of Communication, 47*(4), 27–53.

Barry, A.M.S. (1997). *Visual intelligence: Perception, image, and manipulation in visual communication.* Albany: State University of New York Press.

Bar-Tal, D. (1997). Formation and change of ethnic and national stereotypes: An integrative model. *International Journal of Intercultural Relations, 21*(4), 491–523.

Bartolomé, L. I., & Macedo, D. P. (1997). Dancing with bigotry: The poisoning of racial and ethnic identities. *Harvard Educational Review, 67*(2), 222–245.

Bates, K. G. (1997, September 19). Where's the color on primetime TV? *Los Angeles Times,* sec. B, p. 9.

Beck, B. (1998). Lost & found: Who owns the Amistad? *Multicultural Education, 5*(4), 36–39.

Berdayes, L. C., & Berdayes, V. (1998). The information highway in contemporary magazine narrative. *Journal of Communication, 48*(2), 109–124.

Berger, P. L., & Luckman, T. (1966). *The social construction of reality: A treatise in the sociology of knowledge.* Garden City, NY: Doubleday.

Bernardi, D. L. (1998). *Star Trek and history: Race-ing toward a white future.* New Brunswick, NJ: Rutgers University Press.

Berry, G. L. (1980). Children, television and social class roles: The medium as an unplanned educational curriculum. In E. L. Palmer & A. Dorr (Eds.), *Children and the faces of television* (pp. 71–81). New York: Academic Press.

Berry, G. L., & Asamen, J. K. (Eds.). (1993). *Children and television: Images in a changing socio-cultural world.* Beverly Hills, CA: Sage.

Berry, G. L., & Mitchell-Kernan, C. (Eds.). (1982). *Television and the socialization of the minority child.* New York: Academic Press.

Bettelheim, B. (1976). *The uses of enchantment: The meaning and importance of fairy tales.* New York: Knopf.

Billings, D. B., Norman, G., & Ledford, K. (Eds.). (1999). *Confronting Appalachian stereotypes: Back talk from an American region.* Lexington: University Press of Kentucky.

Bird, S. E. (1996). *Dressing in feathers: The construction of the Indian in American popular culture.* Boulder, CO: Westview Press.

Black, G. D. (1998). *The Catholic crusade against the movies, 1940–1975*. New York: Cambridge University Press.

Black, G. D. (1994). *Hollywood censored: Morality codes, Catholics, and the movies.* New York: Cambridge University Press.

Bogdanovich, P. (1968). *John Ford.* Berkeley: University of California Press.

Boorstin, D. J. (1961). *The image or whatever happened to the American dream?* New York: Atheneum.

Borden, D. L., & Harvey, K. (Eds.). (1998). *The electronic grapevine: Rumor, reputation, and reporting in the new on-line environment.* Mahwah, NJ: Erlbaum.

Bramlett-Solomon, S., & Farwell, T. M. (1996). Sex on the soaps: An analysis of Black, White, and interracial couple intimacy. In V. T. Berry & C. L. Manning-Miller (Eds.), *Mediated messages and African-American culture* (pp. 146–158). Thousand Oaks, CA: Sage.

Brigham, J. C., & Giesbrecht, L. W. (1976). "All in the family": Racial attitudes. *Journal of Communication, 26*(4), 69–74.

Brown, J. A. (1991). *Television critical viewing skills education: Major media literacy projects in the United States and selected countries.* Hillsdale, NJ: Erlbaum.

Bryant, J., & Zillmann, D. (Eds.) (1991). *Responding to the screen: Reception and re-action processes.* Hillsdale, NJ: Erlbaum.

Bullard, S. (1996). *Teaching tolerance: Raising open-minded empathetic children.* New York: Doubleday.

Cairncross, F. (1998). *The death of distance: How the communications revolution will change our lives.* Cambridge, MA: Harvard Business School.

Campbell, C. R. (1995). *Race, myth and the news.* Thousand Oaks, CA: Sage.

Candy, P. C. (1982). Personal constructs and personal paradigms: Elaboration, modification and transformation. *Interchange: A Journal of Educational Policy, 13*(4), 56–69.

Carby, H. V. (1993). Encoding White resentment: *Grand Canyon*— a narrative for our times. In C. McCarthy & W. Crichlow (Eds.), *Race, identity, and representation in education* (pp. 236–247). New York: Routledge.

Caron, A. H. (1979). First-time exposure to television: Effects on Inuit children's cultural images. *Communication Research, 6,* 135–154.

Carson, D., & Friedman, L. D. (Eds.). (1995). *Shared differences: Multicultural media and practical pedagogy.* Urbana: University of Illinois Press.

Casillo, R. (1991). Moments in Italian-American cinema: From "Little Caesar" to Coppola and Scorsese. In A. J. Tamburri, P. A. Giordano, & F. L. Gardaphe (Eds.), *From the margin: Writings in contemporary Italian Americana* (pp. 374–396). West Lafayette, IN: Purdue University Press.

Caso, A. (1980). *Mass media vs. the Italian Americans.* Boston: Branden Press.

Chaffee, S. (1997). The national television violence studies. *Journal of Communication, 47*(4), 170–173.

Chaffee, S. H., & Hochheimer, J. L. (1985). The beginnings of political communication research in the United States: Origins of the "limited effects" model. In E. M. Rogers & F. Balle (Eds.), *The media revolution in America and in Western Europe* (pp. 267–296). Norwood, NJ: Ablex.

Chan, K. (1998). The construction of Black male identity in Black action films of the nineties. *Cinema Journal, 37*(2), 35–48.

Chartock, R. (1978). A holocaust unit for classroom teachers. *Social Education, 42,* 278–285.

Children Now. (1998). *A different world: Children's perceptions of race and class in the media.* Oakland, CA: Children Now.

Chin, F. (1973). Confessions of a number one son. *Ramparts,* 41–49.

Chiong, J. A. (1998). *Racial categorization of multiracial children in schools.* Westport, CT: Bergin & Garvey.

Christenson, P. G., & Roberts, D. F. (1998). *It's not only rock and roll: Popular music in the lives of adolescents.* Cresskill, NJ: Hampton Press.

Cimons, M. (1998, February 2). Some see internet coming of age during Clinton troubles. *Los Angeles Times,* sec. A, p. 5.

Cleland, N. (1998, September 28). O. C. minorities upbeat about future. *Los Angeles Times,* sec. A, pp. 3, 24.

Cockburn, A. (1997, October 2). A big green bomb aimed at immigration. *Los Angeles Times,* sec. B, p. 9.

Cohen, J. (1998). Yiddish film and the American immigrant experience. *Film & History, 28*(1–2), 30–44.

Comstock, G. A. (1978). *Trends in the study of incidental learning from television viewing.* Syracuse, NY: Eric Clearinghouse in Information Resources.

Comstock, G. A. (1977). *The impact of television on American institutions and the American public.* Honolulu: East-West Communications Institute, East-West Center.

Comstock, G., & Cobbey, R. (1979). Television and the children of ethnic minorities. *Journal of Communication, 29*(1), 104–115.

Condit, C. M. (1994). Hegemony in a mass-mediated society: Concordance about reproductive technologies. *Critical Studies in Mass Communication, 11,* 205–230.

Cooper, E., & Jahoda, M. (1947). The evasion of propaganda: How prejudiced people respond to anti-prejudice propaganda. *Journal of Psychology, 23,* 15–25.

Cornbleth, C. (1998). An American curriculum. *Teachers College Record, 99*(4), 622–646.

Cortés, C. E. (1995). Knowledge construction and popular culture: The media as multicultural educator. In J. A. Banks and C.A.M. Banks (Eds.), *Handbook of research on multicultural education* (pp. 169–183). New York: Macmillan.

Cortés, C. E. (1992). Pride, prejudice, and power: The mass media as societal educator on diversity. In J. Lynch, C. Modgil, & S. Modgil (Eds.), *Prejudice, polemic or progress?* (pp. 367–381). London: Falmer Press

Cortés, C. E. (1991). Hollywood interracial love: Social taboo as screen titillation. In P. Loukides & L. K. Fuller (Eds.), *Plot conventions in American popular film* (pp. 21–35). Bowling Green, OH: Bowling Green State University Popular Press.

Cortés, C. E. (1981). The societal curriculum: Implications for multiethnic education. In J. A. Banks (Ed.), *Education in the 80's: Multiethnic education* (pp. 24–32). Washington, DC: National Education Association.

Cortés, C. E. (1979). The societal curriculm and the school curriculum: Allies or antagonists? *Educational Leadership, 36*(7), 475–479.

Cripps, T. (1993). *Making movies black: The Hollywood message movie from World War II to the civil rights era.* New York: Oxford University Press.

Cripps, T. (1978). *Black film as genre.* Bloomington: Indiana University Press.

Cripps, T. (1977). *Slow fade to black: The Negro in American film, 1900–1942.* New York: Oxford University Press.

Cripps, T. (1970). The myth of the southern box office: A factor in racial stereotyping in American movies, 1920–1940. In J. C. Curtis & L. L. Gould (Eds.), *The Black experience in America: Selected essays* (pp. 116–144). Austin: University of Texas Press.

Dann, M. E. (Ed.). (1971). *The Black press, 1827–1890: The quest for national identity.* New York: Capricorn.

Dates, J. L. (1980). Race, racial attitudes and adolescent perceptions of Black television characters. *Journal of Broadcasting, 24*(4), 549–560.

Dates, J. L., & Barlow, W. (Eds.). (1990). *Split image: African Americans in the mass media.* Washington, DC: Howard University Press.

Davies, M. M. (1997). *Fake, fact, and fantasy: Children's interpretations of television reality.* Mahwah, NJ: Erlbaum.

Davis, P. J., & Wendelyn, C. (1998). Does Princess Adelaide really have the whooping cough? *Phi Delta Kappan, 80*(4), 322–325.

Davison, W. P. (1983). The third-person effect in communication. *Public Opinion Quarterly, 47*(1), 1–15.

Deetz, S. A. (1997). Communication in the age of negotiation. *Journal of Communication, 47*(4), 118–135.

DeGaetano, G., & Bander, K. (1996). *Screen smarts: A family guide to media literacy.* Boston: Houghton Mifflin.

Derman-Sparks, L., & Philips, C. B. (1997). *Teaching/Learning anti-racism: A developmental approach.* New York: Teachers College Press.

Desmond, R. J., Singer, J. L., Singer, D. G., Calam, R., & Colimore, K. (1985). Family mediation patterns and television viewing: Young children's use and grasp of the medium. *Human Communication Research, 11*(4), 461–480.

Devine, P. (1989). Stereotypes and prejudice. *Journal of Personality and Social Psychology, 56*, 5–18.

Diawara, M. (Ed.). (1992). *Black American cinema.* New York: Routledge, Chapman, & Hall.

Dorfman, A. (1983). *The empire's old clothes: What the Lone Ranger, Babar, and other innocent heroes do to our minds.* New York: Pantheon.

Dorfman, L., & Woodruff, K. (1998). The roles of speakers in local television news stories on youth and violence. *Journal of Popular Film and Television, 23*(2), 80–85.

Dower, J. (1986). *War without mercy: Race and power in the Pacific war.* New York: Pantheon.

Downing, J.D.H. (1988). "The Cosby Show" and American racial discourse. In G. Smitherman-Donaldson & T. A. van Dijk (Eds.), *Discourse and discrimination* (pp. 46–73). Detroit: Wayne State University Press.

Dresser, N. (1996). *Multicultural manners: New rules of etiquette for a changing society.* New York: John Wiley.

Dyer, R. (1994). Stereotyping. In R. Dyer (Ed.), *Gays and film* (Rev. ed., pp. 27–39). New York: Zoetrope.

Dyer, R. (1986). *Heavenly bodies: Film stars and society.* New York: St. Martin's.

Dyson, M. E. (1993). *Reflecting Black: African-American cultural criticism.* Minneapolis: University of Minnesota Press.

Dyson, M. E. (1989). Bill Cosby and the politics of race. *Z Magazine, 2*(9), 26–30.

Ebo, B. (Ed.). (1998). *Cyberghetto or cybertopia? Race, class, and gender on the internet.* Westport, CT: Praeger.

Efron, S. (1991, December 5). Japanese roots still ignite bias. *Los Angeles Times,* sec. A, pp. 1, 36–38.

Ely, M. P. (1991). *The adventures of Amos 'n' Andy: A social history of an American phenomenon.* New York: Free Press.

Entman, R. M. (1990). Modern racism and the images of Blacks in local television news. *Critical Studies in Mass Communication, 7,* 332–345.

Erben, R., & Erben. U. (1991–1992). Popular culture, mass media, and Chicano identity in Gary Soto's "Living Up the Street" and "Small Faces." *MELUS, 17*(3), 43–52.

Fairchild, H. H., Stockard, R., & Bowman, P. (1986). Impact of "Roots": Evidence from the national survey of Black Americans. *Journal of Black Studies, 16*(3), 307–318.

Fajes, F. (1984). Critical mass communications research and media effects: The problem of the disappearing audience. *Media, Culture and Society, 6,* 219–232.

Farber, P., Provenzo, E. F., Jr., & Holm, G. (Eds.). (1994). *Schooling in the light of popular culture.* Albany: State University of New York Press.

Festinger, L. (1957). *A theory of cognitive dissonance.* Evanston, IL: Row, Peterson.

Fisher, P. L., & Lowenstein, R. L. (Eds.). (1967). *Race and the news media.* New York: Praeger.

Fiske, S. T., & Taylor, S. E. (1991). *Social cognition* (2d ed.). New York: McGraw-Hill.

Forman, H. J. (1933). *Our movie made children.* New York: Macmillan.

Fox, R. F. (1996). *Harvesting minds: How TV commercials control kids.* Westport, CT: Praeger.

Friar, R. E., & Friar, N. A. (1972). *The only good Indian . . . the Hollywood gospel.* New York: Drama Book Specialists.

Friedan, B. (1963). *The feminine mystique.* New York: Norton.

Friedman, L. D. (Ed.). (1991). *Unspeakable images: Ethnicity and the American cinema.* Urbana: University of Illinois Press.

Friedman, L. D. (1982). *Hollywood's image of the Jew.* New York: Frederick Ungar.

Fritz, M. (1998, June 25). With drug arrests, urban grit smudges Amish life. *Los Angeles Times,* sec. A, pp. 1, 12.

Fuchs, C. J. (1993). The buddy politic. In S. Cohan & I. R. Hark (Eds.), *Screening the male: Exploring masculinities in Hollywood cinema* (pp. 194–210). London: Routledge.

Gabler, N. (1988). *An empire of their own: How the Jews invented Hollywood.* New York: Crown.

Gaines, J. (1987). "The Scar of Shame": Skin color and caste in Black silent melo-drama. *Cinema Journal, 26*(4), 3–21.

Gamson, J. (1998). *Freaks talk back: Tabloid talk shows and sexual nonconformity.* Chicago: University of Chicago Press.

Gandy, O., Jr. (1998). *Communication and race: A structural perspective.* New York: Oxford University Press.

Gandy, O, Jr., & Coleman, L. G. (1986). The Jackson campaign: Mass media and Black student perceptions. *Journalism Quarterly, 63*(1), 138–143, 154.

Gans, H. J. (1967). The mass media as an educational institution. *Television Quarterly, 6*(2), 20–37.

Geertz, C. (1973). *The interpretation of cultures.* New York: Basic Books.

Gentner, D., & Stevens, A. L. (Eds.). (1983). *Mental models.* Hillsdale, NJ: Erlbaum.

Gerbner, G., & Gross, L. (1976). Living with television: The violence profile. *Journal of Communication, 26*(2), 173–199.

Gerlander, M., & Takala, E. (1997). Relating electronically: Interpersonality in the net. *Nordicom: Nordic Research on Media & Communication, 181*(21), 77–81.

Gerson, W. M. (1966). Mass media socialization behavior: Negro-White differences. *Social Forces, 45*(1), 40–50.

Getlin, J. (1998, June 30). New life for adage: Never let facts get in way of good story. *Los Angeles Times,* sec. A, p. 5.

Gilman, S. L. (1985). *Difference and pathology: Stereotypes of sexuality, race, and madness.* Ithaca, NY: Cornell University Press.

Giroux, H. A. (1997). *Channel surfing: Racetalk and the destruction of today's youth.* New York: St. Martin's Press.

Giroux, H. A. (1996). *Fugitive cultures: Race, violence, and youth.* New York: Routledge.

Gitlin, T. (1985). *Inside prime time.* New York: Pantheon.

Gitlin, T. (1980). *The whole world is watching: Media in the making and unmaking of the New Left.* Berkeley: University of California Press.

Gitlin, T. (1979). Prime time ideology: The hegemonic process in television entertainment. *Social Problems, 26*(3), 251–266.

Glazer, N. (1997). *We are all multiculturalists now.* Cambridge, MA: Harvard University Press.

Goffman, E. (1974). *Frame analysis.* Boston: Northeastern University Press.

Golab, C. (1980). Stellaaaaaa. . . . . . ! ! ! ! ! ! ! !: The Slavic stereotype in American film. In R. M. Miller (Ed.), *The kaleidoscopic lens: How Hollywood views ethnic groups* (pp. 135–155). Englewood, NJ: Jerome S. Ozer.

Goldberg, J. N. (1983). *Laughter through tears: The Yiddish cinema.* Rutherford, NJ: Fairleigh-Dickinson University Press.

Goldman, E. A. (1983). *Visions, images, and dreams: Yiddish film past and present.* Ann Arbor, MI: UMI Research Press.

Goldstein, N. E. (1998, September 14). My online synagogue. *Newsweek,* p. 16.

Golumbia, D. (1995–1996). Black and White world: Race, ideology, and utopia in *Triton* and *Star Trek. Cultural Critique, 32,* 75–95.

Goodman, M. E. (1952). *Race awareness in young children.* New York: Collier.

Graber, D. A. (1984). *Processing the news: How people tame the information tide.* New York: Longman.

Graves, S. B. (1996). Diversity on television. In T. M. MacBeth (Ed.), *Tuning in to young viewers: Social science perspectives on television* (pp. 61–86). Thousand Oaks, CA: Sage.

Gray, H. (1986). Television and the new Black man: Black male images in prime-time situation comedy. *Media, Culture and Society, 8,* 223–242.

Gray, H. (1995). *Watching race: Television and the struggle for "Blackness".* Minneapolis: University of Minnesota Press.

Greenberg, B. S. (1988). Some uncommon television images and the drench hypothesis. In S. Oskamp (Ed.), *Applied social psychology annual: Television as a social issue* (Vol. 8, pp. 88–102). Newbury Park, CA: Sage.

Greenberg, B. S. (1986). Minorities and the mass media. In J. Bryant & D. Zillman (Eds.), *Perspectives on media effects* (pp. 165–188). Hillsdale, NJ: Erlbaum.

Greenberg, B. S. (1972). Children's reactions to TV Blacks. *Journalism Quarterly, 49*(1), 5–14.

Greenfield, G. M., & Cortés, C. E. (1991). Harmony and conflict of intercultural images: The treatment of Mexico in U.S. feature films and K–12 textbooks. *Mexican Studies/Estudios Mexicanos, 7*(2), 283–301.

Gregg, R. W. (1998). *International relations on film.* Boulder, CO: Lynne Rienner.

Grossberg, L. Wartella, E., & Whitney, D.C. (1998). *Mediamaking: Mass media in popular culture.* Thousand Oaks, CA: Sage.

Hall, S. (1982). The rediscovery of "ideology": Return of the repressed in media studies. In M. Gurevitch, T. Bennet, J. Curran, & J. Woollacott (Eds.), *Culture, society and the media* (pp. 56–90). London: Methuen.

Hall, S. (1981). The whites of their eyes: Racist ideologies and the media. In G. Bridges & R. Brunt (Eds.), *Silver, linings: Some strategies for the eighties* (pp. 28–52). London: Lawrence & Wishart.

Hall, S. (1977). Culture, the media and the "ideological effect." In J. Curran, M. Gurevitch, & J. Woollacott (Eds.), *Mass communication and society* (pp. 315–348). London: Edward Arnold.

Hamamoto, D. Y. (1994). *Monitored peril: Asian Americans and the politics of TV representation.* Minneapolis: University of Minnesota Press.

Harper, C. (1998). *And that's the way it will be: News and information in a digital world.* New York: New York University Press.

Harris, J. R. (1998). *The nurture assumption: Why children turn out the way they do; parents matter less than you think and peers matter more.* New York: Free Press.

Hartmann, P., & Husband, C. (1972). The mass media and racial conflict. In D. McQuail (Ed.), *Sociology of mass communications* (pp. 435–455). Baltimore: Penguin.

Haskell, M. (1987). *From reverence to rape: The treatment of women in movies* (2d ed.). Chicago: University of Chicago Press.

Hatcher, R., & Troyna, B. (1993). Racialization and children. In C. McCarthy & W. Crichlow (Eds.), *Race, identity and representation in education* (pp. 109–125). New York: Routledge.

Hawkins, R., & Pingree, S. (1981). Using television to construct social reality. *Journal of Broadcasting, 25,* 347–364.

Heller, M. A. (1992, November). "Bad news." *Hispanic,* pp. 18–26.

Herman, E. S., & Chomsky, N. (1988). *Manufacturing consent: The political economy of the mass media.* New York: Pantheon.

Higashi, S. (1998). Melodrama, realism, and race: World War II newsreels and propaganda film. *Cinema Journal, 37*(3), 38–61.

Higgins, B. (1997, October 7). The night at a premier and party with Brad Pitt. *Los Angeles Times,* sec. E, p. 2.

Hilmes, M. (1997). *Radio voices: American broadcasting, 1922–1952.* Minneapolis: University of Minnesota Press.

Hines, G. (1998, January 6). Gingrich wants end to bilingual education. *Riverside Press-Enterprise,* sec. A, p. 3.

Hirsch, E. D., Jr. (1987). *Cultural literacy: What every American needs to know.* Boston: Houghton Mifflin.

Hirschfeld, L. A. (1996). *Race in the making: Cognition, culture, and the child's construction of human kinds.* Cambridge, MA: M.I.T. Press.

Hoberman, J. (1991). *Bridge of light: Yiddish film between two worlds.* New York: Museum of Modern Art and Schocken Books.

Holmes, D. (Ed.). (1998). *Virtual politics: Identity and community in cyberspace.* Thousand Oaks, CA: Sage.

Holmes, R. M. (1995). *How young children perceive race.* Thousand Oaks, CA: Sage.

hooks, b. (1996). *Reel to real: Race, sex, and class at the movies.* New York: Routledge.

Hoover, S. M. (1998). *Religion in the news: Faith and journalism in American public discourse.* Thousand Oaks, CA: Sage.

Hornaday, A. (1998, February 6). '97 opens a new frame of reference. *Los Angeles Times,* sec. F, p. 27.

Howard, J., Rothbart, F., & Sloan, L. (1978). The response to "Roots": A national survey. *Journal of Broadcasting, 22,* 279–288.

Hunt, D. M. (1997). *Screening the Los Angeles "riots": Race, seeing, and resistance.* New York: Cambridge University Press.

Huston, A. C., Donnerstein, E., Fairchild, H., Feshbach, N. D., Katz, P. A., Murray, J. P., Rubinstein, E. A., Wilcox, B. L., & Zuckerman, D. M. (1992). *Big world, small screen: The role of television in American society.* Lincoln: University of Nebraska Press.

Huston, A. C., & Wright, J. D. (1996). Television and socialization of young children. In T. M. MacBeth (Ed.), *Tuning in to young viewers: Social science perspectives on television* (pp. 37–60). Thousand Oaks, CA: Sage.

James, J. (1999, February). This Hawaii is not for tourists. *The Atlantic Monthly,* 90–94.

Jarvis, A.R.J. (1991). The Payne Fund reports: A discussion of their content, public reaction, and effect on the motion picture industry, 1930–1940. *Journal of Popular Culture, 25*(2), 127–140.

Jefferson, R. S. (1997, September 21). Confidentially . . . , *Los Angeles Times,* Calendar, p. 87.

Jenkins, H. (1992). *Textual poachers: Television fans and participatory culture.* New York: Routledge.

Jensen, K. B. (1987). Qualitative audience research: Toward an integrative approach to reception. *Critical studies in mass communication, 4,* 21–36.

Jhally, S., & Lewis, J. (1992). *Enlightened racism: "The Cosby Show," audiences, and the myth of the American dream.* Boulder, CO: Westview Press.

Johnson, A. A., & Johnson, R. M. (1979). *Propaganda and aesthetics: The literary politics of Afro-American magazines of the twentieth century.* Amherst, MA: University of Massachusetts Press.

Johnston, J., & Ettema, J. S. (1982). *Positive images: Breaking stereotypes with children's television.* Beverly Hills, CA: Sage.

Jones, S. G. (Ed.). (1997). *Virtual culture: Identity and communication in cybersociety.* Thousand Oaks, CA: Sage.

Jowett, G. S., Jarvie, I. C., & Fuller, K. H. (1996). *Children and the movies: Media influence and the Payne Fund controversy.* Cambridge, England: Cambridge University Press.

Jowett, G., & Linton, J. M. (1980). *Movies as mass communication.* Beverly Hills, CA: Sage.

Kaniss, P. (1991). *Making local news.* Chicago: University of Chicago Press.

Kaplan, J., & Bjorgo, T. (Eds.). (1998). *Nation and race: The developing Euro-American racist subculture.* Boston: Northeastern University Press.

Katz, J. (1997). *Virtuous reality: How America surrendered discussion of moral values to opportunists, nitwits and blockheads like William Bennett.* New York: Random House.

Katz, P. A. (1976). The acquisition of racial attitudes in children. In P. A. Katz (Ed.), *Towards the elimination of racism* (pp. 125–154). New York: Pergamon Press.

Kauffman, J. M., & Burbach, H. J. (1997). On creating a climate of classroom civility. *Phi Delta Kappan, 79*(4), 320–325.

Keen, S. (1986). *Faces of the enemy: Reflections of the hostile imagination.* New York: Harper & Row.

Keever, B.A.D., Martindale, C., & Weston, M. A. (Eds.). (1997). *U.S. news coverage of racial minorities: A sourcebook, 1934–1996.* Westport, CT: Greenwood.

Keyser, L., & Keyser, B. (1984). *Hollywood and the Catholic church: The image of Roman Catholicism in American movies.* Chicago: Loyola University Press.

Kiernan, V. (1998, April 24). Report documents role of race in who uses the worldwide web. *Chronicle of Higher Education,* p. A–38.

Kilpatrick, J. (1995). Disney's "politically correct" *Pocahontas. Cineaste, 21*(4), 36–37.

Kniveton, B. H. (1976). Social learning and imitation in relation to television. In R. Brown (Ed.), *Children and television.* Beverly Hills, CA: Sage.

Kohlberg, L. A., & Ullian, D. Z. (1974). Stages in the development of psychosexual concepts and attitudes. In R. C. Friedman, R. M. Richaret, & R. L. Warde Wiete (Eds.), *Sex differences in behavior* (pp. 209–222). New York: Wiley.

Koppes, C. R., & Black, G. D. (1987). *Hollywood goes to war: How politics, profits and propaganda shaped World War II movies.* New York: Free Press.

Korzenny, F., & Ting-Toomey, S., with Schiff, E. (Eds.). (1992). *Mass media effects across cultures. International and Intercultural Communication Annual, 16.* Newbury Park, CA: Sage.

Kosicki, G. M. (1993). Problems and opportunities in agenda-setting research. *Journal of Communication, 43*(2), 100–127.

Krugman, H. (1971). Brainwave measures of media involvement. *Journal of Advertising Research, 5,* 3–9.

Lalonde, R. N., & Gardner, R. C. (1989). An intergroup perspective on stereotype organization and processing. *British Journal of Social Psychology, 28,* 289–303.

Lamb, B. S. (1975). The convenient villain: The early cinema views the Mexican-American. *Journal of the West, 14*(4), 75–81.

Lazarsfeld, P., Berelson, B., & Gaudet, H. (1944). *The people's choice.* New York: Duell, Sloan, & Pearce.

Leab, D. J. (1975). *From sambo to superspade: The Black experience in motion pictures.* Boston: Houghton, Mifflin.

Lebo, H. (1997). *The Godfather legacy.* New York: Fireside.

Leckenby, J. D., & Surlin, S. H. (1976). Incidental social learning and viewer race: "All in the Family" and "Sanford and Son." *Journal of Broadcasting, 20*(4), 481–494.

Leifer, A. D., Gordon, N.J., & Graves, S. B. (1974). Children's television more than mere entertainment. *Harvard Educational Review, 44*(2), 213–245.

Leiss, W., Kline, S., & Jhally, S. (1986). *Social communication in advertising.* Toronto: Methuen.

Leonard, T. C. (1998). The uncensored war. *Culturefront, 7*(1), 59–62.

Lepore, J. (1996). *The Scarlet Letter* and *Pocahontas. American Historical Review, 101*(4), 1166–1168.

Leslie, E. (1996). Pocahontas. *History Workshop Journal, 41,* 235–239.

Lester, P. M. (Ed.). (1996). *Images that injure: Pictorial stereotypes in the media.* Westport, CT: Praeger.

Lewels, F. J., Jr. (1974). *The uses of the media by the Chicano movement: A study in minority access.* New York: Praeger.

Lewis, A. C. (1997). A new consensus emerges on the characteristics of good professional development. *Harvard Education Newsletter, 13*(3), 2–8.

Leyens, J. P., Yzerbyt, V., & Schadron, G. (1994). *Stereotypes and social cognition.* Thousand Oaks, CA: Sage.

Lichter, S. R., & Lichter, L. S. (1988). *Television's impact on ethnic and racial images.* New York: American Jewish Committee.

Liebert, R. M., & Sprafkin, J. (1988). *The early window: Effects of television on children and youth* (3rd ed.). New York: Pergamon.

Liebes, T. (1997). *Reporting the Arab-Israeli conflict: How hegemony works.* New York: Routledge.

Lind, R. A. (1996). Diverse interpretations: The "relevance" of race in the construction of meaning in, and the evaluation of, a television news story. *Harvard Journal of Communications, 7,* 53–74.

Liss, M. B. (1981). Children's television selections: A study of indicators of same-race preferences. *Journal of Cross-Cultural Psychology, 12*(1), 103–110.

Lourdeaux, L. (1990). *Italian and Irish filmmakers in America: Ford, Capra, Coppola, and Scorsese.* Philadelphia: Temple University Press.

MacBeth, T. M. (1996). Introduction. In T. M. MacBeth (Ed.), *Tuning in to young viewers: Social science perspectives on television* (pp. 1–36). Thousand Oaks, CA: Sage.

MacDonald, J. F. (1992). *Blacks and White TV: African Americans in television since 1948* (2d ed.). Chicago: Nelson-Hall.

Macrae, C. N., Stangor, C., & Hewstone, M. (Eds.). (1996). *Stereotypes and stereotyping*. New York: Guilford Press.

Maeroff, G. I. (Ed.). (1998). *Imaging education: The media and schools in America*. New York: Teachers College Press.

Martindale, C. (Ed.). (1993). *Pluralizing journalism education: A multicultural handbook*. Westport, CT: Greenwood Press.

Matabane, P. W. (1988). Television and the Black audience: Cultivating moderate perspectives on racial integration. *Journal of Communication, 38*(4), 21–31.

Matlin, M. W. (1991). The social cognition approach to stereotypes and its application to teaching. *Journal on Excellence in College Teaching, 2,* 9–24.

McAllister, S. (1997, October 16). Peace prodigy. *Los Angeles Times,* sec. B, p. 5.

McCombs, M. W., & Shaw, D. L. (1993). The evolution of agenda-setting research: Twenty-five years in the marketplace of ideas. *Journal of Communication, 43*(2), 58–67.

McLaughlin, K. A., & Brilliant, K. J. (1997). *Healing the hate: A national bias crime prevention curriculum for middle schools*. Newton, MA: Education Development Center.

McLeod, J. M., & Reeves, B. (1981). On the nature of mass media effects. In S. B. Withey & R. P. Abeles (Eds.), *Television and social behavior: Beyond violence and children* (pp. 17–54). Hillsdale, NJ: Erlbaum.

Media literacy symposium. (1998). *Journal of Communication, 48*(1), 3–120.

Medved, M. (1992). *Hollywood v. America: Popular culture and the war on traditional values*. New York: HarperPerennial.

Medved, M., & Medved, D. (1998). *Saving childhood: Protecting our children from the national assault on innocence*. New York: HarperCollins.

Mehlinger, H. D. (1996). School reform in the information age. *Phi Delta Kappan, 77*(6), 400–407.

Meyer, P. (1999, April 14). Group effort replaces lone reporter of yore. *USA Today,* sec. A, p. 27.

Middleton, R. (1960). Ethnic prejudice and susceptibility to persuasion. *American Sociological Review, 25*(5), 679–686.

Miller, S. M. (Ed.). (1987). *The ethnic press in the United States: A historical analysis and handbook*. Westport, CT: Greenwood Press.

Miller, T. (1998). *Technologies of truth: Cultural citizenship and the popular media*. Minneapolis: University of Minnesota Press.

Minow, N. (1995). *Abandoned in the wasteland: Children, television and the first amendment*. New York: Hill & Wang.

Morris, M., & Ogan, C. (1996). The internet as mass medium. *Journal of Communication, 46*(1), 39–50.

Morse, M. (1998). *Virtualities: Television, media art, and cyberculture*. Bloomington: Indiana University Press.

Myrdal, G. (1944). *An American dilemma: The Negro problem and modern democracy*. New York: Harper & Brothers.

Naficy, H., & Gabriel, T. (Eds.). (1993). *Otherness and the media: The ethnography of the imagined and the imaged.* Langhorne, PA: Harwood Academic Publishers.

Nikken, P., & Peeters, A. L. (1988). Children's perceptions of television reality. *Journal of Broadcasting & Electronic Media, 32*(4), 441–452.

No apology warranted. (1991, December 10). *Riverside Press-Enterprise*, sec. F, p. 7.

Norden, M. F. (1994). *The cinema of loneliness: A history of physical disability in the movies.* New Brunswick, NJ: Rutgers University Press.

Noriega, C. (1988–1990). Chicano cinema and the horizon of expectations: A discursive analysis of recent film reviews in the mainstream, alternative and Hispanic press, 1987–1988. *Aztlán, A Journal of Chicano Studies, 19*(2), 1–31.

Noriega, C. (Ed.). (1992). *Chicanos and film: Essays on Chicano representation and resistance.* New York: Garland.

Nornes, A. M., & Yukio, F. (Eds.). (1994). *The Japan/American film wars: World War II propaganda and its cultural contexts.* Langhorne, PA: Harwood Academic Publishers.

Oakes, P. J., Haslam, S. A., & Turner, J. C. (1994). *Stereotyping and social reality.* Cambridge, MA: Blackwell.

O'Barr, W. M. (1994). *Culture and the ad: Exploring otherness in the world of advertising.* Boulder, CO: Westview Press.

Oldham, J. (1997, December 18). Wiesenthal center compiles list of hate-based web sites. *Los Angeles Times*, sec. A, p. 1.

Pechter, W. S. (1975, March). "Godfather II." *Commentary*, pp. 79–80.

Perkins, T. E. (1979). Rethinking stereotypes. In M. Barrett, P. Corrigan, A. Kuhn, & J. Wolff (Eds.), *Ideology and cultural production* (pp. 135–159). New York: St. Martin's Press.

Perlmutter, D. D. (1997). Manufacturing visions of society and history in textbook. *Journal of Communication, 47*(3), 68–80.

Perloff, R. M. (1993). Third-person effect research 1983–1992: A review and synthesis. *International Journal of Public Opinion Research, 5*(2), 167–184.

Peterson, R. C., & Thurstone, L. L. (1933). *Motion pictures and the social attitudes of children.* New York: Macmillan.

Pettit, A. G. (1980). *Images of the Mexican American in fiction and film.* College Station: Texas A & M University Press.

Pewewardy, C. D. (1999). From la belle sauvage to the noble savage: The deculturalization of Indian mascots in American culture. *Multicultural Education, 6*(3), 6–11.

Phinney, J. S., & Rotheram, M. J. (Eds.). (1987). *Children's ethnic socialization: Pluralism and development.* Beverly Hills, CA: Sage.

Piaget, J. (1932). *The moral judgment of the child* (M. Worden, Trans.). New York: Harcourt, Brace & World.

Piaget, J. (1929). *The child's conception of the world* (J. & A. Tomlinson, Trans.). New York: Harcourt, Brace & World.

Plato. (1968). *The Republic of Plato* (2d ed.; A. Bloom, Trans.). New York: BasicBooks.

Porter, D. (Ed.). (1997). *Internet culture.* New York: Routledge.

Postman, N. (1985). *Amusing ourselves to death: Public discourse in the age of show business.* New York: Viking Penguin.

Postman, N. (1982). *The disappearance of childhood*. New York: Delacorte.

Potter, W. J. (1998). *Media literacy*. Thousand Oaks, CA: Sage.

Rafaeli, S. (1986). The electronic bulletin board: A computer-driven mass medium. *Computers and the Social Sciences, 2*, 123–136.

Ramsey, P. G. (1987). Young children's thinking about ethnic differences. In J. S. Phinney & M. J. Rotheram (Eds.), *Children's ethnic socialization: Pluralism and development*. Newbury Park, CA: Sage.

Rapaczynski, W., Singer, D. G., & Singer, J. L. (1982). Teaching television: A curriculum for young children. *Journal of Communication, 32*(2), 46–55.

Raths, L. E., & Trager, F. N. (1948). Public opinion and "Crossfire." *Journal of Educational Sociology, 21*(6), 345–368.

Real, M. R. (1991). Bill Cosby and recoding ethnicity. In L. R. Vande Berg & L. A. Wenner (Eds.), *Television criticism, approaches and applications* (pp. 58–84). New York: Longman.

Real, M. R. (1977). *Mass-mediated culture*. Englewood Cliffs, NJ: Prentice-Hall.

Reeves, B., & Nass, C. (1996). *The media equation: How people treat computers, television, and new media like real people and places*. New York: Cambridge University Press.

Ríos, D., & Gaines, S. (1997). Impact of gender and ethnic subgroup membership on Mexican Americans' use of mass media for cultural maintenance. *Howard Journal of Communications, 8*(2), 197–216.

Rivers, C. (1996). *Slick spins and fractured facts: How cultural myths distort the news*. New York: Columbia University Press.

Roberts, D. F., & Bachen, C. M. (1982). Mass communication effects. *Annual Review of Psychology, 32*, 307–356.

Rogers, E. M. (1994). *A history of communication study: A biographical approach*. New York: Free Press.

Rogers, E. M., Dearing, J. W., & Bregman, D. (1993). The anatomy of agenda-setting research. *Journal of Communication, 43*(2), 68–84.

Rogin, M. (1996). *Blackface, White noise: Jewish immigrants in the Hollywood melting pot*. Berkeley: University of California Press.

Rosen, I. C. (1948). The effect of the motion picture "Gentleman's Agreement" on attitudes toward Jews. *Journal of Psychology, 26*, 525–536.

Rosen, M. (1973). *Popcorn Venus: Women, movies and the American dream*. New York: Avon.

Rosenberg, H. (1997, October 31). It's beauty and the beast. *Los Angeles Times*, sec. F, pp. 1, 31.

Rosenstiel, T. B. (1989, August 17). Viewers found to confuse TV entertainment with news. *Los Angeles Times*, sec. A, p. 1.

Rosenstone, R. A. (Ed.). (1995). *Revisioning history: Film and the construction of a new past*. Princeton, NJ: Princeton University Press.

Ross, S. J. (1998). *Working-class Hollywood: Silent film and the shaping of class in America*. Princeton, NJ: Princeton University Press.

Rubin, B. (Ed.). (1980). *Small voices & great trumpets: Minorities & the media*. New York: Praeger.

Russo, V. (1987). *The celluloid closet: Homosexuality in the movies* (Rev. ed.). New York: Harper & Row.

Said, E. W. (1978). *Orientalism*. New York: Random House.

Sampedro, V. (1998). Grounding the displaced: Local media reception in a transnational context. *Journal of Communication, 48*(2), 125–142.

Samuelson, R. J. (1998, July 13). Down with the media elite? *Newsweek*, p. 47.

Sardar, Z. (1996–1997). Walt Disney and the double victimisation of Pocahontas. *Third Text*, Winter, 17–26.

Scheufele, D. A. (1999). Framing as a theory of media effects. *Journal of Communication, 49*(1), 103–122.

Schwartz, T. (1973). *The responsive chord*. Garden City, NY: Doubleday.

Schwoch, J., White, M., & Reilly, S. (1992). *Media knowledge: Readings in popular culture, pedagogy, and critical citizenship*. Albany: State University of New York Press.

Seiter, E. (1986). Stereotypes and the media: A re-evaluation. *Journal of Communication, 36*(2), 14–26.

Shaheen, J. G. (1984). *The TV Arab*. Bowling Green, OH: Bowling Green State University Popular Press.

Shaw, D. (1997, June 18). Online magazines on the cutting edge. *Los Angeles Times*, sec. A, p. 19.

Shaw, D. (1997, June 15). Digital age poses the riddle of dividing or uniting society. *Los Angeles Times*, sec. A, p. 25.

Shaw, D. L. (1993). The evolution of agenda-setting research: Twenty-five years in the marketplace of ideas. *Journal of Communication, 43*(2), 58–67.

Shayon, R. L. (1952). *Television and our children*. New York: Longman.

Shenk, D. (1997). *Data smog: Surviving the information glut*. San Francisco: Harper Edge.

Shenk, D. (1997, June 17). No one mingles in "global village." *USA Today*, sec. A, p. 13.

Shipp, E. R. (1998). One movie, different reactions, depending on race. *Columbia University Journalism Alumni Journal*, Winter, p. 5.

Shoemaker, P. J., & Reese, S. D. (1991). *Mediating the message: Theories of influences on mass media content*. White Plains, NY: Longman.

Silver, M. (1997, September 1). Party of five. *Sports Illustrated*, pp. 188–199.

Simon, R. J., & Alexander, S. H. (1993). *The ambivalent welcome: Print media, public opinion and immigration*. Westport, CT: Praeger.

Sklar, R. (1975). *Movie-made America: A cultural history of American movies*. New York: Random House.

Slater, E. (1998, April 18). Family ties put a face on the faceless issue of free speech. *Los Angeles Times*, sec. B, pp. 1, 3.

Small, E. S. (1992). Introduction: Cognitivism and film theory. *Journal of Dramatic Theory and Criticism, 6*(2), 165–172.

Spring, J. (1992). *Images of American life: A history of ideological management in schools, movies, radio, and television*. Albany: State University of New York Press.

Staiger, J. (1992). *Interpreting films: Studies in the historical reception of American cinema.* Princeton, NJ: Princeton University Press.

Stanley, R. H., & Steinberg, C. S. (1976). *The media environment: Mass communications in American society.* New York: Hastings House.

Stedman, R. W. (1982). *Shadows of the Indian: Stereotypes in American culture.* Norman: University of Oklahoma Press.

Stein, J. W. (1979). *Mass media, education, and a better society.* Chicago: Nelson-Hall.

Stephan, W. (1999). *Reducing prejudice and stereotyping in schools.* New York: Teachers College Press.

Stout, D. A., & Buddenbaum, J. M. (Eds.). (1996). *Religion and mass media: Audiences and aspirations.* Thousand Oaks, CA: Sage.

Stroman, C. A. (1991). Television's role in the socialization of African American children and adolescents. *Journal of Negro Education, 60*(3), 314–327.

Subervi-Vélez, F. A. (1986). The mass media and ethnic assimilation and pluralism: A review and research proposal with special focus on Hispanics. *Communication Research, 13*(1), 71–96.

Summerfield, E. (1993). *Crossing cultures through film.* Yarmouth, ME: Intercultural Press.

Surlin, S. H. (1978). "Roots" research: A summary of findings. *Journal of Broadcasting, 22*(3), 309–319.

Surlin, S. H., & Tate, E. D. (1976). "All in the family": Is Archie funny? *Journal of Communication, 26*(4), 61–68.

Tan, A., & Tan, G. (1979). Television use and self-esteem of Blacks. *Journal of Communication, 29*(1), 123–135.

Tasker, Y. (1998). *Working girls: Gender and sexuality in popular cinema.* New York: Routledge.

Tatum, B. D. (1997). *"Why are all the Black kids sitting together in the cafeteria?" and other conversations about race.* New York: BasicBooks.

Taylor, P. S. (1930). *Mexican labor in the United States* (Vol. I). Berkeley: University of California Press.

Teaching Tolerance. (1997). *Starting small: Teaching tolerance in preschool and the early grades.* Montgomery, AL: Author.

Thomas, C. (1998, July 5). Conservatives not surprised by media lies. *Riverside Press-Enterprise,* sec. A, p. 14.

Tichi, C. (1992). *Electronic hearth: Creating an American television culture.* New York: Oxford University Press.

Tilton, R. S. (1994). *Pocahontas: The evolution of an American narrative.* New York: Cambridge University Press.

Tomasulo, F. P. (1996). Italian Americans in the Hollywood cinema: Filmmakers, characters, audiences. *Voices in Italian Americana, 7*(1), 65–77.

Toplin, R. B. (Ed.). (1993). *Hollywood as mirror: Changing views of "outsiders" and "enemies" in American movies.* Westport, CT: Greenwood Press.

Tran, M. T., Young, R. L., & DiLella, J. D. (1994). Multicultural education courses and the student teacher: Eliminating stereotypical attitudes in our ethnically diverse classroom. *Journal of Teacher Education, 45*(3), 183–189.

Trend, D. (1997). *Cultural democracy: Politics, media, new technology.* Albany: State University of New York Press.

Trubowitz, J. (1969). *Changing the racial attitudes of children.* New York: Praeger.

U. S. Indians—new energy sheikhs? (1980, March 5). *Senior Weekly Reader,* pp. 4–5.

Vasey, R. (1997). *The world according to Hollywood, 1918–1939.* Madison: University of Wisconsin Press.

Vidmar, N., & Rokeach, M. (1974). Archie Bunker's bigotry: A study in selective perception and exposure. *Journal of Communication, 24*(1), 36–47.

Volkan, V. (1988). *The need to have enemies and allies: From clinical practice to international relationships.* Northvale, NJ: J. Aronson.

Vygotsky, L. (1986). *Thought and language* (A. Kozulin, Trans.). Cambridge, MA: M.I.T. Press.

Walling, J. I. (1976). The effect of parental interaction on learning from television. *Communication Education, 25,* 16–24.

Wartella, E., & Reeves, B. (1985). Historical trends in research on children and the media. *Journal of Communication, 35*(2), 118–133.

Watson, A. (1998). The newspaper's responsibility. In G. I. Maeroff, (Ed.), *Imaging education: The media and schools in America* (pp. 13–25). New York: Teachers College Press.

Webster, J. G., & Phalen, P. F. (1997). *The mass audience: Rediscovering the dominant model.* Mahwah, NJ: Erlbaum.

Weigel, R. H., Loomis, J., & Soja, M. (1980). Race relations on prime time television. *Journal of Personality and Social Psychology, 39*(5), 884–893.

Wiegman, R. (1989). Negotiating AMERICA: Gender, race, and the ideology of the interracial male bond. *Cultural Critique, 13,* 89–117.

Wilhoit, G. C., & de Bock, H. (1976). "All in the Family" in Holland. *Journal of Communication, 26*(4), 75–84.

Williams, L. (Ed.). (1995). *Viewing positions: Ways of seeing film.* New Brunswick, NJ: Rutgers University Press.

Willis, S. (1997). *High contrast: Race and gender in contemporary Hollywood film.* Durham, NC: Duke University Press.

Wilson, C. C., II, & Gutiérrez, F. (1995). *Race, multiculturalism, and the media.* Thousand Oaks, CA: Sage.

Winn, M. (1977). *The plug-in drug.* New York: Viking Press.

Wong, E. F. (1978). *On visual media racism: Asians in the American motion pictures.* New York: Arno Press.

Worth, S., & Adair, J. (1972). *Through Navajo eyes: An exploration in film communication and anthropology.* Bloomington: Indiana University Press.

Wurman, R. S. (1989). *Information anxiety.* New York: Doubleday.

Ynegar, S., & Kinder, D. R. (1987). *News that matters: Agenda-setting and priming in a television age.* Chicago: University of Chicago Press.

Young guns. (1998, April 20). *Sports Illustrated,* p. 26.

Yum, J. O. (1982). Communication diversity and information acquisition among Korean immigrants in Hawaii. *Human Communication Research, 8*(2), 154–169.

Index

About the Author

Carlos E. Cortés is a Professor Emeritus of History at the University of California, Riverside. Since 1990 he has served on the summer faculty of the Harvard Institutes for Higher Education and is also on the faculty of the Summer Institute for Intercultural Communication.

Among his many honors are the 1980 Distinguished California Humanist Award, the American Society for Training and Development's 1989 National Multicultural Trainer of the Year Award, and the California Council for the Social Studies' 1995 Hilda Taba Award. A consultant to many government agencies, school systems, universities, mass media, private businesses, and other organizations, he has lectured on diversity throughout the United States, Latin America, Europe, Asia, and Australia and has written film and television documentaries.